THE GERMAN DEMOCRATIC REPUBLIC

WESTVIEW PROFILES · NATIONS OF CONTEMPORARY EASTERN EUROPE

†Available in hardcover and paperback.

ABOUT THE BOOK AND AUTHOR

This important new overview of the German Democratic Republic focuses on the country's search for identity and legitimacy throughout its history. Dr. Henry Krisch analyzes major aspects of East German life—political, economic, cultural, and societal—to answer the fundamental question of the nature of the GDR. Arguing that East Germany has been shaped by history to an unusual degree, he explores the country's historical background, including the Soviet Zone, the origins of the GDR, and the leadership of Ulbricht and Honecker, and examines the role and structure of the party, state, and military and security forces. The main emphasis of this book, however, is upon current problems and on likely responses to them in the near future. Issues such as the viability of communist politics in a technologically advanced society, the relationship of the GDR to a common German heritage and a competing West German state, and the country's role within the Soviet alliance system are examined in detail, and current social concerns, including the peace movement, cultural trends, the role of women and youth, and the prime importance of sports, are discussed.

Dr. Henry Krisch is associate professor of political science at the University of Connecticut. He is the author of *German Politics Under Soviet Occupation* (1974) and is most recently a contributor of a chapter on the GDR armed forces in *Soviet Allies*, edited by Daniel Nelson (Westview, 1984).

The center of East Berlin includes the old city hall (*Rotes Rathaus*), restored St. Nikolai church, and new buildings in the background. Photo courtesy of the GDR Embassy, Washington, D.C.

THE GERMAN DEMOCRATIC REPUBLIC

The Search for Identity

Henry Krisch

Westview Press / Boulder and London

Westview Profiles/Nations of Contemporary Eastern Europe

Copyright © 1985 by Westview Press, Inc.

Published in 1985 in the United States of America by Westview Press, Inc.; Frederick A. Praeger, Publisher; 5500 Central Avenue, Boulder, Colorado 80301

Library of Congress Cataloging in Publication Data
Krisch, Henry.
  The German Democratic Republic.
  (Westview profiles. Nations of contemporary Eastern
Europe)
  Bibliography: p.
  Includes index.
  1. Germany (East). I. Title. II. Series: Nations
of contemporary Eastern Europe.
DD280.6.K75 1985   943.1   85-11508
ISBN 0-89158-850-7

Printed and bound in the United States of America

10   9   8   7   6   5   4   3   2   1

Contents

Illustrations

For my mother
and in memory of my father

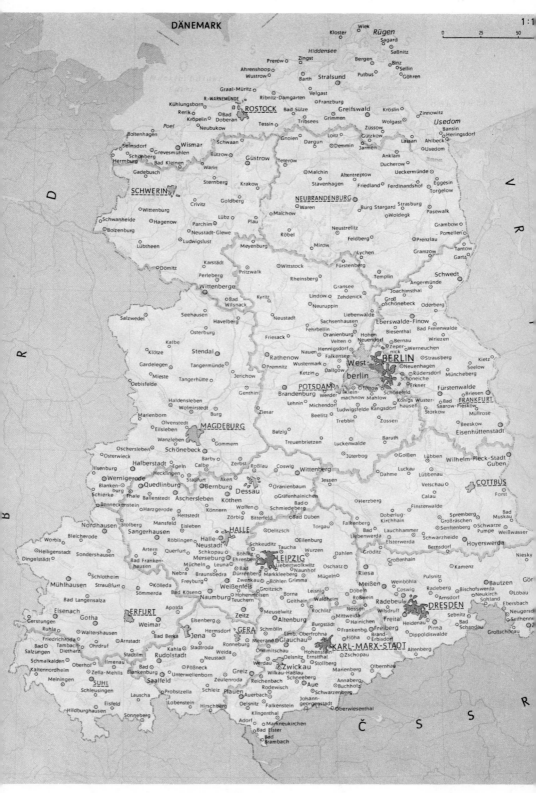

The German Democratic Republic.

1

The GDR
in Time and Place

THE HISTORICAL BACKGROUND
OF THE GDR (BEFORE 1945)

Although it is a small country, celebrating (in 1985) only its thirty-sixth anniversary, the German Democratic Republic (GDR) is the product of over a thousand years of German and European history. That history, furthermore, took place over a larger geographical territory than that of today's GDR. To understand the GDR, therefore, one must consider its politics and society against this historical and territorial background.[1]

The dominant theme of German history has been the search for a secure communal identity and for political and territorial arrangements that would reflect and secure this identity. Other problems, such as foreign affairs and social relations, important in themselves, have been shaped by this central drive. The questions of what is Germany and who are the Germans influence the rate and direction of social change in the two German states, the nature of German culture in all of its manifestations, and the relations of the two German states to the world at large, to their respective alliances, and, not least, to each other.

Despite a long and glorious record of cultural achievement, Germans in modern times are bitterly aware of their historical inability to establish a single state resting on a social and political consensus. There have been many lines of cleavage in German history, beginning with the conflicts between the Holy Roman Empire and territorial sovereigns and between the Empire and the Papacy—two dichotomies that by the end of the Middle Ages left "Germany" a political mosaic of varied jurisdictions. Colonization and eastward expansion laid the foundation for later tensions with Poles and Czechs.

The religious conflicts of the early modern period (i.e., the sixteenth and seventeenth centuries) divided the German lands into Catholic and Protestant areas (with neither denomination sufficiently in the majority to impose a settlement on the other) and further divided the Protestants into Lutheran, Calvinist, and other groups. These manifold religious

1

divisions of Germany in the sixteenth and seventeenth centuries were intertwined with dynastic and social conflicts and were further complicated by the interventions of such foreign powers as Spain, Sweden, and France. These interventions exacerbated Germany's political and religious struggles and helped to bring on the paroxysm of the Thirty Years War (1618–1648), which, in turn, left the German people and states economically and demographically devastated, politically more divided than ever, and helpless on the international level.

In the eighteenth century, German economic backwardness and military weakness reached their apogee, and language and culture were strongly under foreign, especially French, influence. Ironically, it was during this same century that Germany began its recovery—politically and militarily through the rise of Prussia, and culturally through the emergence of distinctively German music, literature, and art, culminating in the early nineteenth-century Romantic movement. The ultimately successful response to French pressure in the Napoleonic era demonstrated this renewed German vitality.

From a later German perspective, a crucial aspect of this resurgence was the link between internal reform, central political authority, and external success. The drive for administrative efficiency and rationality under such Prussian rulers as Frederick William (the Great Elector, from 1640–1688) and Frederick II (the Great, from 1740–1786), as well as the reforms of state and society at the time of the "War of Liberation" against the French (1813–1815), provided the precedents for the assertion of German power under Bismarck.

The Bismarckian state was both the product and the generator of an economic advance that by 1900 made Germany the premier economic power of Europe. Germany's strength was mobilized by an authoritarian regime that had its origins in the defeat of the liberal and largely middle class movement for national unity and political reform symbolized by the Frankfurt Assembly of 1848, and, more particularly, Bismarck's defeat of the Prussian parliamentary opposition of the early 1860s. The resulting regime of "Blood and Iron" used Germany's growing strength against the major enemies of a German national state—France and Austria— in the three famous victorious wars (of 1864, 1866, and 1870–1871) that led to the formation of the German Empire in 1871.

This "Second Reich" seemed to provide a solution to Germany's historical dilemmas of disunity and weakness, but at the cost of forfeiting the chances for democratic political life. Even so, it could not overcome a number of problems that confronted Germany in the late nineteenth century, and this failure led to the regime's downfall in 1918. These problems had a common theme—namely, the question of German identity and its proper political, social, and national expression. Germany was faced by a double social cleavage: between the regime and the minority Catholic population of the Reich, and between the regime and the growing and ever more organized industrial working class. Its authoritarian political system came under increasing attack, particularly the three-class voting system in Prussia and the absence of cabinet responsibility to the legislature at the national level. Finally, the Imperial regime was unable, especially after Bismarck's dismissal in 1890, to secure for Germany a peaceful place in the European state system. The exclusion of the German population of Austria in 1871 from the German national state left both Germany and Austria vulnerable to a dynamic German nationalism; it also tied Germany to the continued existence of the multiethnic Hapsburg state—a connection fateful for the prospects of European peace. (Germany itself had to deal with a Polish minority resulting from the partitions of Poland.)

Bismarck's Germany might, in time, have dealt successfully with these problems, but the regime did not (and perhaps could not) avoid involvement in World War I; the result, of course, was Germany's defeat (1918) and the collapse of the Imperial regime. Although from the perspective of many Germans in 1945 the period under Bismarck's rule was seen as a time of German power and prosperity, its legacy to postwar Germany was one of unresolved social, national, and political questions.

The Weimar Republic that emerged in place of Bismarck's Germany faced many of the same problems as those of its predecessor, but with a smaller margin of popular support. Its ultimate failure should not obscure its many accomplishments. Weimar Germany, especially during its era of relative stability (1924–1930), experienced an extraordinary and still influential flowering of the arts. Less appreciated is Weimar's record of social and political innovation. For previously disadvantaged groups, such as women and Jews, the Weimar era was one of liberation. Weimar's political structure and the social legislation it produced were among the most progressive in the world.

The Weimar legacy also included political flaws that served as negative examples to postwar Germans. Many lessons were drawn from the inability of the Weimar Republic to defend itself against its enemies. For the Social Democrats and Communists especially, a critical aspect of the Weimar record (and of particular importance to the politics of postwar Germany) was the disastrous internecine warfare within the working-class movement, followed by the failure of that movement, including its trade union component, along with the failure of the liberal bourgeoisie to save the Weimar Republic from its enemies.

Although the Weimar Republic preserved a united German national state, its ability to promote national interests was limited by its weak international position. Excluded initially from the ranks of the Great Powers, it could not exercise German sovereignty over the Saar or the Rhineland, was unable to secure self-determination for the German populations of Austria, South Tyrol, and the Sudetenland, and had difficulty in asserting German interests in Polish border areas.

Although Weimar Germany did not suffer from religious conflict to nearly the extent that the Empire had, social conflicts grew worse.

The majority of industrial workers, organized through the Social Democratic party (SPD), now had a powerful voice in state and society, but the SPD was challenged by the breakaway of more radical groups, which eventually formed the Communist party of Germany (KPD). The Weimar Republic seemed at the mercy of economic fortune: the social and political stability of the mid-1920s ended in the turmoil of the Wall Street crash and the subsequent Great Depression.

In the years of economic distress that followed, the Weimar Republic was faced by a growing and increasingly Soviet-dominated Communist party, which to the end of the republic—and, indeed, beyond—was a bitter enemy of the parliamentary order. More deadly yet was the menace of the swiftly growing Nazi movement. Between September 1930 and the summer of 1932, the Nazis became the largest German political party and Adolf Hitler emerged as a charismatic enemy of German democracy. In the face of the Nazi menace, the republic suffered from weak, if not malevolent, leadership; its institutions were turned against its own survival. After July 1932, an absolute antirepublican majority paralyzed its legislature; from 1930 on, its government tended more and more to rule through abuse of the infamous Article 48, which gave presidential decrees the force of law. The president from 1925 on was former Field Marshal Paul von Hindenburg, a weak and faint-hearted, if very correct, defender of the republic. Acting on the advice of antirepublican intriguers, he appointed Adolf Hitler head of the German government on January 30, 1933.[2]

The fundamental cause of the Weimar Republic's collapse was the lack of a democratic and republican political culture in Germany: Weimar was known as "the Republic without Republicans." Although some of the stability of the Hitler regime undoubtedly stemmed from the widespread political terror employed by the Nazis, there can be little doubt that the Hitler regime could impose its political will on Germany because it seemed to end social conflict and restore prosperity at home while successfully asserting German national interests abroad.

Although there was some domestic opposition to the Hitler regime, especially as the war turned against Germany, it is clear that only the victory of the Grand Alliance did in fact put an end to the Nazi order. The heroism of individual Communists notwithstanding, there is no basis for the later GDR claims of continuous and effective Communist resistance. Thus the legacy of the Empire, the Weimar Republic, and the Third Reich to postwar Germany was one of political and moral failure, social and economic conflict, war and international ostracism.

With the unconditional surrender of German forces in 1945 there came the famous "Year Zero," from which contemporary German politics is dated. German borders in the east were pushed back to the point at which they had rested centuries before. It was significant for the future GDR that German territories in East Prussia, Silesia, and Pomerania, including the mouth of the Oder River and the port of Stettin (in Polish,

Szczecin), were assigned to Poland and to the USSR. Frontier adjustments were also made on Germany's western and northern borders. Long-time German inhabitants were forcibly expelled from eastern Europe. German sovereignty in every part of the remaining territories passed into the hands of the occupying powers, who limited and strictly supervised every kind of political activity. The country's economic life was shaped, as well, to suit the victors' needs and plans.

It was in these circumstances of political and social disaster, amid physical and human ruin unmatched in German history since 1648, that the future GDR had its origins. Awareness of this humble beginning has been kept alive for future generations, as evidenced by the opening line of the country's anthem: "Arisen from ruins."

THE SOVIET ZONE AND
THE ORIGINS OF THE GDR (1945–1949)

The German Democratic Republic was an unintended polity. Fore-seen neither in the postwar plans of the governments of the anti-Hitler coalition nor in the thinking of German politicians during and immediately after World War II was the partition of Germany into two states—one tied to the Soviet Union, the other allied to the Western powers.[3]

It was at the wartime summit conferences of the Soviet, British, and U.S. leaders, especially at Yalta (January 1945) and Potsdam (July–August 1945), that the practical preparations for Allied control of Germany were made, based on the assumption of joint administration of a united country. It was this detailed but supposedly provisional demarcation of the occupation zones that in time became the basis for the division of Germany. The present borders of the GDR were determined by these Allied agreements, according to which the prewar German state lost territory while it absorbed German refugees. Some three million of those "new settlers" (as they were euphemistically known) were living in the Soviet Zone in 1946. Subsequently, many of them joined the flight of population to the West.[4]

The most consequential line of division was that established between the occupation zone allotted to the USSR and those allotted to the Western powers. The diplomatic history of the creation of these zonal borders shows that they were drawn largely for the military-administrative convenience of the occupying powers. As a result, the main inland waterways of the GDR, the Elbe and Oder Rivers, reach the'sea after leaving GDR territory (in the FRG and Poland, respectively). The complications arising from the location of West Berlin amidst GDR territory are notorious.

In the final demarcation of the occupation zones, the Soviet Union received an area equivalent to about one-fifth of prewar Germany but over one-third of the Germany of 1945. The municipality of Greater Berlin was given special "four-power" status and was occupied by all of the Allied powers.[5] In accordance with Allied agreements, the U.S. forces withdrew at war's end from those areas of the present-day GDR in which they found themselves as a result of military operations, and they were replaced by Soviet troops; at the same time (July 1945), Western forces entered Berlin and occupied their assigned sectors. At the Potsdam Conference, the Allied powers agreed to treat Germany as an economic unity. Each occupation power was to be sovereign in its own zone, but questions affecting Germany as a whole were to be settled by the occupation commanders meeting as the Allied Control Council for Germany. Soviet actions at this time make it clear that Soviet measures were intended to apply to all of Germany, with control of the Soviet Zone of Occupation (SBZ) at best a minimum position.[6]

The Soviet authorities were the first to permit the formation of political parties and trade unions (June 10, 1945) in their zone. The structure and program of these organizations were clearly all-German in scope. The Communist and Social Democratic parties were established on June 15, with the Christian Democrats (CDU) and Liberal Democrats (LPD) following a few weeks later. A new trade union federation (the Freier Deutscher Gewerkschaftsbund, or FDGB) and various cultural organizations were also founded at this time. As early as July 27, the Soviet Military Administration for Germany (SMAD) arranged for the creation of eleven "Central Administrations." These agencies were de facto ministries for social and economic matters. Five of them—including those for education, labor, finance, and agriculture—were headed by Communists. The Central Administrations (including several more added over the next few years) were later transformed into the government ministries of the GDR.

Immediately after the war, most Germans assumed that Germany would continue to be a united national state and persisted in this expectation after prospects for German unity had begun to fade. But regardless of what the expectations both of the Germans and of their conquerors may have been, within three years of the war's end Germany's division had become a central fact of European and Great Power politics.

Within the wider context of clashing Soviet and U.S. political and economic needs and interests, there occurred a number of specific developments that led to the eventual division of Germany into two states.[7] In 1945–1946, when East-West hostility was not yet so great as to prevent some agreement on all-German matters, the French blocked such initiatives as licensing political parties on an all-German basis.

Another cause for the breakdown of all-German arrangements was the inter-Allied wrangling over reparations. A particularly thorny subject was the 10 percent of industrial production of the Western zones to be added to the amount due the USSR and to be paid for mainly through agricultural commodities from the Soviet Zone. Disputes over this arrangement led to the U.S. decision of 1946 to suspend deliveries to the Soviet Zone, thus leading directly to the creation of the joint British-

American economic zone ("Bizonia") at the end of 1946 and eventually to the introduction of separate currencies for the western zones and West Berlin in 1948. The result was the Soviet blockade of Berlin in 1948 and the creation of two German states in 1949.

Long before that, however, the Soviet authorities had undertaken measures (or supported those of their German clients) that were designed to project Soviet political power across all of Germany while at the same time ensuring that the social, economic, and political arrangements of the SBZ conformed to the Soviet pattern. These activities prepared the ground for the formation of the GDR as a Soviet-style state, with economic and social systems based on the Soviet model.

Politically the most important move was the unification of the Communist and Social Democratic parties in the Soviet Zone (April 1946) to form the Socialist Unity Party of Germany (Sozialistische Einheitspartei Deutschland, or SED), the present-day ruling party of the GDR. Although this unification was in part a response to long-held and deeply felt German desires, it was accomplished in such a way (with massive Soviet pressure on behalf of the KPD) as to limit it to the Soviet Zone and establish a still-relevant hostility between the West German SPD and the SED.

The position of the SED was strengthened by the establishment of a "Bloc of Antifascist Democratic Parties," which served to limit the freedom of action of the non-Communist parties. Moreover, the SMAD severely curtailed the ability of the CDU and LPD to organize, particularly at the regional and local levels. The political outcome of these developments was made manifest in the results of the Soviet Zone elections of October 1946. The SED, while winning pluralities in all state legislatures, was hard pressed to command majorities, and did so only with the help of representatives put forward by extraparty organizations, such as the trade unions. In Berlin, where free elections were held under four-power auspices, the SED did poorly, especially by contrast with the SPD (led in Berlin by people who had opposed the April 1946 merger with the KPD). The SPD won over 48 percent of the vote; the SED was a distant third.

Such political obstacles were not allowed to interfere with the social and economic transformation of the Soviet Zone. Going beyond the Allied agenda of demilitarization and de-Nazification, the Soviet occupation authorities carried out a series of measures designed to break up the social structure not only of Hitler's Germany but of Imperial and Weimar Germany as well.

Important early steps in this effort included the proclamation of land reform (1945), the reform of the schools (1945), the revamping of the judiciary and police (1945–1946), and the nationalization of industrial property belonging to "Nazis and war criminals" (1945–1946). In Saxony, voters approved this latter measure (by 77.6 percent) in a referendum of June 1946. Under the SMAD's aegis, approximately 2.5 million hectares of land were redistributed from some seven thousand landowners to half a million smallholders or landless peasants.

The educational and judicial reforms struck at two sets of officials—judges and school teachers—who were seen as reactionary opponents of socialism and democracy. This was part of a broader and more rigorously applied purge of the bureaucracy, and it resulted not only in the removal of numerous Nazi officeholders but also in the destruction of the old administrative machinery of the state. Of course, not all former officeholders—indeed, not all former Nazis—were necessarily purged. Some, especially if they had essential skills, such as military ones, were retained; usually in such cases the persons involved had undergone political "re-education," often in the "Antifa" schools in Soviet POW camps.

These and other measures of radical social and economic reform met with the approval not only of Socialists and Communists, but also of many Germans who were convinced that such measures were necessary to ensure the emergence of a truly democratic Germany. From the Soviet and German Communist perspectives, they laid the foundation for the transformation of German society into a Soviet-style one. Whatever the motives, the effect was to finish what Hitler and the war had only begun: the breakup of the aristocratic-bourgeois order that had dominated Bismarck's German nation-state and had defeated the reform efforts of the Weimar republicans.[8]

These measures of social transformation were accompanied by a steady radicalization of SBZ political life. This radicalization had two dimensions: the consolidation of the SED's position as a ruling party, and movement away from any accommodation with West German forces in the interest of national unity.[9]

The goal of German unity had not lost any of its normative power, however, and German politicians in both East and West continued their verbal support of such unity. When formal interzonal German meetings failed to produce any accord (as occurred in 1947, with the Munich conference of German state administrative chiefs), both sides resorted to the easier, albeit less effective, weapon of proclamations. In this regard, the SED leaders were at a great advantage. Calls for joint action by all Germans could be issued in the secure knowledge that oppositional political activity in the SBZ was becoming steadily more difficult. In 1947, large-scale arrests of Social Democrats and other enemies of the SED began, often carried out by the Soviet authorities directly. As Soviet control over political life in the SBZ tightened, and as more leeway for political activity was granted to Germans in the Western zones, the early Soviet political advantage in competititon for German favor faded. In circumstances of deepening cold war, Soviet influence was increasingly limited to the Soviet Zone itself.

In 1948, in the wake of the Soviet-Yugoslav dispute, the SED was forced onto a path that led away from all-German, generally democratic appeals. Back in 1946, in a key ideological move within the struggle to unite the SPD and KPD, the Communist theoretician and party official Anton Ackermann asked, "Is there a special German road to socialism?" He answered his own question in the affirmative, declaring that the special circumstances of postwar Germany made a peaceful and parliamentary path to socialism possible.[10] Now, in September 1948, Ackermann was forced to withdraw his thesis. This ideological shift marked a shift in the nature of the SED as such; it now became a "party of a new type." This meant the elimination of all Social Democratic influence in the party. The SED began to purge "Titoists," "Zionists," and persons who had simply spent the Hitler years in Western exile. (Unlike parallel processes in the Hungarian, Czechoslovak, and other parties, the East German purges did not result in death sentences.)

To cement the SED's hold on Soviet Zone politics, the SMAD and SED saw to the establishment of subservient parties designed to mobilize specific social strata behind the zonal authorities. These were the National Democratic party (NDPD) and the Democratic Peasants' party (DBD). The former was founded to recruit right-wing nationalists and especially former rank-and-file Nazis; the latter was aimed especially at the peasant beneficiaries of the earlier land reform. With the admission of these parties into the "Antifascist Bloc," the SED's control over the formally multiparty political system of the SBZ was complete.

As the East-West struggle over Germany intensified with the collapse of four-power control in March 1948 and the imposition in June of the Berlin Blockade, each Great Power sponsored German representative assemblies to advance its cause. In the SBZ, this was the German People's Congress (*Deutsche Volkskongress*). The sessions of this "Congress," which always had some West German members, were the counterpart of the Parliamentary Council in the Western zones, and, as such, they prepared the way for the establishment of a separate German state.

The decisive steps were taken at the sessions of the Third *Volkskongress* in May 1949. In the elections to this body, the voters had been asked in an advisory referendum whether they desired a united Germany and a German peace treaty. A "yes" vote for this attractive proposition was also counted as a vote for a single-list slate of candidates. Even so, only 66.1 percent of the valid votes were cast in favor. The session then elected a 330-member People's Council (*Volksrat*), in which the SED and mass organizations subservient to it held 210 seats. The *Volksrat* then prepared a constitutional draft and took other steps to prepare for the founding of an East German state.

In response to the emergence of the West German Federal Republic (FRG), the *Volksrat*, on October 7, 1949, constituted itself as a provisional *Volkskammer* (People's Chamber), while on October 10 the legislatures of the five *Laender* elected delegates to a provisional upper house. The two chambers, meeting jointly, proclaimed the German Democratic

Republic, adopted its constitution, selected Otto Grotewohl (in 1945–1946 the leader of the SPD in the Soviet Zone) as the provisional chairman of the Council of Ministers, and a day later elected the veteran Communist, Wilhelm Pieck, as the provisional president of the republic (and thus head of state). Elections, which were put off until 1950, were then held for a single list of candidates, with seats distributed in advance among the parties and mass organizations.

What Stalin's long-term expectations for Germany were remain unclear.[11] Certainly he could not have been too hopeful that the Western powers would abandon German resources to him. Nevertheless, the postwar Soviet position in Europe was sufficiently strong as to make some hope of political gain seem reasonable. All-German institutions had been established under Soviet tutelage in the old German capital. The economic future of the Western zones, with their large concentrations of industrial workers, was widely thought to be bleak. Until the collapse of four-power administration in Germany in 1948–1949, Soviet policy focused on all of Germany and retained a measure of non-Communist support for its policies.

Thus, while the existence of the GDR in one sense signaled the failure of Soviet policy on an all-German basis, it was not until the mid-1950s that the Soviet leadership abandoned any but extremely long-term hopes for such an extension of Soviet power.

THE CONSOLIDATION OF THE GDR (1949–1971)

At its beginnings in 1949, the GDR was an unusually provisional political entity. It lacked substantial legitimacy for many of its people; its relationships to the one-time united Germany, as well as to the other, also newly-formed, West German state were unclear; and its field of action was severely restricted by the power of its sponsor and occupier, the USSR. Internationally, it was recognized by only a small number of Communist states; its very existence as a sovereign entity was denied by the Western powers.

Fourteen years later, the GDR was a member of the United Nations and generally recognized by other states; its relationship with the USSR was that of a valued junior partner in economic and military alliances, and its relationship with West Germany was regulated by treaty; its economic successes were considerable, and its political system was stable and at least acceptable to the bulk of the population. We must now review the development of this remarkable record of the consolidation of a state.

The consolidation of the GDR was accompanied by a narrowing of political focus from an all-German to an East German field of action. For the leaders of party and state who dominated the GDR in its early years, it was self-evident to think in all-German terms. A unitary German republic had been an important ideological goal for Socialists and

Communists before and during the Hitler era; their plans for the future had been drawn with all of Germany in mind.

Moreover, just as political leaders in Bonn presented the West German state as the only legitimate German state, with its democratic political system as a model for all of Germany, so did the political leaders in East Berlin present their state as a German core territory and the social and economic institutions emerging in the GDR as a model for all of Germany.[12]

During the first years of the GDR, however, these two aspects of its policy—the national and the social—came increasingly into conflict with one another. Stalinist policies rendered the GDR less attractive to many Germans, East or West. Moreover, the increasing social differentiation of the two Germanies dampened hopes for speedy reunification. Crucial in this regard was the decision of July 1952 (at the SED Second Party Conference) to proceed with the "construction of socialism in the GDR." Although this turning point in the social development of *one* part of Germany was depicted as fostering the attainment of a united, independent, peace-loving, and democratic Germany, it was clearly a step that impeded any uniform development for the country as a whole. In any case, the circumstances of increasing cold war made the all-German objectives recede as feasible goals. In domestic as in foreign policy, assumptions based on German unity and autonomy had to be abandoned.

Thus the GDR's leaders had to choose between their all-German ambitions and the preservation of their power over the limited territory of their country. During successive crises, the GDR leadership was divided on this fundamental issue; in each case, the political outcome was to strengthen those forces that stressed the security of the GDR at the expense, if necessary, of all-German appeals. In each case, this choice paralleled, and was made possible by, a similar Soviet decision. In this historical-national context, what was at stake in the crises of 1953, 1956, 1961, and 1971 was the very existence of the GDR.[13]

Crises (1953–1971)

The 1953 crisis was brought on by the shift of Soviet policy in the wake of Stalin's death—a shift, that is, toward the "New Course" of ameliorating living standards and revoking some of the worst political and judicial abuses of Stalin's last years. In the GDR, this New Course meant a reduction of the political stature of the SED leaders, an improvement in living standards, and a lessening of the political hostility expressed against such groups as intellectuals, peasants, and artisans— in short, a slowing of the 1952 campaign of "building socialism." An increase in work norms on construction projects was not revoked, however, thus leading on June 16 and 17 to strikes and demonstrations. Eventually, the unrest in Berlin and in a number of other GDR cities had to be put down by Soviet armed force.

June, 1953: Construction workers from Stalinallee (now Karl Marx Allee) march toward the center of East Berlin. Photo courtesy of the German Information Center, New York.

The 1956 crisis was also brought on by Soviet developments—specifically by the beginning of de-Stalinization in the wake of the CPSU Twentieth Congress. In the GDR, unrest was especially widespread among intellectuals, but not within the working class, which had gained some concessions from the regime. Within the party leadership a struggle emerged concerning the proper conclusions to be drawn from de-Stalinization. As in 1953, a faction in the party leadership wished for greater liberalization, partly in order to appeal to West Germans; once again, more conservative elements, pointing to dangers for the political security of the regime, gained Soviet backing and won out.

Similar forces were at work in the next great crisis of the GDR's consolidation—namely, the internal and external pressures that led to the building of the Berlin Wall on August 13, 1961. Internally, the regime's grandiose economic goals led to severe shortfalls in the planned growth of industrial production in 1959–1960; this period was also the height of the crisis over collectivization. Moreover, beginning in November 1958, the Soviet Union, under Khrushchev's leadership, tried to settle the Berlin question on Soviet terms. The possibility of drastic change, especially in access to West Berlin or in the use of the transit routes across the GDR, had an extremely unsettling effect on large numbers

June, 1953: Demonstrators burn an official propaganda kiosk near the Potsdamer Platz, East Berlin. Photo courtesy of the German Information Center, New York.

June, 1953: Soviet forces intervene—the officer in the tank is Soviet General Kutzoba. Photo courtesy of the German Information Center, New York.

June, 1953: Freedom fighters make a futile effort against the Communist regime's oppression (East Berlin). Photo courtesy of the German Information Center, New York.

of East Germans. A frantic rush to leave the country ensued. The numbers of refugees had always reflected either a sense of crisis or one of relative well-being in the GDR; in the panicky atmosphere of early 1961, monthly refugee totals rose toward 50,000 (the entire number for 1960 had been just under 200,000). Something clearly had to be done, as a disproportionate share of those fleeing were young people, some with important technical skills, needed for the labor force.

This "something" was the closing off of access to West Berlin by transforming the sector lines into a formal frontier. A meeting of Soviet-bloc first-secretaries in Moscow (August 3–5, 1961) approved the decision to seal off the border. The Berlin Wall closed off a chapter in GDR and postwar German history. It physically symbolized the apparent per-manence of those "provisional" arrangements made at the war's end. In West Germany it was taken to mean that the Allied commitment to German unification was only verbal, whereas in the GDR the Wall represented the end of all hopes for all-German political action.

For the final consolidation of a separate East German state there remained the routinization of its relationship to West Germany and to the remaining symbol of all-German politics, West Berlin. Once again, the primary impulse for change came from Soviet sources (this time together with West Germany's "new Eastern policy").[14] The de facto acceptance of the existing European interstate relations came at the expense of the GDR. The GDR's ability to exert pressure on Berlin and the Federal Republic was reduced, and its prior conditions for an East-West accommodation (such as formal recognition) were pushed aside.

As before, the GDR leadership was divided in its response to this new situation. Soviet pressure helped to install a leadership that accepted the new situation. With the conclusion of the treaties between Bonn and the Soviet, Polish, and GDR governments, as well as the Four-Power Agreement on Berlin (1971–1973), the GDR was established as an East German state. It drew the appropriate policy consequences—specifically, the policy of "demarcation" (*Abgrenzung*) from the West. The GDR would now be a state oriented toward participation in a Soviet-dominated commonwealth. Its contacts with the Federal Republic would be as commonplace as its diplomacy could arrange. Indeed, the GDR's chief contact with things German came to focus on the German past, on the GDR's German heritage (*Erbe*).

Political Leadership

More than most states, the German Democratic Republic is the creation of its political leadership. If it was said of Prussia that it represented "an army that had a state," so may it be said of the GDR that it was formed by a "party that has a state." The consolidation of the GDR as an East German successor state of the pre-1945 Reich cannot, therefore, be understood apart from the development of the SED as a ruling party. Each stage in the establishment of the GDR was paralleled by conflicts within the party; the consolidation of the GDR was paralleled by the consolidation of the party's position in society.

The transformation of the SED into a Soviet-style party after 1948–1949 increased the power of the party apparatus, and thus also the power of the chief manipulator of that apparatus and the most important actual leader of the party, Walter Ulbricht.[15] One-time non-Communist elements were eliminated: the leader who led the SPD into the unity party, Otto Grotewohl, was by 1950 one of only three former Social Democrats remaining in the leadership.

The consolidation of Ulbricht's leadership within the SED meant that, as in other East European Communist parties, groups of Communists were singled out for political suppression. These included those party workers who had been in exile in the West, Communists who had had contact with Noel Field, the American relief administrator and OSS contact during the war, and (in 1952–1953) several leading Jewish Communists. It must be noted that, unlike Hungary or Czechoslovakia, East Germany had no late-Stalinist show trials, and none of the leading intraparty oppositional figures was executed.

When in early 1953 Ulbricht succeeded in undermining the position of his chief rival within the Politburo, Franz Dahlem, it seemed that Ulbricht's position as effective head of the SED (he had become general secretary of the Central Committee in 1950) was secure. The SED seemed ready to be used for the "building of socialism" in the GDR. Both this policy and Ulbricht's leadership underwent a severe crisis, however, in the period of the early post-Stalin "thaw." For Ulbricht and the SED, the New Course, and the workers' uprising of June 17, 1953, marked a challenge to the party's position in society and to Ulbricht's leadership of the party. The SED responded to this crisis by mandating material concessions to the population and (in early 1954, when the storm had abated) by instituting a purge of the SED membership. Ulbricht in July 1953 beat back the opposition led by Wilhelm Zaisser, the head of the security police; Rudolf Herrnstadt, editor of the party daily, *Neues Deutschland*; and others. It is noteworthy that Ulbricht's position was saved in part by the fact that Zaisser had had close ties to the Soviet secret police chief, Lavrenti Beria. It was later alleged that Beria, as part of his drive for power in Moscow, was prepared to make concessions on the German question in dealing with the West. In any case, when Beria was removed from power in June 1953, his SED contacts lost their positions as well. In Beria's disgrace lay Ulbricht's salvation.

After the denunciation of Stalin at the CPSU's Twentieth Congress (February 1956), the party's leading role in society and Ulbricht's leading role within the party came under renewed attack by party leaders and membership. The crisis over de-Stalinization led to an attempt to replace Ulbricht with a more "liberal" leadership. The leading figures in this conspiracy were Karl Schirdewan, a powerful Politburo member and party secretary, and Ernst Wollweber, Zaisser's successor as security chief. Once more Ulbricht's enemies seemed to have Soviet backing; but in the winter of 1956–1957, with Khrushchev's power temporarily in eclipse, Ulbricht was able to save his position. He declared calls for reform—and especially calls for postponement of full socialism in the GDR to keep alive a last chance at German unity—to be a form of revisionism, then the main ideological enemy. In 1957–1958, the anti-Ulbricht group was denounced and removed from party positions, and its supporters were purged. By the SED's Fifth Congress (July 1958), Ulbricht's position was secure and remained so for thirteen more years.

Party leaderships increasingly consisted of long-time allies and younger followers. The Politburo members elected at the Sixth and Seventh SED Party Congresses (in 1963 and 1967, respectively) consisted of old Communist allies, a very few docile former SPDers, and a large number of younger protégés, including Ulbricht's eventual successor, Erich Honecker.

Walter Ulbricht. Ulbricht's power within the party and state stemmed from several factors.[16] His own considerable skills at political manipulation helped to bring him to the top and to keep him there. Until the very end of his career, he was devoted to Soviet interests and managed to retain Soviet support; it is significant that in the crisis of 1960–1961, which culminated in the building of the Berlin Wall, there was no thought given to replacing Ulbricht.

The political history of Communist states is in large measure the history of particular leaders. Power in the GDR has been in the hands of two such leaders: Walter Ulbricht (to 1971) and Erich Honecker (1971 to present). The power of each has rested above all on control of the ruling party, the SED. Both have counted on at least toleration by Soviet leaders. Both added to their party functions the supervision of the armed forces and a formal role as head of state. In this latter capacity, they have conducted foreign policy in the personalized style so common today.[17]

Ulbricht's early life and political career bridge the nineteenth-century world of Central European Social Democracy and the contemporary era of a superpower world and a divided Europe. Along with others in the left wing of the prewar SPD, he joined the German Communist movement, which, in the 1920s, was the largest Leninist party outside the Soviet Union. Ulbricht's career in the KPD was marked by two qualities that were to become notorious in the postwar days of his power: loyalty to Soviet wishes and dedication to administrative detail.

As "Comrade Cell," Ulbricht gained a deserved reputation as an organizational technician. Until 1958–1960, however, he was always in the shadows of power, allowing others to have a more public role. His notoriously humorless and unremitting attention to cadre policy, while it kept him from attaining personal popularity within the party, made him the master of its bureaucracy and, hence, of the party itself.

Ulbricht's survival in the crises of 1953 and 1956–1957 was due in part to this coolness and political daring, his understanding that his first concession would signal to an irresolute majority in the SED leadership that he could be defeated, and his manipulation of the Soviet and SED leaders.

In the last decade and a half of his power, Ulbricht demonstrated that he could even use deviation from Soviet aims to maintain and expand his own power. Cleverly assuming the post-Stalin line of "many roads to socialism," he defended any divergence from Soviet policy as a legitimate adaptation to GDR-specific conditions. Moreover, he wanted to be a notable theoretician. Such interesting notions as that of a Socialist community in a long, historically autonomous period of socialism and that of the building of socialism in the GDR as providing a generally valid example of socialism under conditions of mature technology and industry were the ideological adornments of the deliberate glorification of Ulbricht typical of the 1960s.

During the 1960s, Ulbricht became the formal head of state of the GDR and, in the propaganda of the time, an avuncular elder statesman. In the face of renewed pressure for de-Stalinization after 1961, for example, his position was defended by Honecker and other party subordinates with the public avowal, "*Ulbricht—das sind wir alle*" ("We are all Ulbricht").

Yet, despite his service and his standing, Ulbricht could not survive the crisis of 1970–1971. His ideological posturing and failures in his economic policy had alienated both internal rivals and the Soviet leadership. When he became an obstacle in the way of Soviet–West German détente, he was removed from the party leadership in May 1971. (He was given an honorific party post and allowed to remain as head of state until his death in August 1973.)

The years of Ulbricht's ascendancy saw the completion of the basic structure of a Socialist society in the GDR. In politics this meant the consolidation of Ulbricht's hold on a relatively stable party leadership. In economics, the years from 1958 to 1970 saw the final triumph of nationalized industry as the main employer of labor and in control of productive resources; the remaining private enterprises, including retail trade and artisan workshops, were phased out. The system of national economic planning was firmly established. Finally, a massive propaganda and harassment campaign between late 1959 and June 1960 resulted in the complete collectivization of agriculture.

Many important GDR social policies originated in this period. They include the comprehensive ten-year secondary school, the general support and preferment of youth, the public subsidy and control of sports, the stress on the utility of science and technology, and the development of an indigenous GDR culture.

Erich Honecker. With Honecker's accession to the party leadership, the GDR entered a new stage of its history—one in which it still finds itself today. Characteristic of this era is a shift in policy focus both at home and abroad. From setting the foundations of the political and social order and achieving international recognition, the regime's attention has turned to solving the problems arising from the existence of a socialist order at home to conducting an active foreign policy in Soviet bloc affairs toward the Third World and in inter-German relations.

Along with the other East European regimes and the USSR itself, the GDR has experimented with reform of the planning system; it has also sought to satisfy an increasing demand for consumption, incurring a growing hard-currency debt in the process. In common with other Communist states, the GDR has dealt with the regulation of culture, a task made especially difficult for it by the fact of common language and literary heritage with West Germany.

In recent years, the GDR has become a Soviet-bloc military power. Its armed forces have assumed an increasingly important role within the Warsaw Treaty Organization (they participated in the 1968 invasion of Czechoslovakia), and it has actively projected its military power into the Third World.

Politically, the system of Communist party–state rule has been maintained. Since 1956, none of the political storms that have affected, say, Poland or Czechoslovakia have occurred in the GDR. Even the replacement of Ulbricht by Honecker in 1971 had few immediate repercussions in the structure or personnel of power in the GDR. The GDR has become a stable, effectively governed, economically viable state.

Throughout this latest era of GDR history, Erich Honecker has been its political leader. He has faced problems quite different from those that confronted his predecessor. The very successes of the GDR before Honecker put dramatic social transformation out of Honecker's reach. It achieved a breakthrough to general international recognition and UN membership in 1971–1973, at the very start of the Honecker era. Honecker's tasks are thus very different from those that confronted Ulbricht; Honecker's rise to power was necessarily different from Ulbricht's; and finally, by all accounts, Honecker's less driven, less forbidding personality is certainly different from Ulbricht's.

Born on August 25, 1912,[18] Honecker became politically aware in the post–World War I period, when German radicals, especially in the Saar and adjacent Rhineland, fought "French imperialism" as enthusiastically as they had fought German capitalism. Later in his career, he reacted vehemently to the suggestion of French control of the Saar. When Hitler came to power, Honecker was, like Ulbricht, a party *aparatchik* (of a lower rank), but unlike him he spent most of the twelve years of the "Thousand Year Reich" within Germany and, indeed, in jail. After some adventurous underground years, Honecker was arrested in Berlin in 1935 and two years later was sentenced to prison, from which he was not finally freed until the coming of Soviet forces in May 1945.[19]

Honecker greets a group of youngsters. Photo courtesy of the GDR Embassy, Washington, D.C.

An important aspect of Honecker's early political activity concerns the enormous impression left on him by the experience of common struggle and sacrifice among his fellow foes of Hitler. Honecker feels (or now affects to feel) a strong bond to those days of struggle. Thus he briefly relaxed the de facto house arrest of the dissident physicist Robert Havemann, so that the latter could attend the celebration of the thirty-fifth anniversary of their liberation from Brandenburg prison; he also arranged for his biographer and one-time youth group collaborator, Heinz Lippmann, to receive official materials regarding Honecker's early life—an extraordinary concession to a defected former GDR official.

Honecker's attitude to the political past is an intriguing one. In his memoirs he mentions in a matter-of-fact (and occasionally favorable) way a number of Soviet and GDR political leaders of the past who were purged. For many years, the one leader rarely mentioned in the Honecker era was Walter Ulbricht; in 1983, however, even he achieved an honorable public rehabilitation,[20] thus expanding the historical foundations of the present regime.

Another important aspect of Honecker's early career is that he met many important GDR leaders while he himself was still in his twenties. They include the present Defense Minister Heinz Hoffmann, chief party ideologue Kurt Hager, and (until 1983) the party security overseer Paul Verner. Honecker, now in his seventies, is thus a personal link to the older generation of German communism, although he also represents, and is related to as a patron by, many of the younger state and party leaders (due especially to his leadership of the youth organization).

Finally, Honecker's career shows a strong connection with, and a marked predilection for, the Soviet Union. Honecker visited the USSR for a year (1930–1931) as a student at the cadre school of the Communist Youth International. His experiences there (including a volunteer stint in Magnitorgorsk) left him with a lasting and favorable impression of the "heroic age" of Soviet industrialization. In 1947, Honecker led a GDR youth delegation to the USSR—the first official contact with other countries allowed the Germans after the war. The scenes of wartime devastation, still visible in the Soviet cities and countryside, left an indelible impression on Honecker, whose steadfast commitment to GDR-Soviet ties was sealed at that time.

Honecker's postwar career took place entirely within the youth group (FDJ) and party hierarchies. He headed the FDJ between 1946 and 1955, and during those years was also active in party affairs—in particular, as a Politburo candidate member after 1950. Throughout this period, Honecker had no direct experience of the administration of affairs; he was always the organizer, agitator, and supervisor. His success was due in equal measure to his own abilities and to the patronage of Ulbricht (the most important political decision of his life was to side with Ulbricht against intraparty rivals). This sort of career may carry with it the disadvantage of not dealing with administrative problems (as a youth leader Honecker was apparently notoriously lax in office routine), but it perhaps gives a person a surer feel for the political adjustments needed to maintain support from diverse constituencies.

Honecker's career as a rising party leader included as an important step his third visit to the USSR. From mid-1955 to mid-1956, he attended the Higher Party School of the CPSU in Moscow. Honecker returned to the GDR to side with Ulbricht in 1956–1958, and he emerged from that crisis, in effect, as Ulbricht's deputy for party affairs, charged with supervision of the military and security forces. He was "Crown Prince" unless he blundered—and this he did not do. When internal and external pressures led the Soviet Union to favor a change in GDR and SED leadership, Honecker was the obvious choice as party leader. As party first-secretary (and then general secretary), Honecker gradually assumed the same positions of power that Ulbricht had held. In addition to becoming party leader in 1971, he also took control of the National Defense Council; in 1976 Honecker became head of state as well.

In office, Honecker has stressed themes and activities that marked his earlier career: fidelity to the Soviet Union; ideological conformity modified by a desire to win over key social groups (exemplified by the fluctuations of his cultural policy); primacy of the party in political life and a gradual strengthening of his position within the party while avoiding demotions of opponents; a clear priority for GDR stability over riskier closeness to West Germany and to all-German themes; and close attention to the material and ideological foundations of the GDR armed forces.

The major policy innovation of the Honecker regime has been the stress on consumerist and welfare issues, especially housing and family services. Not unlike other industrially developed East European regimes, the GDR under Honecker has become a country where economic advance, social security, and reward for achievement are made the basis for regime legitimacy. The GDR's main task in the 1980s is to ensure, despite less favorable external conditions, that economic and social progress continue through technological intensification. The party and FDJ leader has become the enthusiast for microprocessors and industrial robots. In this, Honecker personifies the planned and hoped-for transition of the GDR from an embattled ideological outpost to a secure, modern, and accepted state.

In foreign affairs, Honecker has found opportunities for a prominent personal role. Beginning with his appearance at the 1975 Helsinki Conference (seated between Schmidt and Ford) and, subsequently, while visiting states in Africa, the Middle East, and the Orient (Japan, India, the Philippines), traveling to Austria, Cyprus, Mexico, and receiving Schmidt in the GDR, Honecker has had a chance to enhance his personal leadership and to identify himself in the minds and on the television screens of the GDR population with the emergence of the GDR to accepted world status.

In his eighth decade, Honecker has become the dominant figure of GDR politics, with his position marked by growing personal acclaim. His position within the SED is supreme, especially following the personnel changes in the party leadership in 1983–1984. After years of close relations with Leonid Brezhnev, he negotiated the transition to the Andropov regime with some success. Under Chernenko, Honecker's policies (especially in inter-German affairs) were seemingly set back, as in the cancellation of Honecker's visit to West Germany planned for September 1984. It is too early to tell how he will fare under Gorbachev— but the observable continuities between the latter's policies and those of Andropov bode well for Honecker.[21]

THE GEOGRAPHY OF THE GDR

Almost unique among developed industrial states, the German Democratic Republic exists without regard either for natural or historical regions or for the cultural or political heritage of a particular territory. The GDR is, rather, the result of historical and political forces external to Germany. The most important of these events and forces were the military defeat of the unitary German nation-state in its Nazi incarnation and the occupation of an east-central portion of the country by the armed forces of the Soviet Union.

The city of Stralsund lies in the Baltic region of the GDR. Photo courtesy of the GDR Embassy, Washington, D.C.

Territories to the east of today's GDR were lost to Poland and to the USSR; Austrian lands to the south resumed their separate identity; a similarly truncated and occupied German state emerged to the west, with the Saar territory possibly lost to France. This Federal Republic of Germany (FRG), however, acknowledged itself from the beginning to be the legal successor to a German national state that had emerged in 1871, whereas the GDR sees itself as a newly created, socially quite different, and juridically totally separate state.

Territory and Borders

The present territory of the GDR encompasses some 108,910 square kilometers, slightly less than half the area of the Federal Republic of Germany and something like one-fifth of the Germany of 1937.[22] Its northern portion consists of parts of the North German plain and the Baltic coastal regions, including sections of the former provinces of Mecklenburg and the old Brandenburg heart of Prussia. To the south are the mountainous province of Thuringia and the historically important and socially and economically developed lands of Saxony. These areas form an agglomeration of regional units without common focus or history (although, of course, particular areas, such as Saxony, do have their traditions).

The northern frontier of the GDR is the Baltic Sea coast from which there are ship and ferry ties to Scandinavia; a direct sea link is being built from the Baltic island of Rügen to the Lithuanian coast of the USSR. To the east is the Oder-Neisse frontier with Poland; from 1972 to 1980 this was almost a control-free border for GDR citizens, but in 1980–1981, as in 1956, it became a sealed and politically sensitive frontier. To the south and southeast is the border with Czechoslovakia, where a similar fluctuation of controls has occurred. To the west and southwest is the long border with the Federal Republic. It is important to note here that the entire 1381-kilometer border has been closed since 1952, and that it has become the most heavily controlled and fortified border in the world. Along its eastern edge, in the GDR, lies a security zone larger than Luxembourg, counting the 275-meter-wide mined and plowed strip, the 500-meter-wide guarded strip, and the 5-kilometer-wide restricted access area.[23]

Population

The population density of the GDR is between 155 and 160 persons per square kilometer.[24] Aside from heavily settled territory around the port and shipping areas of the Baltic coast, the bulk of the GDR population lives in and around East Berlin and in the industrial and urban centers of Saxony and Thuringia. The population of the GDR as of 1980 stood at 16,737,204, of which 53 percent is female. After a slight rise in the years between 1946 and 1948, due largely to an influx of refugees from Eastern Europe, the GDR has steadily lost in population, although the birth rate has risen slowly since 1974 and in 1980 stood at 14.6 live births per thousand of population. The 1983 figure was 14.0, with 233,736 live births in 1983.

The demographic situation in the GDR is complicated by the effects of large-scale migration to West Germany on the age structure and fertility of the population. The GDR is one of the world's few advanced countries in which migration played an important role in population change. Between 1950 and 1975, some 2.5 million persons, or 13 percent of the 1950 population, left the country. Especially prior to 1961, those fleeing to West Germany were very often young people in the economically most productive age groups, thus contributing to the marked shortage of males in crucial military and industrial age cohorts.

Moreover, the years of dictatorship and war, and especially the dislocations of the war's final months, had a profound effect on the social composition of the population of the future GDR. The influx of refugees from further east, the evacuation of people from major cities to escape bombing raids, and shifts in the location of productive facilities all helped to uproot many people from traditional regional and local social settings. The substantial Jewish population, especially the Jewish people in Berlin, vanished almost entirely. Finally, unlike the former united Germany, the GDR became overwhelmingly Protestant.

These basic demographic conditions underlie many particular GDR problems and developments, including the building of the Berlin Wall; the extraordinarily high percentage of women in the labor force (in the early 1970s, over 80 percent of all women between the ages of 18 and 60 were employed); a variety of pronatalist policies; emotional and biological pressures on single women; and the use of East European foreign labor (chiefly Polish and Hungarian) on a project-contract basis.[25]

The GDR is an urbanized society; a quarter of the overall population lives in the fifteen cities in the GDR with populations exceeding 100,000. Leipzig and Dresden number over a half-million each and East Berlin—or "Berlin the Capital City" ("Hauptstadt Berlin"), as it is officially termed—has more than one million inhabitants.

The Natural Resource Base

The GDR as a society reflects the physical basis of its geography.[26] In an echo of one aspect of the German past—that of Prussia—the GDR has become a highly developed society despite its poor endowments of natural resources for industry and agriculture.

With regard to fuel, the GDR has no economically significant anthracite deposits and only negligible amounts of bituminous coal. Its chief domestic fuel resource is lignite, of which the GDR is the world's largest producer. Lignite is increasingly being used for generating electricity; its extraction has brought with it extensive problems of land despoliation through open-pit mining and excessive demands on water supply. There are no useful indigenous oil sources and only small amounts of natural gas. It is undoubtedly significant in this context that the GDR has extensive plans for generating electric power from nuclear reactors.

Perhaps typical of GDR development is the growth of an extensive iron and steel industry without significant deposits of iron ore and inadequate supplies of coking coal.[27] Reserves of such nonferrous metals as copper, zinc, lead, and tin are small, and production has remained steady in recent years; yet these modest extractions, largely from familiar mining areas—and including those that gave the mountains of the southwestern GDR their name of "ore mountains" (Erzgebirge)—are important to domestic industry as well as to trade within the CMEA community. Finally, the GDR's extensive chemical industry uses important domestic raw materials, especially potash.

Special mention should be made of the extensive deposits of uranium ore near the Czech border.[28] With an estimated annual production of 5,000 tons of uranium oxide, the GDR ranks as one of the world's major uranium producers; since 1947, all uranium production has been in the hands of a special (and since 1954 a joint GDR-Soviet) company, Wismut AG. All of the ore produced apparently goes to the USSR. An indication of the importance of this enterprise is that its SED party organization has a status equivalent to that of a regional (Bezirk) committee.

Resources for Agriculture

Agricultural production is ultimately dependent on soil, climate, and water. The GDR's climate is a mixture of cool and wet winters along the Baltic coast and drier weather in the southern uplands. In any case, the weather is not an obstacle to effective agriculture.

A major problem does exist, however, in the loss of arable soil to urban and industrial uses; annually this amounts to about 10,000 hectares.[29] Compounding the problem is the fact that the best stretch of agricultural land, running southeast from Magdeburg to Dresden, is also the site of important industries, with all their heavy demands on water supplies. This situation has led to a campaign to improve soil quality and ensure adequate water supplies, although the amount of acreage irrigated and drained, after rising in the early and middle 1970s, dropped toward the end of the decade.

This brief survey of the GDR's natural resources indicates the extent to which the GDR's economic progress is dependent on a skilled labor force and technical innovation and efficiency, and why it is that precisely these factors should have come to the forefront of economic discussion in the GDR in the 1980s.

NOTES

1. An excellent introduction to modern German life and politics is Gordon A. Craig, *The Germans* (New York: Putnam, 1982). Notable among the many narrative accounts of German history are Geoffrey Barraclough, *The Origins of Modern Germany*, 2nd ed. (Oxford: Basil Blackwell, 1949); Frederick Heer, *The Holy Roman Empire* (New York: Praeger Publishers, 1968); Hajo Holborn, *A History of Modern Germany*, 3 vols. (New York: Alfred A. Knopf, 1959–1969); Golo Mann, *The History of Germany Since 1789* (New York: Praeger Publishers, 1968); and Gordon A. Craig, *Germany, 1866–1945* (New York: Oxford University Press, 1978).

2. There have been many studies of the collapse of German civilization into the Third Reich. Of those in English, some of the more important are Ralf Dahrendorf, *Society and Democracy in Germany* (New York: Norton, 1979); Karl Dietrich Bracher, *The German Dictatorship* (New York: Praeger Publishers, 1970); Peter Gay, *Weimar Culture: The Outsider as Insider* (New York: Harper & Row, 1968); and Alan Bullock, *Hitler: A Study in Tyranny* (Oxford: Oxford University Press, 1957). Two provocative studies of Germany's contentious role in world affairs are Fritz Fischer, *Germany's Aims in the First World War* (New York: Norton, 1967); and David Calleo, *The German Problem Reconsidered* (New York: Cambridge University Press, 1978).

3. There is a truly enormous literature on the wartime and postwar diplomacy relating to the future of Germany, as well as on the domestic origins of postwar German politics. A discussion of the expectations of postwar German foreign relations held by political actors in the Soviet Zone of Occupation is in Henry Krisch, "Vorstellungen von künftiger aussenpolitischer Orientierungen der SBZ bis 1947 und ihre Auswirkungen auf die spätere Aussenpolitik der

DDR," in Eberhard Schulz, ed., *Drei Jahrzehnte Aussenpolitik der DDR* (Munich: R. Oldenbourg, 1979), ch. 1.

4. Roy E. H. Mellor, *The Two Germanies: A Modern Geography* (New York: Harper & Row/Barnes & Noble, 1978), pp. 153–154.

5. The zonal borders, and thus the present East–West German border, largely followed existing internal German administrative divisions. Since 1972, a joint East–West German commission has been marking the frontier but has been unable to agree on its location along a section of the Elbe River. The western side wants it to run along the GDR bank, corresponding to a former internal German border; the GDR side wants the border drawn at midstream or midchannel, which would follow general international practice and thus (presumably) enhance the interstate nature of the frontier. A lengthy polemical exchange on this point has taken place since Honecker forced the issue in his Gera speech of October 1980. See, for example, *Frankfurter Allgemeine Zeitung*, 7 May 1981, p. 6.

6. Two monographs on related aspects of this topic are Henry Krisch, *German Politics Under Soviet Occupation* (New York: Columbia University Press, 1974); and Gregory W. Sandford, *From Hitler to Ulbricht* (Princeton, N.J.: Princeton University Press, 1983).

7. For a discussion on the breakdown of Allied unity, see F. Roy Willis, *The French in Germany* (Stanford, Calif.: Stanford University Press, 1962); and John H. Backer, *The Decision to Divide Germany* (Durham, N.C.: Duke University Press, 1978), especially chs. 3, 4, and 7.

8. For an excellent survey as well as documentation of this early period, see Hermann Weber, *Kleine Geschichte der DDR* (Cologne: Edition Deutschland Archiv, 1980), ch. 1.

9. The following discussion is based in part on Weber, *Kleine Geschichte*, chs. 2 and 3; and Dietrich Staritz, *Sozialismus in einem halben Land* (Berlin: Verlag Klaus Wagenbach, 1976). A GDR account is Rolf Badstubner and Heinz Heitzer, eds., *Die DDR in der Übergangsperiode* (Berlin: Dietz, 1979). See also Stefan Doernberg, *Die Geburt eines neuen Deutschlands, 1945–1949* (Berlin: Dietz, 1959).

10. Anton Ackerman, "Gibt es einen besonderen deutschen Weg zum Sozialismus?" *Einehit* 1 (February 1946):23–32; Krisch, *German Politics*, pp. 143, 191–194. One of the earliest Western discussions of this issue appears in Melvin Croan, "Soviet Uses of the Doctrine of the 'Parliamentary Road' to Socialism: East Germany, 1945–1946, *American Slavic and East European Review* 17 (October 1958):302–315.

11. Krisch, *German Politics*, pp. 200–210; Alexander Fischer, "Aussenpolitische Aktivität bei ungewisser Sowjetischer Deutschlandpolitik (bis 1955)," in Schulz, ed., *Drei Jahrzehnte*, pp. 51–84. Stalin's congratulatory telegram to the new GDR leadership is reprinted in Weber, *Kleine Geschichte*, p. 53.

12. Wilhelm Bleek, "Einheitspartei und Nationalfrage," in *Der X. Parteitag der SED. 35 Jahre SED Politik-Versuch einer Bilanz* (Cologne: Edition Deutschland Archiv, 1981).

13. Weber, *Kleine Geschichte*, chs. 2 and 3; Ilse Spittmann and Karl Wilhelm Fricke, eds., *17. Juni 1953. Arbeiteraufstand in der DDR* (Cologne: Edition Deutschland Archiv, 1982); and Jürgen Rühle and Gunter Holzweissig, eds., *13. August 1961. Die Mauer von Berlin* (Cologne: Edition Deutschland Archiv, 1981). These sources contain analyses, documentation, narrative accounts, and some contemporary reactions.

14. See Honore M. Catudal, Jr., *The Diplomacy of the Quadripartite Agreement on Berlin* (Berlin: Berlin Verlag, 1978). See also Lawrence L. Whetten, *Germany East and West* (New York: New York University Press, 1980); and N. Edwina Moreton, *East Germany and the Warsaw Alliance: The Politics of Détente* (Boulder, Colo.: Westview Press, 1978). For Honecker's own account of his role as operational head of the Wall enterprise, see his memoirs entitled *From My Life* (London: Pergamon Press, 1980), pp. 203–207.

15. For details on party development, and especially on its factional struggles, see Carola Stern, *Porträt einer bolschewistischen Partei* (Cologne: Verlag für Politik und Wirtschaft, 1957); and Hermann Weber, *Die Sozialistische Einheitspartei Deutschlands, 1946–1971* (Hannover: Verlag für Literatur und Zeitgeschehen, 1971).

16. Carola Stern, *Ulbricht. Eine politische Biographie* (Cologne: Kiepenheuer & Witsch, 1964). A GDR work is Heinz Vosske, *Walter Ulbricht. Biographischer Abriss* (Berlin: Dietz, 1984).

17. Ulbricht and Honecker exemplify the relevance, in the GDR, of the generalization advanced for Soviet party leaders by Archie Brown. Each successive party leader becomes more powerful as his tenure of office lengthens; each is at all times less powerful than his predecessor. Archie H. Brown, "The Powers of the General Secretary," in T. H. Rigby, Archie Brown, and Peter Reddaway, eds., *Authority Power and Policy in the USSR* (New York: St. Martin's Press, 1980), ch. 8.

18. An excellent biography of Honecker, by a former close collaborator, is the late Heinz Lippmann's *Honecker. Porträt eines Nachfolgers* (Cologne: Verlag Wissenschaft und Politik, 1971). The details on Honecker's career in this present chapter are based on Lippmann's book, as well as on the Honecker memoirs cited later in this note. The Lippmann work has been published in English as *Honecker and the New Politics of Europe* (New York: Macmillan, 1972). Honecker has published his memoirs in German as *Aus meinem Leben* (Berlin: Dietz Verlag, 1982), and in English as *From My Life* (London: Pergamon Press, 1980). See also Weber, *Kleine Geschichte*, chs. 6 and 7.

19. Considerable attention has been paid to a murky episode in Honecker's last days in prison. Assigned to outside work repairing bomb damage, he escaped and hid with a succession of politically reliable friends. He eventually returned to the work detail, was luckily not otherwise punished, and was subsequently liberated by the Red Army. Honecker's inability to find secure refuge is reasonable in the days of heavy Allied air bombardment; his fear of being found at large is understandable, given the fact that SS commandos were roaming the city and shooting deserters on the spot.

20. See the stories in *Neues Deutschland*, 30 June 1983, pp. 1–2, and 1 July 1983, p. 1, as well as those in *Frankfurter Allgemeine Zeitung*, 1 July 1983, p. 5.

21. An interesting, if speculative, reconstruction of the SED's relationship with successive Soviet leaders is Fred Oldenburg, "Im Dienste der eigenen Sache: Die SED und die Wahl Tschernenkos," *Deutsche Studien* 23, no. 85 (March 1984):97–106.

22. For basic geographical data, see the most recent volume of the *Statistisches Jahrbuch der Deutschen Demokratischen Republik* (Berlin: Staatsveralg der DDR); another excellent source of data and analysis is Roy E. H. Mellor, *The Two Germanies: A Modern Geography* (New York: Harper & Row, 1978).

23. See Mellor, *The Two Germanies*, pp. 138–141. For a vivid account of the physical feel of the intra-German border, see Anthony Bailey, *Along the Edge of the Forest* (New York: Random House, 1983).

24. Geoffrey Baldwin, "Population Estimates and Projections for Eastern Europe: 1950–2000," *East European Economic Assessment, Part 2: Regional Assessments* (Washington, D.C.: Government Printing Office [for U.S. Congress, Joint Economic Committee], 1981), p. 198; *Neues Deutschland*, 20–21 January 1979, p. 1, and 25 January 1980, p. 3; Mellor, *The Two Germanies*, p. 358. Between 1975 and 1981, the ratio of live births per thousand had risen from 181 to 237.5. See *Neues Deutschland*, 5 March 1982, p. 3. Figures for 1983 are from *Statistisches Taschenbuch der DDR 1984* (Berlin: Staatsverlag der DDR, 1984), p. 145.

25. Peter C. Ludz et al., *DDR Handbuch*, 2nd ed. (Cologne: Verlag Wissenschaft und Politik, 1979), p. 425.

26. For a survey of climate and soil conditions, see Eugene K. Keefe, ed., *East Germany: A Country Study* (Washington, D.C.: Government Printing Office, 1982), pp. 53–56.

27. Mellor, *The Two Germanies*, p. 376.

28. Ludz et al., *DDR Handbuch*, pp. 54–55.

29. Mellor, *The Two Germanies*, pp. 394–396.

2

The Political System
of the GDR

THE RULING PARTY

The most important political institution in the GDR—and one characteristic of it and of Soviet-style polities generally—is the ruling party, the Socialist Unity party of Germany (SED). As "the conscious and organized vanguard of the working class and toiling people of the socialist German Democratic Republic,"[1] it is the "leading force in the creation of the developed socialist society."[2] Its function is to guide the social development of the GDR, a function that must be enhanced in the future to ensure through deliberate action the party's leading role in all spheres of social development.[3]

The institution that is self-entrusted with this vital function must be studied from the triple perspective of membership, organization, and operation.

Party Membership

Possibly as a consequence of its origin in the unification of the Communists with a larger group of Social Democrats, the SED, to this day, has a relatively large membership (2,238,283 as of mid-1984) in proportion (13 percent) to total population. Every sixth GDR citizen over eighteen is an SED member, or 17 percent of the population over the minimum age of party membership. The "vanguard of the working class and toiling (*werktätigen*) people" includes in its ranks workers (57.8 percent), collective farm peasantry (4.7 percent), employees, or *Angestellte* (8.5 percent), intellectuals (22.3 percent), and "others" (6.7 percent). Workers and employees, together with apprentices, constituted 89.4 percent of the GDR population in 1979.[4]

Age and gender data, especially when taken together, provide an instructive profile of SED membership. As noted, almost 17 percent of those over eighteen are party members. Of the women who are over eighteen, however, only 10 percent are in the SED, whereas 45 percent of the men above eighteen are party members. Party membership of women has increased, however, reaching the highest level ever—34.4 percent (including candidate members). Of that active segment of the population between thirty and forty years of age, the party enrolls 19.1 percent.

In the period between the Ninth and Tenth Party Congresses (1976–1981), the SED accepted 351,953 new members; this represented a substantial increase over the corresponding period between previous party congresses. Of that number, 263,920, or almost three-fourths, were workers. This desire to remain the vanguard of a class-conscious proletariat conflicts with the party's need to incorporate highly educated and trained personnel in order to control scientific and technical affairs effectively. The party resolves this conflict by recruiting a greater proportion of the skilled and trained personnel of the country than of workers and peasants.

The relative stability, with slow growth, of the party under Honecker has not excluded the familiar ritual of the party membership purge (also known as the "exchange of party cards"). The last such combing out of SED members was held in March and April 1980, at which time just under 4,000 members were expelled (as compared to some 3,000 a decade earlier). No special ideological or factional grouping seems to have been the target for this particular operation.[5]

Local Party Organizations

Like the other ruling Communist parties, the SED is organized according to a "territorial-industrial" principle; its basic units, called Grundorganisationen (GOs), are organized primarily at places of work, but each succeeding higher level, up to the national, corresponds to a geographical-administrative unit of the state.[6] These units are organized on a hierarchical basis, with the work of each subordinate party organization subject to supervision and control by a superior one. These restrictions and duties are balanced in theory by the right of discussion and the election of all party bodies. The two features comprise the famous four characteristics of "democratic centralism."

A Grundorganisation must be established when at least 3 party members are present in a given work place; where there is a work place with more than 150 party members, sections (Abteilungen) may be formed. The duties of these groups entail inclusion and expulsion of members and encouragement of higher productivity, greater civic consciousness, and strengthened ideological awareness. They thus occupy a key position in implementation of the party's program.

There are two kinds of GOs worthy of special note: those in government ministries and those in the armed forces. Such "government" GOs are responsible to the party level encompassing the entire ministry or regional government; for their supervision of the work of the agencies themselves, however, the GOs report to the appropriate geographical (local, district, or national) party authority (Leitung). In this way the ability of the party to maintain control over the activities of the state organs is greatly enhanced.[7] Party organizations in units of the armed forces "work according to special instructions" from the Central Committee. These organizations are in fact guided by political officers and are controlled by the Secretariat's department of security affairs, and ultimately by the secretary in charge of these matters. From 1958 to 1971, that secretary was Erich Honecker; from 1971 to late 1983 it was Paul Verner; and since then it has been the former FDJ head, Egon Krenz.

In 1983, there were 57,782 GOs plus another 26,386 Abteilungsorganisationen (AbtOs) for a total of 77,608.[8] No figures are available as to the number of GOs and AbtOs with substantial memberships. The official view is that these basic units secure the party's "political-ideological influence . . . in all spheres of social life"; for the individual member they are "a political home in which the member is firmly rooted and in whose communist atmosphere he feels at home and from which he draws new strength."[9]

Judging by the directives issued for the election of party organization leaderships in the fall of 1983,[10] the chief task of party groups at the lower levels is to secure the achievement of economic goals. Although the "heart and soul of party work" are proclaimed to be "political and ideological work with people," the "criteria . . . for judging the results of political leadership" by party organizations deal exclusively with detailed economic matters.

Regional and National Organizations

The party organizations are organized territorially, first into local units, then into district (Kreis), region (Bezirk), and national bodies. Party organizations in especially important political or economic institutions are given territorially equivalent status. Thus the SED organization in the Ministry for State Security is equivalent to a Kreis organization, and that of the uranium-mining complex at Wismut is equivalent to a Bezirk.

At each of these levels, the party committees, "elected" from below, are led by bureaus (Leitungen) headed by one or more secretaries. The 261 Kreis first-secretaries represent an important line of policy implementation.[11] In recent years, Honecker has delivered an annual talk to a closed session of Kreisleiter. Such sessions, attended by most Politburo and central Secretariat members, are devoted mainly to economic themes, and Honecker's speeches are reported only indirectly and in excerpts. The function of these meetings is apparently to inform the responsible party officials at this level of impending policy developments and to secure energetic compliance in policy execution.[12]

Above the Kreise are the Bezirke: fourteen in number, plus East Berlin and the party organizations of the Wismut district. These sixteen party leaders are key figures in securing implementation of policies in their districts, providing a pool of talent for higher party positions, and forming the factional political basis for a given political leadership. All of these men are members of the Central Committee. Although only one (Konrad Naumann, Berlin) is a full Politburo member (one other, Werner Walde, Cottbus, is a candidate member), past service as a *Bezirk* first-secretary has often led to a higher position. Of the fifteen members of the Politburo other than Naumann, for example, seven were at one time regional party leaders; three other former *Bezirk* leaders now head the trade unions, the national legislature, and the highest party school.

In recent years the career stability of *Bezirk* first-secretaries has been striking. Of the nineteen persons who held one of these positions since Honecker replaced Ulbricht in May 1971, seven were already in office at that time (two of them since the 1950s). Five of these men are still in office and the other two (from the 1950s) were replaced only in 1979 and 1980. Four more assumed their positions on the eve of the SED's Eighth Congress and in four cases replaced incumbents who were promoted at the time of Honecker's ascension. Thus only eight of the present incumbents are products of the Honecker era, and at least two of these new appointments resulted from the filling of positions vacated by the sudden deaths of their occupants.[13]

In asserting his will within the party, therefore, Honecker has had to rely on the acquiescence of party officials who do not owe him their careers. Whether out of inclination or inability to do so, Honecker has not overturned the important regional bureaucracy of the party.

Until late 1983, the Politburo and Secretariat presented a rather similar picture. Seven Politburo members elected at the party congress in 1981 were already members before 1971. In November 1983, Egon Krenz was made a full member of the Politburo as well as a secretary of the Central Committee. Seven months later, at the 8th Plenum in May 1984, two long-time Politburo candidate members, Werner Jarowinsky and Guenther Kleiber, were raised to full membership, as was candidate member Guenther Schabowski; Berlin Bezirksleitung (BL) first-secretary and Politburo member Konrad Naumann became a secretary (while apparently retaining his Berlin position); Paul Verner left both his Politburo and Secretariat jobs; and, finally, Herbert Häber, a veteran staff expert on West German affairs, became a full member of the Politburo and a secretary of the Central Committee. Jarowinsky and Kleiber are experts in economic matters; Schabowski is editor of the party daily, *Neues Deutschland*.[14] These moves have apparently strengthened Honecker's position in the party leadership.

It is significant that six individuals who are currently members of the Politburo and Secretariat rose from the ranks of Honecker's long-time bailiwick, the FDJ (Axen, Felfe, Herrmann, Naumann, Krenz, Lange). Five of these men became Politburo members under Honecker; in all, of the Politburo members other than Honecker himself, nine became full members after his assumption of command in 1971.

The other central locus of party power, aside from the Politburo, is the party Secretariat. The head of this body, the general secretary (termed the "first-secretary" before 1976), is the effective political leader. There are currently eleven secretaries in addition to the general secretary; *all* are full or candidate members of the Politburo.

The Central Committee (Zentralkomitee, or ZK), on which this leadership is based, is elected by the party congress and according to party statute is required to meet at least twice a year (in the 1976–1981 intercongress period, it met fourteen times). The size of the Central Committee has grown from 181 members in 1963, to 190 at the time of Honecker's replacement of Ulbricht (1971), to 213 at the last party congress in 1981. This growth has kept pace with the growth of the party.

The criteria used to select members of the Central Committee are not made public. An examination[15] of the ZK membership shows that the 213 members and candidates of the ZK elected in 1981 may be divided functionally as follows: 40 members each from the central and regional party apparatus; 59 representatives of the state apparatus; 27 from mass organizations (trade unions, youth groups, etc.); 19 from industry and construction; 16 representatives of culture and science; 9 from agriculture; and 3 party veterans. Thus members of the party apparatus constitute over one-third of the membership of the body that controls and judges their actions. These 80 party bureaucrats include the important party officials previously discussed (Politburo members and *Bezirk* first-secretaries, as well as prominent officials in the media, the arts and sciences, and foreign affairs).

Judging by the topics discussed at recent ZK plenary sessions, the leadership uses these meetings for relatively frank expositions of the economic and diplomatic problems confronting the country and, in the process, informs the officials who will have to implement or supervise the implementation of the leadership's decisions as to their content.

The "highest organization" of the party, according to its statute, is the party congress; since 1971, congresses have been held every five years. (The Eleventh Party Congress is scheduled for April 1986.) Although in theory the party congress is the body that sets party policy and elects the leadership, it is in reality more a gathering of the important and the symbolic to hear the leadership's account of its policies, accept its choices for replacement or co-optation, engage in corridor lobbying and gossip, and perform those public acts that serve to legitimize the party as a mass movement, in the eyes of both the party's rank-and-file membership and, not least, those of the top leadership as well.

The 1981 Tenth Party Congress followed this tradition. Of just under 2,700 delegates, 1,950 held some sort of party leadership spot, from GOs to the Secretariat of the Central Committee. Equally significant is the fact that 1,728 delegates were attending their first party congress. This combination of party functionaries and novices helps to ensure that congresses are run according to the leadership's schedule.

Of recent SED congresses, the most dramatic was the Eighth Congress in 1971. It was at this congress that Honecker formally succeeded

Walter Ulbricht as leader of the party and first enunciated his own policy line. Although the leadership change had been announced at a ZK meeting prior to the congress, the attentive public in the GDR was notified through changes in the congress agenda and in relevant terminology, as well as through the noticeable absence of Ulbricht from the proceedings. Although given an ad hoc honorary position ("Chairman of the Party"), he was not allowed to attend the congress of the party he had done so much to create and lead.

The SED under Ulbricht's successors has not been a markedly different party; in many significant ways, it is Ulbricht's party still (although his fame is much diminished these days). The structure and social composition of the party, with its stress on recruitment of skilled personnel, is the same; the concentration of power in the party leader is, not surprisingly, unchanged as well.

Although there has been a remarkable stability within the SED's top leadership, substantial renewal has occurred among the party workers who execute the leadership's commands. The emphasis on economic and technical leadership has meant a more educated party bureaucracy (and membership); most strikingly, the formative years for increasing numbers of party workers are those of the relatively stable GDR of the Honecker era, rather than the difficult early period.[16]

In short, the central role of the party in the political and social system of the GDR is upheld as firmly as ever: "The growing role played by the party in socialist construction is not only an objective necessity, but a process to be guided consciously."[17]

THE SOCIALIST STATE

"The socialist state," Erich Honecker has declared, "is the chief instrument" for executing the public policy of the "toiling masses under leadership of the working class." The most recent party congress had decided, he went on, that "the all-around strengthening of the socialist state" is an important task for the 1980s.[18] A few months later, *Neues Deutschland* declared editorially that "the all-around strengthening of the socialist state is and remains for our party a basic issue of the revolution. . . . Without a strong and well-functioning socialist state there can be no socialist achievements for the people."[19] In keeping with the Soviet pattern, SED leaders in power begin to appreciate both the utility of the state apparatus and the charm of state trappings for officeholders. Thus, although state bureaucrats are but scantily represented on the Politburo, the role of the state apparatus has steadily increased.

The state machinery of the German Democratic Republic,[20] like that of other Communist states, can best be understood when divided into three categories: constitutional prescriptions, administrative machinery, and representative channels. The constitutional documents of

1949, 1968, and 1974 represent the regime's programmatic notions as to the nature and future prospects of the country; the administrative machinery is the vital instrument for implementation of increasingly complex policies; and it is through representative channels that the regime generates legitimation.

Thus the formal institutions of the state, while not the main centers of political power, are of considerable political importance. Moreover, the GDR has inherited the German tradition of using the state administration to bring about social and economic change. Although the early history of the GDR was marked by revolutionary hostility to past German and Prussian bureaucracies, the recent upgrading of Prussia's historical reputation suggests that the GDR may have entered a stage in which enhancement of the power and image of the state machinery is an important tool of statecraft.

The GDR Constitution

The constitution adopted at the founding of the GDR in 1949 was largely a democratic one. It copied many features of the Weimar constitution, emphasized the supremacy of the legislature, and guaranteed traditional individual liberties. Germany was declared to be a unitary and democratic republic. The ostensibly cabinet-parliamentary structure of the government was crowned by a ceremonial president as head of state. Of special interest is Article 6, which potentially criminalized expressions of opposition to the new political order.[21]

During the following two decades, great changes in society and politics took place in the GDR. Property in both industry and agriculture was effectively nationalized; the five existing states were abolished in 1952 and replaced by the current fifteen-district system (*Bezirke*); a military service obligation was introduced in 1955 and made compulsory in 1962; and the presidency was replaced (after Pieck's death in 1960) by a collective head of state, the State Council (*Staatsrat*). In keeping with Communist doctrine that constitutional changes should reflect prior socioeconomic change, the SED undertook to give the GDR a new "socialist" constitution, which was adopted in 1968.[22]

This constitution outlines the GDR notion of a "socialist democracy." In it, the political hegemony of the ruling party is established, and its exercise of power is legitimated by the ascribed task of furthering the "developed socialist society." In keeping with the generally declamatory nature of Communist constitutions, the reality of the official "actual socialism" (*real existierendes Sozialismus*) is baldly asserted—as, for example, in describing the relationship between the working class and other "toiling strata," or in assuming the achievement of such stated goals as "further increases in . . . living standards." Political rights such as those of speech or assembly are "guaranteed" so long as their exercise does not conflict with the party's goals and its ruling position.

The 1968 constitution described the GDR as a "socialist state of the German nation," and, generally throughout the document, the GDR's commitment to some future united Germany is clearly maintained. Six years later, the regime suddenly propagated a series of constitutional amendments that systematically eliminated all references to a common German identity. The GDR was now described as a "socialist state of workers and peasants" and declared to be "eternally and irreversibly" linked to the USSR. These new formulations provided the constitutional reflection of the consolidation of the GDR as a separate East German state in 1971–1973.

Administrative Structure
at the National Level

The centerpiece of the GDR state apparatus is the State Council (*Staatsrat*)—originally a powerful body used by Ulbricht to consolidate his power, but with a political importance now somewhat less than in the late 1960s. Aside from its formal duties as a collective head of state (such as receiving ambassadors' credentials), the State Council carries out such functions of administrative control as are delegated to it (at the party's discretion) by the legislature (*Volkskammer*), which nominates the State Council's members for five-year terms.

The current *Staatsrat* consists of twenty-six members, including a chairman (Honecker) and nine deputy chairmen, the representatives of four "satellite" parties, and five important SED Politburo members. Of the other members, in addition to the non-SED members and the heads of important social organizations such as trade unions and women's organizations, there are no fewer than ten active SED leaders.[23]

Under Honecker, the State Council has lost many of its supervisory functions to party bodies or to the Council of Ministers. Nonetheless, it remains available for use by an ambitious party leader or head of state as a vehicle for personal political aggrandizement.

The Council of Ministers (*Ministerrat*) is the government of the GDR. It guides the execution of policies, verifies fulfillment of economic plans, and directs the activities of central ministries and the executive organs of the regions. At the head of the Council of Ministers is the chairman, along with a number of deputy chairmen; together they form the Council's Praesidium. The leadership of this council has been marked by an exceptional continuity: in the entire history of the GDR, there have been only three chairmen. From 1949 to 1964, the position was filled by Otto Grotewohl. From 1964 (and de facto for some time prior to this, due to Grotewohl's ill health) to 1973 and since 1976, the chairman has been Willi Stoph. (Horst Sindermann held this post in 1973–1976.) Thus, for sixteen of the GDR's first thirty-four years, Stoph has run the government.

There are at present two first-deputy chairmen and nine deputy chairmen; the latter include four representatives of parties other than the SED: the ministers of justice (Liberal Democrats), of environment and water use (peasants' party), and of post and telecommunications

(Christian Democrats), and the head of the arbitration commission (National Democrats). Of the forty-plus ministers, six were at one time members of the Nazi party.[24]

The size of the Council of Ministers has resulted from the practice of establishing ministries to deal with specific portions of the national economy. Hence, aside from such traditional ministries as those of foreign affairs, defense, and finance, there are, for example, eleven ministries dealing with particular industrial sectors. A special feature of the GDR cabinet is that among its members are a number of officials holding what would normally be considered noncabinet positions. They include the mayor of East Berlin, the chairman of the State Planning Commission as well as his chief deputy, the head of the Office for Youth Affairs, the president of the State Bank, the state secretary in the Ministry of Foreign Trade (along with the minister himself), the GDR's CMEA representative, and the heads of the wage office and of the price office.[25]

The membership of the Council of Ministers has remained quite stable over the past decade. In comparing the 1981 and 1976 membership, we find that of forty-two positions, thirty-six were unchanged in 1981. The ministers in the ministries of finance, light industry, heavy machinery, and coal and energy as well as the head of the workers'-peasants' inspection were replaced. The lengthy tenure of many (especially key) members of the council and its long-term leadership by the clearly trusted and administratively talented Stoph have imparted to GDR policy implementation a sense of continuity, authority, and expertise.

Regional and Local Government

Regional and local government in the GDR is structured such that each of fifteen regions, including East Berlin, revolves around a major urban industrial center. Below this level (*Bezirke*) there are districts (*Kreise*) and, at the lowest level, communes (*Gemeinde*). Larger cities may be further subdivided into urban boroughs (*Stadtbezirke*). There are somewhat more than 200 districts and about 9,000 communes. Each local and regional government has a council or steering committee, and each also appoints standing committees.

Although local governments have in recent years displayed initiative in such areas as use of resources and satisfaction of local cultural needs, and despite being strengthened by 1973 legislation, they remain essentially executive organs of a unitary state. Their chief political function is to enlist the citizenry in performance of public tasks (e.g., urban beautification) and to provide a demonstration of participatory legitimacy to the political system as such.

Representative Channels:
The **Volkskammer,** Elections, and the National Front

The political system of the GDR combines elaborate and ostensibly genuine forms of participation with centrally directed control and supervision of the resulting institutions and processes, as exemplified by the elections to, and work of, the national legislature.

Commenting on the *Volkskammer* elections of June 14, 1981, *Neues Deutschland* noted that candidates both before and after their elections had to maintain close contacts with their constituents; the overwhelming vote for the candidates of the official list was acclaimed as representing the "political-moral unity" of the people and a commitment to the policies of the party. The party daily repeated Honecker's assertion that it was Western-style elections that were without meaning and could well be dispensed with.[26]

The significance of the *Volkskammer* may be judged by the extraordinary infrequency of its sessions: the five years from 1976 to 1981 saw only thirteen plenary sessions. The typical *Volkskammer* session lasts a day or two at the most, although committee sessions add considerably to the length of time during which deputies are engaged in their work. (It may be added that, in the GDR view, the time spent by deputies in information sessions with their constituents is an important part of their task.) On one occasion, the *Volkskammer* did record votes against a government proposal—specifically, when CDU deputies in 1972 voted against liberalization of rules for abortions.

Nominations for the *Volkskammer* originate with social collectives (such as factories and universities) and the parties of the National Front; the actual decisions are made by the ruling party and ratified at local and regional National Front meetings. More candidates are nominated than there are positions to be filled, but no one has ever been rejected; the extra candidates are available to fill seats vacated by death or resignation and may take part in *Volkskammer* committee work.

The electoral process, with its elaborate system of meetings and discussions, is an effective tool of socialization and legitimation. There are almost 200,000 deputies at all levels, from the local to the national. In addition, there are 268 electoral commissions (primarily nominating agencies) with over 2,800 members; over 24,000 electoral groups (*Wahlvorstand*), with over 250,000 participants, run the elections.

The typical electoral commission is designed "in its political as well as social composition to be representative of the broad spectrum of socialist society." In one GDR town, the commission included representatives of the party and army, members of the trade unions and of a nearby collective farm (who were female), as well as a lab assistant from the CDU and a self-employed artisan who was a National Democrat.[27]

The *Volkskammer* consists of 500 members elected for a period of five years. During the elections of 1981,[28] there were 500 candidates; all were elected. The participation rate reached 99.2 percent; and the unitary list of candidates received 99.86 percent of the vote. The vote for members of the *Volkskammer* is a vote for a single list set up by the National Front. As was the case in a number of East European states, the GDR retained the outward forms of a multiparty system to which it added societal organizations as constituent members of a coordinating front organization.

The National Front of the GDR grew out of the People's Congress movement of 1947–1948. It was originally designed as a lodestone for all-German support. Its present functions, for the most part, involve organization of economic and civic improvement campaigns by its approximately 340,000 volunteers and nomination of candidates for the single-list elections.

Just how many nominees each group shall place on the National Front list is arranged in advance. At the last election, the SED was awarded 127 seats (about a fourth of the total *Volkskammer* membership); the other parties had 52 seats each; and the social organizations received 68 seats for the trade unions, 40 for the youth organization, 35 for the womens' organization, and 22 for the Cultural League.[29] Originally, the SED controlled the legislature through its control of the mass organizations. However, the other parties now dutifully express the SED's policy line. Their internal life is largely controlled by the SED.

Mass Participation?

An important issue in considering the political system of the GDR is the extent and quality of mass participation in politics. The restrictions on free expression of political opinion and the hegemonic position of the SED may make the question of participation seem a rather academic one; however, we may distinguish between participation in selection of decisionmakers and in shaping the structure of problem solving. The former is clearly absent in the GDR; the latter, given its possibilities for lay participation in the work of economic and social institutions, is present and may well represent to many GDR citizens a satisfying form of participation relevant to their daily lives.

Moreover, such forms of participation are considered from the GDR perspective to be an essential feature of socialist democracy, an example of the people "securing its interests through collective and organized action."[30] As evidence, GDR writers cite such forms of participation as these:

- 450,000 participants in the committees of representative bodies at all levels;
- over 300,000 lay judges and members of arbitration bodies;
- 340,000 volunteer activists in the National Front;
- over 200,000 participants in the work of the Workers' and Peasants' Inspection;
- members of the trade unions engaged in discussion of economic plans;
- various hundreds of thousands active in youth, women's, sports, and other social groups;
- almost two million industrial "innovators"; and

The annual rally in the center of East Berlin is an illustration of the mass organization in the GDR. Photo courtesy of the GDR Embassy, Washington, D.C.

- over 600,000 in the equivalent of parent-teacher groups.[31]

The growth of membership in approved mass organizations, and especially the proportion of the relevant constituency drawn into membership, is cited in the GDR as evidence of meaningful participation. Of course, we may question the significance of such membership; nevertheless, it must mean something (if only in disposition of free time) when two-thirds of the people in the GDR aged fourteen to twenty-five belong to the FDJ, or over one-third of the population fourteen years and over belong to the Society for German-Soviet Friendship (see Table 2.1).[32]

By these various means, the regime draws large numbers of otherwise perhaps unpolitical persons into activity that furthers its goals while (self-)legitimating the political structure of the country.

THE ARMED FORCES

The armed forces of the GDR—principally the National People's Army (Nationale Volksarmee, or NVA)—are an increasingly important

TABLE 2.1
Trends in Membership of Selected Mass Organizations in the GDR (1971-1981)

Organization	1971 (a)	1981 (b)	% b/a	% Relevant Population
FDGB (trade unions)	7,241,000	9,100,000	25.7	97.2
FDJ (youth)	2,100,000	2,300,000	9.5	67.7
DFD (women)	1,300,000	1,400,000	7.7	18.9
KB (intellectuals)	194,469	235,007	20.8	2.2
DSF (GDR-Soviet)	3,500,000	6,000,000	71.4	35.8
DTSB (sports)	2,233,628	3,239,210	45.0	19.4
KdT (technology)	192,996	246,000	27.5	17.4
VKSK (gardening)	968,437	1,170,000	20.8	7.0

FDJ population = 14-25 years old; DFD = women, 14+; DSF, KB, VSKS = population 14+; VKSK: Verband der Kleingärtner, Siedler und Kleintierzüchter (private vegetable gardens and small animals).

Source: Adapted from Wolfgang Quitt, "Der Auftrag der Kommunisten in den Massenorganizationen," Neuer Weg 37, 10 (1983): 375-377.

NOTE: The VdgB (Vereinigung der gegenseitigen Bauernhilfe), a peasant mutual aid organization, had over 420,000 members as of early 1984, according to Werner Felfe, CC secretary in charge of agriculture (Neues Deutschland, 28 May 1984, p. 3).

instrument of the regime's statecraft in both the foreign and domestic policy arenas.[33] In origins, structure, and purpose, the NVA is a product of several factors—in particular, German military traditions and history, Soviet security and foreign policy interests, and typical Communist patterns of civil-military relations. The GDR armed forces are declared to be different from German armies of the past and from their West German counterpart, yet much of their ceremonies and material symbols evoke the German past. After difficult and unsure beginnings, the NVA has become a politically reliable army whose values and needs are propagated throughout the society by the regime itself.

Alone among the member states of the Warsaw Treaty Organization (WTO), the GDR did not possess armed forces at the time of its accession to the WTO (January 1956). Nevertheless, the regime in East Berlin did command military forces, for as far back as 1946, Soviet authorities had authorized creation of a "barracks" police force, the Kasernierte Volks-polizei (KVP). By 1950, the KVP consisted of some 50,000 men and included both tanks and artillery. In 1952, reacting to the planned incorporation of West German units into the European Defense Community force, the KVP was designated the "national armed forces" of a democratic Germany. When the NVA was formally established, following the Federal Republic's admission to NATO and the GDR's entry into the WTO (January 19, 1956), the KVP consisted of 100,000 men in addition to security and border guard detachments.

The NVA:
Structure, Equipment, and Military Role

The personnel strength of the armed forces totals 167,000, of which 116,000 soldiers represent the NVA. There are an additional 70,000 to 75,000 soldiers in border, security, transport, and other special formations, plus about 350,000 in factory militias (*Kampfgruppen der Arbeiterklasse*); the latter train with mortars, machine guns, and armored tracked vehicles, but they are not full-time military personnel.[34]

About 60 percent of the NVA consists of conscripts (the naval and air units also have conscript troops), whose term of service is eighteen months. Reservists have active-duty obligations until the age of fifty (sixty upon declaration of an emergency). Women are exempt from compulsory service but may be called up for various support as well as possible combat service (since 1982) under emergency conditions.

The NVA consists of two armored and four motorized infantry divisions, as well as artillery, surface-to-surface missile, and other ancillary formations. The armored force disposes of about fifteen hundred T-54/55 and T-72 tanks; the naval forces have two frigates as their largest vessels and are primarily coastal patrol and landing-support formations; the air force has thirty-five MiG-17s, twelve MiG-21s, and twelve MiG-23s.

The heavy equipment of the GDR armed forces (tanks, planes, etc.) is exclusively Soviet in origin. The GDR produces and equips its forces

GDR military units parade in the Marx-Engels-Platz in East Berlin (1969). Photo
courtesy of the German Information Center, New York.

with small arms, coastal vessels, all manner of quartermaster stores,
and various specialized electronic and optical gear (some of the latter
is supplied to the Soviet space program as well).

A special feature of the GDR military establishment is its extraordinary degree of integration into Soviet and Soviet-directed military
commands. The entire NVA, unique in Eastern Europe, is in peacetime
under the direct command of the WTO commander-in-chief. GDR naval
forces (*Volksmarine*), along with some Polish and Soviet units, are under
the operational command of the Joint Baltic Fleet headquartered in
Leningrad. Air and air defense forces are integrated with the air arm
of the Soviet forces, the "Group of Soviet Forces in Germany" (GSFG)
and the WTO air defense command in internal crisis situations, without
prior GDR approval.[35]

The close relationship between the NVA and the Soviet forces in
Germany extends to the small-unit level, where joint military exercises
and mixed recreational and ideological sessions are quite common. At
the other end of the military scale, over 2,500 NVA officers have had
training at Soviet military schools.[36]

In WTO military planning, the GDR armed forces have been
assigned an important role. Together with the Soviet forces in the GDR
and Polish units, they form part of the WTO's first echelon in that

corridor of the North European plain where armed conflict with NATO would most likely take place. The geopolitical significance of the GDR has been underlined by the stationing in the fall of 1983 of Soviet rocket units in the GDR in response to NATO's missile deployment.[37]

Armed Forces, Party, and Society

The impact of the armed forces on the society of the GDR is best measured along three dimensions: the economy, the political relations of armed forces and party, and the position of the armed forces in the larger society.

The burden of defense expenditures on the GDR economy is difficult to determine with satisfactory accuracy. Judging by Western estimates, GDR defense expenditures are equivalent to between 4 percent and 6 percent of GNP.[38] The military budget of the GDR, especially the cost of heavy equipment, is subject to direct GDR-Soviet negotiations. Since 1958, the USSR has foregone troop stationing payments from the GDR.

In recent years, GDR defense expenditures have risen steadily. In many crucial categories, such as military expenditure per capita, it ranks second to the USSR within the WTO (see Table 2.2).

These commitments add a burden to the GDR's economy and make it more difficult to meet social policy goals. Official sources have made it clear that these military needs will be met, however reluctantly. In a blunt message to economic officials, a military professional declared that "The people's economy is to be planned and led in such a way that the economic foundations of the national defense are secure at all times."[39] Compliance with procurement directives is an obligation both for individual enterprises as well as for the industrial branch as a whole: failure to comply must be reported and then, if need be, corrected within four weeks time by action of the Council of Ministers.

Economic pressure is compounded by demographic constraints. Despite the small size of the eighteen-year-old cohort, the GDR has some 8 percent of military-age males under arms (not counting factory militias), a higher proportion than in Poland, Czechoslovakia, or the USSR. As a consequence, military reservists will have to provide more service in the decades ahead.

The personal and institutional arrangements to secure party control over the armed forces fall into a familiar Soviet pattern: effective party controls at every level of the military command structure and high-ranking party personalities in key positions of general military policymaking.

It would be misleading, however, to picture party-military relations in an entirely adversarial light. To a greater extent than in the armies of other East European states, the NVA is a creation of the party regime rather than an autonomous representative of national values. The military plays a valuable role in foreign policy and as an instrument of domestic

TABLE 2.2
GDR Military Expenditures

I. Defense expenditures, by year (in millions of local currency)

1971	1976	1979	1980	1981
7,200	10,223	13,060	13,100	14,100

II. Military expenditures in 1980 prices, in millions of U.S. dollars, by year:

1973	1976	1979	1980	1981	1982
2,467	2,887	3,325	3,604	3,907	4,130

III. Military expenditures per capita (in current dollars and percentage of GNP

	% GNP	per capita
1971	5.6	342
1980	5.7	451

Sources: U.S. Arms Control and Disarmament Agency, World Military Expenditures and Arms Transfers, 1971-1980 (Washington, D.C.: Government Printing Office, 1983); International Institute of Strategic Studies, The Military Balance, 1983-1984 (London: IISS, 1983); Stockholm International Peace Research Institute, World Armaments and Disarmament: SIPRI Yearbook 1983 (New York: International Publications Service/Taylor & Francis, 1983).

legitimation. For these reasons it is more appropriate to think in terms of a party-military symbiosis; the party is clearly in charge, but its goals and those of the politically reliable and technically proficient officers are largely the same.[40]

Formal direction of the armed forces is centered in the State Council, but actual direction is vested in the National Defense Council, which is headed by Honecker, with the NVA chief of staff, General Streletz, as secretary. Administrative control of the armed forces is exercised through the Ministry of National Defense, which has had only two heads since its creation in 1956: Willi Stoph until July 1960 and Heinz Hoffmann since. (Stoph, as minister of the interior, had previously controlled the KVP.) Hoffmann, a veteran of the Communist movement, has been a Politburo member since 1973.

These *governmental* agencies are subordinate to the party leadership: Honecker, Stoph, and Hoffmann are all Politburo members, as is Egon Krenz, who, like Honecker, is a Secretariat member as well as party secretary in charge of security matters. The operative head of the Secretariat's security department is a career officer and Central Committee member, Horst Scheibe. The number of professional military officers in central policymaking structures is quite limited. For example, both Stoph and Hoffmann are essentially civilian party politicians, although Stoph served in the Wehrmacht and Hoffmann fought in Spain with the International Brigades.

In the Central Committee of the SED, membership by military officers has never exceeded the current level of 4 percent of the total membership. The eight military members, or candidates, of the Central Committee, aside from Hoffmann, are either concerned with the political relationship of party and armed forces or, except for one staff officer, are the formal commanders of the border troops, naval, air, and ground forces.[41]

Within the NVA itself, an astounding 99 percent of the officers are SED full or candidate members—what amounts to the highest total in the WTO.[42] These officers are, of course, expected to be highly qualified military professionals, but they must also display a conscious political commitment and "devotion" (*Ergebenheit*) to the "Marxist-Leninist party." Of course a military career has its rewards: according to Scheibe, it is a "many-sided, interesting and pleasant career, with good opportunities for advancement."[43]

The officer corps of the NVA was recruited originally from two sources: veterans and reliable young civilian officials. According to Hoffmann, of the twenty-nine generals and admirals who occupied "leading positions" in the GDR armed forces as of March 1, 1956, seven had served with the International Brigades in Spain, and twenty-one had "actively" opposed Hitler in World War II, either in a military capacity or while imprisoned. These veterans were assigned the task of rapidly training their successors; the new officers were "young workers, members and officials of the Free German Youth, who in the 1950s had volunteered for . . . the KVP."

The average age of these newcomers was 27.7 years; 78.7 percent of them had had no more than an eighth-grade education, and 82 percent came from a proletarian background. Such politically reliable volunteers still represent the bulk of the NVA officers corps; at the apex of the GDR armed forces are veterans of the Wehrmacht. Half of the military officers elected to the Central Committee in 1981 had served in Hitler's army, and one had belonged briefly to the Nazi party.[44]

In addition to careful selection of officers, the SED has established a hierarchy of party control units throughout the military. Basic party organizations were established down to the battalion level and sections down to the platoons; each commander (at company levels and higher) had a political deputy; finally, a central party political leadership was set up to watch over the political activities of officers and men "down to a very low organizational level."[45]

In recent years, the two main issues confronting this system of indoctrination and control have been a reluctance on the part of young males to undertake military service and the soldiers' ambivalent image of the enemy—especially the West Germans. The first of these issues, already observable at the founding of the NVA, is apparently still a problem today; as a consequence, the military and party are striving to encourage a positive attitude toward military service. School, work place, and family—and especially the female friends of recruits—are all being exhorted to encourage potential enlistees. Indeed, "socialist military training" has been made compulsory in the last two years of secondary school, despite the opposition of certain parents and of the Evangelical Church. In the GDR, there "is no room for pacifist beliefs."[46]

Inculcating the desired attitude toward a possible West German enemy became more difficult in the wake of the inter-German agreements of the 1970s. As early as 1972, Honecker warned East German troops that for them the Federal Republic was "not only a foreign country, but an imperialistic foreign country at that."[47] This theme has been repeated often and in many versions since that time. A recent NVA manual declares that it matters not what language an enemy speaks, what uniform he wears, or even what class he comes from: "whoever serves Imperialism with arms is our enemy."[48]

From this viewpoint, it makes sense to regard military duty not only as an obligation—both to the GDR and to the entire socialist community—but also, in fact, as a "right," albeit one that, for males, is difficult *not* to exercise. Commenting on the 1982 military service law, *Neues Deutschland* declared that the GDR may properly demand "from every male citizen . . . that he be ready at any time to perform his service," in what, at the celebration of the NVA's twenty-fifth anniversary, it called "the only German army deserving that name."[49]

As military service becomes an ever more integral part of life in the GDR, it follows that the armed forces should become an ever more ubiquitous presence in GDR society. Military units have been linked quite systematically to schools, factories, and local governments in "patron" relationshps. Officers are encouraged to participate in local community affairs. The military has become a presence in the life of the community, encouraging enlistments and applications for officers' training and propagating desired values regarding the WTO and NATO—in short, doing much of the work of political socialization that had once been largely the domain of the party. In return, social institutions are required by law to "prepare citizens for military service," with specific prescriptions as to how schools, factories, and individual citizens are to implement this end.[50]

How this increasing amalgamation of political and military leadership will be received by a citizenry exhorted to struggle for peace remains to be seen. As an instrument of statecraft, however, the armed forces of the GDR remain strong and firmly in the party's hands.

NOTES

1. *Statut der Sozialistischen Einheitspartei Deutschlands* (Berlin: Dietz Verlag, 1976), p. 5.

2. *Programm der Sozialistischen Einheitspartei Deutschlands* [SED] (Berlin: Dietz Verlag, 1976, p. 93.

3. Manfred Herold, "Die allgemeingültigen Gesetze der sozialistischen Revolution und ihre schöpferische Anwendung durch unsere Partei," *Einheit* 37 (January 1982):7–14. A veteran party leader has written that "the more extensive and complicated the tasks of guiding and planning . . . social processes become, the more important becomes the role of the political leadership of society by the marxist-leninist party." See Erich Mückenberger, "Fest mit den Massen verbunden und ihnen voran," *Einheit* 38 (September 1983):816.

4. See the figures in *Neuer Weg*, 38, no. 17 (1983) on the inside back cover; for additional data, see also *Neues Deutschland*, 19–20 February 1983, pp. 1–2. The membership figure comes from Kurt Hager's report to the Eighth Central Committee (CC) Plenum in May 1984 (see *Neues Deutschland*, 25 May 1984, pp. 6–7); the partial breakdown by social class given in that report differs inconsequentially from the numbers cited in the text.

5. *Frankfurter Allgemeine Zeitung*, 23 May 1980, p. 7.

6. For this account of the party's basic structure, I have used as a reference source the edition of the statutes cited in Note 1 of this chapter.

7. Heinz Puder, "Grundorganisationen—Fundament der Partei," *Einheit* 35 (September 1980):964; Heinz Hirtschin, "Grundorganisationen-Kampfkollektive zurverwirklichung unserer Politik," *Einheit*, 38 (September 1983):827–833.

8. *Neues Deutschland*, 5 December 1983, p. 1. Some 2,052 more GOs were added in the first months of 1984; see Hager's report in *Neues Deutschland* 25 May 1984.

9. Puder, "Grundorganisationen," p. 963, quoting from *Programm der SED*, p. 98.

10. "Direktive des Zentralkomitees der Sozialistichen Einheitspartei Deutschlands für die Durchführung der Parteiwahlen 1983/84," *Neuer Weg* 38, no. 17 (1983): Beilage.

11. Kurt Sontheimer and Wilhelm Bleek, *Die DDR. Politik, Gesellschaft,* 4th ed. (Hamburg: Hoffmann und Campe, 1975), p. 81; Peter C. Ludz et al., *DDR-Handbuch,* 2d ed. (Cologne: Verlag Wissenschaft und Politik, 1979), pp. 948–952.

12. *Neues Deutschland,* 13–14 February 1982, pp. 1–2; *Frankfurter Allgemeine Zeitung,* 15 February 1982, p. 2; Hannsjörg F. Buck and Johannes Kuppe, "SED Bericht 'zur Lage.' Honecker vor den 1. Sektretären der Kreisleitungen," *Deutschland Archiv* 15 (April 1982):392–401. The practice was continued in similar form in 1983; see *Neues Deutschland,* 19–20 February 1983, pp. 1–2.

13. This stability extends to the *Bezirksleitungen* (BL) as a whole. Of ninety-seven positions on the BL, only twelve (including just two second secretaries) were given to new persons in the party elections of early 1984. See "Kaum Veränderungen nach Parteiwahlen," *Frankfurter Allgemeine Zeitung,* 21 February 1984, p. 5.

14. *Neues Deutschland,* 25 May 1984, p. 1; *Frankfurter Allgemeine Zeitung,* 26 May 1984, pp. 1–2.

15. Categorized on the basis of the Central Committee roster; see *Neues Deutschland,* 24 May 1976, pp. 3–5, for data as of the SED Ninth Congress; and *Neues Deutschland* 17 April 1981, pp. 3–5, for data after the SED Tenth Congress. See also Günther Buch, ed., *Namen und Daten wichtiger Personnen der DDR,* 3d ed. (Berlin: Verlag J.H.W. Dietz Nachf., 1982); and "East European Leadership Rosters," RFE-RL Research, *RAD Background Report/Supplement* (May 16, 1983), pp. 11–14.

16. Only about 10 percent of the party cadre (!) have been in their positions longer than a decade (whether or not their current position is the first and only one is unclear). Most have gained all of their substantial experience since the SED Eighth Congress in 1971; that is, they are products of the Honecker era and do not know much about the "difficult period of our advance." Indeed, in the party staff for the *Bezirksleitung* Berlin, every fifth party worker was born after 1945. See Helmut Müller, "Kaderarbeit heisst Erziehung zur parteilichen Haltung," *Neuer Weg* 37, 17(1982):641–646.

17. Kurt Tiedke, "Die marxistisch-leninistische Lehre von der Partei im Klassenkampf unserer Zeit," *Einheit* 39 (September-October 1984):859.

18. *Neues Deutschland,* 20–21 June 1981, p. 1.

19. *Neues Deutschland,* 15 January 1982, p. 1.

20. For background, see Sontheimer and Bleek, *Die DDR,* ch. 4; Günter Erbe et al., *Politik, Wirtschaft und Gesellschaft in der DDR,* 2d ed. (Opladen: Westdeutscher Verlag, 1980), pp. 129–136.

21. Hermann Weber, *Kleine Geschichte der DDR* (Cologne: Edition Deutschland Archiv, 1980), pp. 52–55.

22. For the current text, see *Verfassung der Deutschen Demokratischen Republik* (Berlin: Staatsverlag der DDR, 1975). A synoptic edition of the 1968 and 1974 texts is in *Deutschland Archiv* 7 (November 1974):1188–1223.

23. The symbolic value of *Staatsrat* membership is shown by the elevation of Egon Krenz and Günter Mittag to the position of deputy chairman, and Konrad Naumann to the level of membership at the legislative session of June 1984.

24. This latter point is based on biographical data in Buch, *Namen und Daten.*

25. The most recent convenient roster in English is in "East European Leadership Rosters," RFE-RL Research, *RAD Background Report/Supplement* (Sep-

tember 12, 1983), pp. 13–14. See also *Neues Deutschland* 2 November 1976, and 27–28 June 1981.

26. *Neues Deutschland,* 11 June 1981.

27. Günther Fleischmann, "Eine Million Ehrenamtliche . . . ," *Neues Deutschland,* 13 June 1981, p. 9.

28. *Neues Deutschland,* 17 June 1981, pp. 1–5.

29. *Neuer Weg,* 37 (1982), p. 264.

30. Wolfgang Weichelt, "Politische Macht und Demokratie in unserer Gesellschaft," *Einheit* 37 (July-August 1982):768.

31. Ibid., pp. 770–771.

32. Wolfgang Quitt, "Der Auftrag der Kommunisten in den Massen organisationen," *Neuer Weg,* 37 (1982), pp. 375–377. See the similar argument of Horst Sindermann, "Mensch und Macht in unserer Gesellschaft," *Einheit* 39, nos. 9, 10 (September-October 1984):785–791. Sindermann stressed the participation of mass organizations and their memberships in formulating legislation.

33. Joachim Nawrocki, *Bewaffnete Organe in der DDR* (Berlin: Verlag Gebrüder Holzapfel, 1979); Studiengruppe Militärpolitik, *Die Naitonale Volksarmee* (Hamburg: Rowohlt Taschenbuch Verlag, 1976); Thomas M. Forster (pseud.), *The East German Army* (London: Allen & Unwin, 1980); Dale M. Herspring, "GDR Naval Buildup," *Problems of Communism* 33 (January-February 1984):54–62.

34. This and the following three paragraphs are based on International Institute of Strategic Studies, *The Military Balance, 1983–1984* (London: IISE, 1983), pp. 21–22; and Stockholm International Peace Research Institute, *World Armaments and Disarmament: SIPRI Yearbook 1983* (New York: International Publications Service/Taylor & Francis, 1983), pp. 297–298. See also Eugene K. Keefe, ed., *East Germany: A Country Study,* 2d ed. (Washington, D.C.: Government Printing Office, 1982), pp. 218–232.

35. Studiengruppe Militärpolitik, *Die Nationale Volksarmee,* pp. 54–55; Karl Wilhelm Fricke, "Okkupanten oder Waffenbrüder?" *Deutschland Archiv* 15 (March 1982):270–271.

36. Heinz Hoffmann, "Die Nationale Volksarmee—eine moderne sozialistische Verteidigungsmacht," *Einheit* 36 (February 1981):144.

37. See Henry Krisch, "German Democratic Republic," in Daniel N. Nelson, ed., *Soviet Allies* (Boulder, Colo.: Westview Press, 1984), ch. 6.

38. SIPRI estimates are for 4.3 percent of GNP in 1980 (*SIPRI Yearbook 1983,* p. 171); 5.7 percent of GNP for 1980 is cited in U.S. Arms Control and Disarmament Agency, *World Military Expenditures and Arms Transfers 1971–1980* (Washington, D.C.: Arms Control and Disarmament Agency, 1983), p. 49.

39. (Col.) Willy Meinert, "Zuverlässiger Schutz des Sozialismus," *Die Wirtschaft,* no. 5 (1982), p. 21.

40. For a typical example of the military as an instrument of the legitimization of civil-political leadership, see the story of a visit by the party leadership to troop exercises, "Soldaten des Arbeiter—und-Bauern-Staates verteidigen Frieden und Sozialismus," *Neues Deutschland,* 22 June 1984, pp. 1–4. This visit, during which Honecker played the role of commander-in-chief, was also the lead item on the evening television newscast.

41. Dale R. Herspring, "Die Rolle der Streitkräfte in der Aussenpolitik der DDR," in Eberhard Schulz, ed., *Drei Jahrzehnte Aussenpolitik der DDR* (Munich: R. Oldenbourg, 1979), p. 318; Ulrich Rühmland, "Wehrverfassung und Befehls—

und Kommandogewalt in der DDR," *Deutsche Studien* 9, no. 73 (March 1981):34–43.

42. Gero Neugebauer, "25 Jahre Nationale Volksarmee," *Deutschland Archiv* 14 (March 1981):272. See Dale R. Herspring, *East German Civil-Military Relations* (New York: Praeger Publishers, 1973), ch. 2.

43. Horst Scheibe, "Sozialistischer Offizier—Klassenauftrag und Verpflichtung," *Einheit* 36 (February 1981):149.

44. The data in this paragraph are derived from Hoffmann, "Die Nationale Volksarmee"; Schiebe, "Sozialistischer Offizier"; and Buch, *Namen und Daten.*

45. Herspring, "Die Rolle der Streitkräfte," p. 314.

46. For antimilitary service sentiment in the 1950s, see Scheibe, "Sozialistischer Offizier," p. 150. A most revealing source book for current attitudes, and the campaigns to shape them, is Werner Hübner and Willi Effenberger, *Wehrpolitische Massenarbeit unter Führung der Partei* (Berlin: Dietz Verlag, 1982), especially pp. 7–12, 39–50.

47. *Neues Deutschland*, 7 January 1972, p. 1.

48. Quoted from *Vom Sinn des Soldatseins. Ein Ratgeber für Soldaten* (Berlin, 1979), in Michael Richter, "Kann man Frieden kriegen?" *Deutschland Archiv* 16 (March 1983):259. The GDR book is a manual distributed to new NVA recruits.

49. *Neues Deutschland*, 26 March 1982, p. 3, 29 March 1982, p. 2 (editorial), and 17 February 1981, p. 1 (anniversary headline).

50. The relevant passage in the law is in *Neues Deutschland*, 27–28 March 1982, p. 9; a comprehensive discussion, with details, can be found in Hoffmann, "Die Nationale Volksarmee." See also Hübner and Effenberger, *Wehrpolitische Massenarbeit*, especially pp. 37–39. Hoffmann has written recently that "since the SED founded and has guided the NVA as part of the process of building a socialist society, it is only proper that all party and state organizations, all social institutions—including education—help with socialist military education and military recruitment." Heinz Hoffmann, "Wir schützen Sozialismus und Frieden," *Einheit* 39, nos. 9, 10 (September-October 1984):835.

3

The GDR in the World

THE ROLE OF FOREIGN POLICY

With respect to foreign policy, few countries in the world are as bound up with fundamental questions of national identity and state interests as the GDR. To understand the foreign policy of the GDR, therefore, one must see it primarily as a policy instrument employed to secure the existence and development of the GDR, to obtain for it an accepted place in the community of states, and to preserve an international environment favorable to its interests.[1]

From this perspective, it is not surprising that the most important feature of the GDR's foreign policy should be the country's relationship to the power that made the GDR possible, that both sustained and limited its existence, and that dominates the economic and military alliances modulating the GDR's international presence—the Soviet Union. This GDR-Soviet relationship brings with it a GDR–East European relationship that constitutes a subsidiary but distinct aspect of foreign affairs. The other pole of GDR foreign policy is its relationship with "Germany." By this is meant its relationship both with the Federal Republic of Germany and with the German past. As the GDR is uniquely lacking in national legitimation, its relationship to the past is, in effect, a crucial external determinant of its identity and legitimacy.

Beyond these two essential relationships, GDR foreign policy is prompted mainly by two additional motives, which are important in its relations with the Third World and the industrial democracies: economics, including the question of access to crucial raw materials, and questions of prestige. Even today, more than a decade since most nations recognized the GDR, its leadership remains extraordinarily sensitive to routine international protocol; for example, the official media prominently records routine exchanges of messages with foreign heads of state.

Before considering GDR foreign policy in detail, we must review its development and the means by which it is currently carried out.

For most of the first quarter-century of its existence, the GDR had almost no foreign relations. Indeed, as far as most of the international

53

community was concerned, the GDR was not a legitimate state in international life. The reasons for this anomalous state of affairs, in which a territory and population were effectively governed by a regime that was officially ignored by all but a dozen other states, lie in the circumstances of the GDR's birth. Throughout the cold war years of the 1950s and 1960s, the Western powers were seeking to cement their ties to the Federal Republic. They followed Bonn's lead in denying all legitimacy to the GDR, and most other countries followed suit. The GDR was, of course, recognized by Communist states, beginning with the USSR. In its search for wider recognition, the GDR turned early toward the Third World. GDR relations with liberation movements— continuing today in the form of close ties to the South-West Africa People's Organization (SWAPO), the Palestine Liberation Organization (PLO), the African National Council (ANC), and others—were established long before formal diplomatic ties existed; they have paid off in good relations with countries subsequently ruled by such movements, including Angola and Mozambique. The ultimate result of this courtship was recognition of the GDR by Third World governments during the 1960s (see Table 3.1).

General recognition, however, remained blocked until after the signing of the treaties between Bonn and the Soviet and Polish governments, as well as the Four-Power Agreement on Berlin. In effect, the West Germans were able to act as gatekeepers of the international community against the GDR.

The GDR is thus very sensitive to changes in the international environment, for it owes its international acceptance to a favorable configuration of European and world affairs. This perception influenced its behavior at a time of worsening international relations in the period from 1982 to 1984.

Instruments and Personalities in GDR Foreign Policy

The foreign policy of the GDR is decided on and carried out in a manner typical of Communist states; the basic decisions are made by the party leadership in the SED Politburo and Secretariat and carried out by the Council of Ministers, the Ministry for Foreign Affairs, and the members of the diplomatic service.[2]

The execution of GDR foreign policy is not the exclusive province of the diplomatic services; it is carried out by military personnel (especially in the Third World), by foreign trade emissaries, by the security services, and by party and public organizations, including trade unions, journalists' associations, and youth groups. The latter are especially important in relations with the Third World; the SED maintains ties to political organizations, primarily non-ruling Communist parties, in various countries.

At the apex of political power in the GDR, both foreign policy formulation and implementation are the prerogative of a small number

TABLE 3.1
Growth in Diplomatic Recognition of the GDR (1949-1974)

1949-1954	USSR Bulgaria Poland CSSR Romania Hungary China (People's Republic) North Korea Albania North Vietnam Mongolia
1955-1960	Yugoslavia
1960-1965	Cuba
1965-1970	Cambodia Iraq Sudan Syria South Yemen Egypt Congo (Brazzaville) Somalia Central African Republic Algeria Maldives Sri Lanka Guinea
1971	Chile Equatorial Guinea Chad
1972	24 countries
1973	46 countries
1974	11 countries, including the United States
NOTE:	Relations with the Federal Republic were established, in accordance with the Basic Treaty between the two states, upon its ratification in 1973. By inter-Allied agreement, both Germanies were granted UN membership in September 1973.

Source: Adapted from Eberhard Schulz, ed., Drei Jahrzehnte Aussenpolitik der DDR (Munich: R. Oldenbourg, 1979), pp. 857-859.

of leading persons. Chief among these is Erich Honecker. As party leader and head of state, he dominates both foreign-policymaking and implementation. As is true of many chief executives, Honecker conducts personal diplomacy in a self-confident and wide-ranging fashion.

Honecker's personal diplomacy included his more than forty meetings with Brezhnev between 1971 and 1982 (as well as his meeting with Andropov in spring 1983); he has met with the political leaders of West Germany, beginning with the Helsinki Conference on Security and Cooperation in Europe (CSCE) in 1975 and highlighted by Helmut Schmidt's official visit to the GDR in December 1981. In 1982–1984, Honecker received a steady succession of both government and opposition leaders from the Federal Republic in East Berlin.

Honecker's personal diplomacy has not been limited to those traditional poles of GDR attention, Moscow and Bonn. Beginning in 1979, he visited some sixteen capitals in just over five years, including the Far East (Japan, India, the Philippines), the Middle East (Libya, Syria, Kuwait, Cyprus, Ethiopia, Algeria, South Yemen), southern Africa (Angola, Zambia, Mozambique), as well as Finland, Mexico, and Austria. At home, in the two months of October and November 1982, for example, Honecker made the front page of the party daily no less than ten times in the process of receiving foreign politicians, including the Yugoslav prime minister, Polish foreign minister, Angolan officers, and various Communist party or government leaders.

Other than Honecker, the Politburo leaders involved in foreign relations are Hermann Axen, who supervises interparty relations, chief ideologue Kurt Hager, and economics expert Günter Mittag. The government leader, defense minister, and security chief (Stoph, Hoffmann, and Mielke) combine Politburo membership with ex-officio governmental responsibilities in foreign affairs.

The detailed formulation of the SED's foreign policy line is the work of the departments of the Secretariat. The departments relevant to foreign policy include those for international information (which is headed by Honecker's brother-in-law, Manfred Feist), propaganda, international relations, friendly parties, security matters, and the department that deals with Western ("Imperialist") countries in general. With the promotion of Herbert Häber to the Secretariat, a department dealing with West Germany now presumably exists. Aside from Honecker himself, Secretariat members Hermann Axen, Herbert Häber, Günter Mittag, and Joachim Hermann supervise departments handling foreign relations.[3]

It is the task of the state apparatus to put GDR foreign policy into effect. Here, too, Honecker, as head of the State Council, plays the leading role. The tasks of detailed coordination and supervision of routine diplomatic activity, external propaganda and cultural work, and foreign affairs research and publication are handled by the Ministry of Foreign Affairs, which supervises the training of future foreign policy personnel, especially through the Institute for International Relations in Potsdam-

Babelsberg. This institute administers a five-year training course for future diplomats, journalists, specialists in foreign trade, and scholars of international affairs.[4]

The four GDR foreign ministers form a varied quartet. The first, Georg Dertinger, served from 1949 to his arrest for espionage in January 1953 and subsequently spent a decade (1954–1964) in jail before being pardoned. Lothar Bolz was a Communist sympathizer who spent the war years in the USSR and served as foreign minister from October 1953 to January 1965. Otto Winzer, a veteran Communist who had returned to Germany from the USSR with Ulbricht in 1945, served until shortly before his death in early 1975. The current foreign minister, Oskar Fischer, served in the German army and was taken prisoner on the Russian front. Fischer, an early SED member, served in various FDJ offices from 1947 to 1955 (i.e., during the period of Honecker's control of the FDJ apparatus).

Fischer, like Winzer—and like Soviet professional diplomats before Gromyko—has not risen higher in party ranks than the level of membership in the Central Committee (1971). Thus he presumably plays a lesser role in foreign policy formulation than do Politburo members; in fact, he is especially disadvantaged in that Defense Minister Hoffmann, who is very active in Third World diplomacy, is a full member of the Politburo. Moreover, within the Council of Ministers, Fischer is flanked not only by Hoffmann but also by the GDR's permanent CMEA representative, Gerhard Weiss (who technically outranks Fischer as a deputy chairman in the Council of Ministers), as well as Foreign Trade Minister Horst Sölle and Sölle's deputy Gerhard Beil.

The instruments available to the GDR leadership for the execution of foreign policy include several mass and "public" organizations, which maintain ties to corresponding target groups abroad. Among the most important of these are the trade union and youth organizations. They allow the GDR to conduct an active foreign policy at many levels; in the years before the GDR achieved general diplomatic recognition, such contacts were a valuable channel of influence.

Examples of recent trade union and FDJ activity will serve to illustrate these functions. The GDR trade union organization (FDGB) held a series of conferences with West European trade unions to propagate the GDR view that there is a "close connection between the aggressive policy of Imperialism and the dismantling of social benefits. . . ." In the Third World, the FDGB helps fledgling union organizations, especially in those countries that have embarked on a "Socialist" path.[5]

A particular commitment of the FDJ is to send youthful work teams (*Jugendbrigaden*) to various countries, especially in southern Africa. Such brigades are also a prominent feature of contemporary GDR-Soviet relations. The *Soiuz* pipeline, for example, was built with the help of FDJ labor on the Orenburg-Ushgorod segment at the Soviet-Czechoslovak border.

LINKS TO THE SOVIET UNION
AND EASTERN EUROPE

"We pledge that . . . we will preserve friendship and cooperation between the GDR and the Soviet Union and between the SED and the CPSU, as something of priceless value."[6] In this declaration is expressed the fundamental fact of GDR foreign policy. The relationship of the GDR to the Soviet Union goes to the heart of the regime's legitimacy. The Soviet Union is officially credited with having provided the external factor necessary for the establishment of the "first workers' and peasants' state on German soil."[7] Moreover, the GDR-Soviet tie is seen as guaranteeing the continued existence of the GDR, and it is thus one aspect of the fundamental socioeconomic and political order. This connection between sovereignty, society, and foreign policy limits the extent to which the regime can base itself on German nationalism as such.[8]

Until sometime into the mid-1950s, the very existence of the GDR was at stake in Soviet maneuvering on the field of Central European politics.[9] Thereafter, the GDR underwent systematic integration into the economic and military alliances of the Council for Mutual Economic Assistance (CMEA) and the WTO; the GDR also signed a series of bilateral treaties with the USSR and several other East European regimes. The GDR-Soviet relationship, however, remained tied to the unresolved conflicts regarding the status of Berlin and Germany.

For the Soviet Union, the dominant considerations were the strategic balance in Europe, the Soviet relationship to West Germany, and the status of the GDR—in roughly that order. For the GDR leaders, understandably, the priorities were reversed. At each crisis of German affairs, therefore, Soviet and GDR interests coincided to a considerable extent, but at some point they diverged—and each time, at that point, Soviet interest took precedence.

In the crisis of the Berlin Wall, for example, minimal GDR needs were met by the sealing off of the intra-urban border, but GDR actions were clearly limited by Soviet perceptions as to the limits of U.S. forbearance. How quickly Soviet pressure could force a GDR retreat on this issue was shown in March 1969 at the time of the election of the West German president in Berlin, when larger concerns for a possible arrangement with Bonn, as well as the sudden escalation of tension on the Sino-Soviet border, brought the crisis to an end.

The classic confrontation between the GDR and the Soviet Union over the German problem took place in 1969–1971.[10] The GDR's fundamental strategy had been to secure its own needs by making them the collective priority demands of the USSR and of its allies. The GDR wanted international recognition, acceptance of its successor-state status by West Germany, and access to international markets; it also wanted its allies to make realization of these demands a prior condition for other agreements in which their own economic or diplomatic arrangements were being made with the Western powers, especially the Federal Republic. In short, it would have preferred to be the Soviet bloc's only Germany.

The pacification of Central Europe between 1969 and 1973 did not meet these maximum GDR goals. For a dozen years, therefore, the post-Ulbricht GDR leadership abandoned all thought of divergence from Soviet decisions and strove to identify its policies, especially those on defense and foreign affairs, as closely as possible with those of the USSR.

This assimilation of GDR policy to a Soviet model became a dominant motif in all aspects of GDR life, not only in the areas of foreign and military policy but also with respect to the ever closer degree of cooperation in economic, personal (e.g., tourism), technical, and political arrangements. These ties found their formal expression in three documents of the mid-1970s characterizing the status of GDR-Soviet relations in that period.

First, there was the unexpected 1974 revision of the GDR constitution. The new Article 6 contained the assertion that the GDR would be "forever and irreversibly allied with the Soviet Union"; such ties were said to guarantee to the people of the GDR "further progress on the road to peace and socialism."[11]

One year later (October 1975), the still-valid GDR-Soviet treaty of 1964 was replaced by a pact that declared that the "all-around strengthening" of GDR-Soviet relations would serve the "further assimilation [Annäherung] of the socialist nations." Language equivalent to the Brezhnev Doctrine pledged the GDR to intervene to halt undesirable political development elsewhere in Eastern Europe. In the area of specific military obligations, the treaty (in Article 8) committed the GDR to aid the USSR with all means, including military, if the latter is attacked by "any state or group of states." Unlike the WTO obligation, therefore, this pledge is not limited to Europe.[12]

To give these formal acts a suitable ideological foundation, the SED program adopted in 1976 declared that the "most important" task in foreign affairs was the "development of all-around fraternal relations between the GDR and USSR," based on the "law-determined qualities [Gesetzmässigkeiten] of the flowering and assimilation [Aufblühen und Annäherung] of socialist nations."[13]

Firmly anchored in the Soviet foreign policy sphere, the GDR, throughout the 1970s and early 1980s, assumed the role of the USSR's military and diplomatic surrogate and crucial economic partner. Moreover, the GDR's good relations with Moscow were not damaged in the transition from Brezhnev to Andropov. The continuity of policy in this regard was signaled by the lavish reception accorded Honecker on an official visit to Moscow and Central Asia in May 1983 and in the official communiqué issued at its close. One month later, the long-time Soviet envoy in East

Berlin, Pyotr Abrassimov (1962–1971 and 1975–1983), was replaced by
V. I. Kotchemassov, a diplomat whose ties to Honecker (through youth
organization work) go back to the 1940s.[14] The transition to Chernenko
seems more problematical, as the early months of the latter's tenure
coincided with an episode of strained GDR-Soviet relations.

This conflict had its roots in the divergent Soviet and GDR reactions
to the deployment of U.S. missiles in West Germany in late 1983.[15] In
some ways, the more recent dispute parallels that of 1970–1971. Then
it was the Soviet Union that favored détente with Bonn while the GDR
hung back. Now it is the GDR that strove to insulate its increasingly
good ties (especially, but not exclusively, economic) with the FRG from
superpower tensions, while the USSR, faced with the failure of its
campaign either to block missile deployment or to induce West German
divergence from NATO policy, looked with disfavor on GDR-FRG ties.

The initial GDR response to the missile deployment, as expressed
by Honecker at the Seventh CC Plenum in November 1983, was much
milder than the predeployment statements would have led one to expect.
Honecker spoke of "limiting the damage" done to détente and inter-
German relations by the deployment; it was better, he said, to negotiate
ten times than to shoot once.[16]

What the Soviet reaction might have been had Andropov lived we
cannot know, although GDR and Soviet views diverged from the start.[17]
A dispute arose in the months just after Andropov's death—a dispute
conducted in a manner typical of such inter-Communist disputes, by
means of esoteric messages, indirect attacks, and the use of third-party
statements. Thus a Hungarian-Czechoslovak controversy about the role
of small states in world affairs and the limits of national divergence
from general Communist policies (in which the Hungarians singled out
GDR foreign policy as praiseworthy) was the first sign of trouble.
However, after Honecker's visit to the USSR and his talk with Chernenko
in June 1984, the GDR leadership must have thought its policies had
met with Soviet approval, for not only did Honecker repeat his moderate
reaction to missile deployment and his willingness to work with the
West Germans in seeking a solution to these issues but the GDR, for
the second year in a row, arranged a large-scale, government-guaranteed
bank credit from West Germany.

This second bank credit seems to have crystallized a Soviet perception that the GDR was pursuing a foreign policy line independent
of larger Soviet strategy. The Soviet response was to work at worsening
the relationship between Bonn and East Berlin by accusing the FRG of
"revanchist" and aggressive designs, and by reminding Honecker of all
the unfulfilled GDR demands made since 1980 and of all of his statements
hostile to the Bonn regime. The heart of Soviet concern was revealed
by a *Pravda* editorial that specifically complained about Bonn's use of
economic inducements to interfere in GDR internal affairs; expansion
of contacts between the Germanies was seen as an attempt to gain
ideological and political influence.[18]

The GDR responded to such signs of Soviet displeasure by formally restating its commitment to negotiations about missiles and economic cooperation with Bonn in a formal interview that Honecker gave to the GDR press in mid-August.[19] Although he made some concessions to Soviet sensitivities (such as declaring that "uniting capitalism and socialism . . . is like uniting fire and ice"), he also reiterated the basic themes of GDR policy over the past nine months—namely, that it was important to limit the damage done to détente; that the GDR "did not desire" Soviet counterdeployment; and that a reduction of Western deployment might bring a retraction of WTO countermeasures.

Sometime in the following month, however, a stern, albeit private, Soviet warning to the GDR must have occurred, for on September 5, 1984, Honecker's long-awaited visit to West Germany was canceled by the GDR, and in September–October 1984, GDR rhetoric regarding West Germany grew notably harsher. Moreover, the economic agreement signed in October for GDR-Soviet cooperation to the year 2000 (discussed later in this chapter) may have been structured in a pro-Soviet manner as a result of this crisis. Nonetheless, the GDR's efforts to maintain Western ties continue, and East Berlin is careful to insist that the Honecker visit is only postponed but not canceled. Honecker's talk at the official GDR thirty-fifth anniversary celebration was carefully balanced between criticism of Bonn and a restated commitment to negotiating the arms race.[20] The transition to Gorbachev, with its implied resumption of Andropov's policies, must have suited the GDR leadership, judging by such events as Honecker's successful visit to the Soviet Union and his meeting with Gorbachev in 1985.

This controversy illustrated the current limits of GDR policy in relation to the Soviet Union. As before, no GDR interest is allowed to get in the way of overriding Soviet strategic concerns—whether those concerns relate to the United States or to the Soviet hold on Eastern Europe. On the other hand, Soviet pressure has only slowed the improvement of GDR relations with the West. As of the year's end (1984–1985), Honecker is still in place as leader, and his basic economic and social programs, as well as his diplomatic initiatives toward Western Europe, are still GDR policy.

Economic Ties

The importance of its economic ties to the USSR for the GDR lies both in their extent and their content. Each country is the other's largest trading partner. For the Soviet Union, this means that some 9 percent of its foreign trade is with the GDR and over a third of the GDR's foreign trade is with the USSR, whereas the next largest volume of trade, that with Czechoslovakia, amounts to only 7 percent of the total.[21]

Moreover, the goods exchanged in GDR-Soviet trade are items mutually important for economic growth. The GDR was the leading foreign supplier to the USSR of industrial machinery in 1979; in 1980,

TABLE 3.2
Critical Items in GDR–Soviet Trade (1980)

	GDR Percentage of Soviet Imports
Oil refining equipment	65%
Construction cranes	62
Railway cars	98

	Soviet Percentage of GDR Imports
Oil	87%
Natural gas	100
Cotton	88
Rolled steel	78
Iron ore	77

Source: Neuer Weg 37, 2 (1982): 64.

the GDR supplied significant quantities of Soviet imports of oil-refining equipment, railway cars, agricultural equipment, and construction cranes. In turn, the USSR supplied all of the GDR's imports of natural gas, just under 90 percent of its oil imports, and major proportions of cotton, iron ore, and rolled steel (see Table 3.2).[22]

This trading relationship is linked to a broader pattern of GDR-Soviet economic cooperation. Operating through the vehicle of the Joint GDR-USSR Governmental Commission, the two countries have coordinated their economic plans, research projects, the production and exchange of technologically advanced items, and joint investment projects; both countries also share in the development of specialized, high-technology goods. There are currently over 160 agreements on the state level, and they embody 37 so-called main directions (*Hauptrichtungen*) for future cooperation.[23]

The closeness of the two countries' economic cooperation may also be seen in the extraordinary degree of interenterprise specialization. Soviet and GDR factories, particularly in high-technology fields, are producing specific parts of the same piece of equipment, thus allowing profitable utilization of specialized equipment on a large scale.[24]

At the GDR's thirty-fifth anniversary celebration, Honecker and Soviet foreign minister Andrei Gromyko signed an agreement for economic and technical cooperation to run to the year 2000 (replacing a Honecker-Brezhnev agreement that had been set until 1990!).[25] The provision of this agreement shed some light on the nature of the economic ties between the GDR and its Soviet partner. Aside from general exhortations for closer cooperation, the program states that the "main direction" for solving energy problems is "conservation and rational use" of energy and raw materials. For "continuation of deliveries of important fuel and raw materials" by the USSR, the GDR pledges itself to undertake necessary investments in "reconstructing and modernizing" its industrial plant so as to ensure continued shipment of "high quality consumer appliances, . . . chemicals, . . . modern high-productivity machinery and world-class equipment" to the USSR. Moreover, the GDR was to continue its "participation in constructing [Soviet] facilities for fuel and raw material extraction"; increased use of nuclear power for energy generation is to be furthered jointly; and GDR-Soviet trade is to be redirected toward high-technology items.

A good example of the intertwined political and economic aspects of the GDR-Soviet relationship is the participation of GDR youth brigades in the construction of the Urengoi-Ushgorod natural gas pipeline. GDR workers on this project, the total number of whom is projected to reach 5,000, are to lay 126 kilometers of pipeline in addition to related work. They will be rewarded with material preferences upon their return home; for the present, they are publicized as personifying GDR-Soviet collaboration.[26]

Whatever the outcome of future and particular transactions between the GDR and its Soviet partner might be, the mutually beneficial relationship between the two most technically advanced members of the CMEA economic community will almost certainly be retained, if only because so great a portion of GDR industrial capacity is based on production for Soviet markets.[27]

Military Ties

The GDR's military establishment and its relationship to the Warsaw Treaty Organization as well as to the Soviet forces in the GDR have already been described. In the context of GDR-Soviet relations generally, these ties are rather more political and geographical than specifically military.

From the Soviet standpoint, the GDR is the physical, territorial basis of its first-echelon military force directed against NATO in Europe. The GDR is thus directly in the line of fire in any conceivable Soviet war planning. The East German response to this has been enthusiastic acceptance of a closely integrated military role in the WTO's "Northern Tier." Given the circumstances, there is probably little choice involved. In any case, the regime has "fled forward" to embrace its military-strategic role within the larger WTO structure.[28]

Despite this regime policy, it might be noted that the GDR receives Soviet weapons in types and quantities that do not single it out as a preferred recipient.[29] Two cases in point are the Soviet-made MiG 23/ 27 (by now the standard WTO fighter aircraft) and the T-72 main battle tank.

The GDR and Eastern Europe

The GDR's relationship to the other East European states that constitute its partners in the CMEA and WTO are less important to it than its ties to Moscow. These relationships have been primarily economic: roughly one-fourth of GDR foreign trade is with the five Communist states of the region.[30] Political relations have been significant in three cases particularly: Romania, Czechoslovakia, and Poland. Relations with Romania have fluctuated from a common foreign policy line, especially in the wake of the 1967 decision in Bucharest to establish diplomatic ties to Bonn. Although GDR-Romanian relations are no longer as strained as they had been at that time, they do tend to be cool and correct. Between 1977 and 1980, for example, Romanian and GDR party leaders met only once.

The GDR leadership watched with misgivings the cultural and then political liberalization of Czechoslovakia between 1962 and 1968. The assembled evidence suggests that GDR pressure contributed to the Soviet decision to intervene against the Dubcek regime in August 1968.[31] In recent years, however, relations between the two regimes have been uneventful. Husak and Honecker, who came into office at about the same time, share a common interest in political stability and economic collaboration. In 1972, Poland and Czechoslovakia were objects of the GDR's policy of encouraging an eastward orientation of its citizens by removing visa restrictions on travel between the three countries. Difficulties regarding currency, consumer goods, and the Polish crisis led later to the reimposition of travel controls.

The GDR response to the campaign for Polish "renewal" in 1980– 1981 was predictably hostile. Aside from particular difficulties, such as shortfalls in Polish deliveries, the rise of Solidarity was viewed by the East Berlin leadership as a consequence of foolish weakness by Polish party leaders. Throughout the turbulent political struggle that ended with the imposition of martial law in December 1981, the GDR took the side of conservative elements in the Polish party (granting such groups access to GDR media, for example) and identified reform elements with Western subversion.

Honecker himself remained restrained in his public comments, but other officials, as well as rank-and-file party members and nonparty workers, were allowed to be more outspoken. An unfortunate consequence of the official hostility to Polish developments was the revival of ethnic prejudice against Poles among some elements in the GDR population. Since December 1981, the GDR has publicly backed the Warsaw military regime, with Honecker becoming the first East European leader to visit Poland since December 1981.[32]

RELATIONS WITH THE FIRST AND THIRD WORLDS

We now turn to an increasingly important, if still relatively small, part of GDR foreign policy: its relations with the Third World, the industrial democracies, and the international organizations. Common to all of these arenas of external activity are two factors in particular: economic interests and the GDR's search for prestige and stature.

The GDR and the Third World

In its relations with the countries of the Third World, the GDR plays the roles, in Michael Sodaro's apt words, of "supplicant and surrogate."[33] Initially, the GDR was a supplicant for diplomatic recognition; more recently it has been a supplicant for access to non-Soviet energy and raw material (especially oil) resources. At the same time, it has acted as the Soviet Union's surrogate—or, more precisely, as its junior partner—in dealing with Third World states and political "liberation" movements.

In playing these roles, the GDR and its leadership have gained important *domestic* political benefits. Third World activity provides a non–Central European dimension to the GDR's place among the world's states as well as an arena for individual and collective accomplishment; it is a source of prestige and recognition, and thus a positive legitimating factor for the East Berlin regime.

As a Soviet junior partner, the GDR supplies economic, political, military, and other technical assistance to Third World states and political movements, sometimes in the form of training, refuge, medical aid, and education in the GDR. Especially noteworthy has been the GDR's commitment to revolutionary movements, often long before these movements attain power: examples include Angola's MPLA and Mozambique's FRELIMO. Such possible future ruling parties as Namibia's SWAPO and South Africa's ANC are being supported now. Such contacts may be continued after a particular movement has come to power; in the case of Ethiopia, for example, interstate contacts are supplemented by formal ties between the SED and the recently established Ethiopian Party of Labor.[34]

GDR support for certain Third World countries takes three forms. First, there is general political support, such as that expressed during UN debates. Second, there is material aid and training of personnel. Direct governmental aid by the GDR is directed chiefly at politically favored states. The exact amount of such aid is difficult to estimate, given that it includes direct grants, trade preferences, training costs, and so on. According to the GDR Foreign Ministry, the aid constituted .79 percent of produced national income in 1983.[35] The GDR is said to have undertaken over 650 industrial projects since 1970 and to have agreements for scientific-technical cooperation with some twenty-seven less developed countries.[36] Considerable aid is channeled directly to both governments and movements through GDR "social organizations" in addition to the direct transfer of funds collected through public appeals in the GDR (which in 1978 alone amounted to some 200 million Mark).

The most controversial GDR activity in the Third World concerns the provision of military equipment, training, and possibly direct combat support. The central role of Third World armies has long been recognized by GDR observers, who stress the state-building function of armies and security forces. According to one NVA source, the GDR and other Communist countries give five types of aid:

1. supplying weapons and technical equipment;
2. training military cadre;
3. helping to build up an armaments industry;
4. licensing local production of advanced weapons; and
5. engaging in field training of military forces.

In addition, there is the "temporary presence in a few liberated countries of troop contingents from particular socialist states," which has been the subject of particularly "malevolent slander"; in fact, all such troop contingents are there by host government invitation and in accord with Article 51 of the UN Charter.[37]

Although there are undoubtedly GDR military personnel in several states of sub-Saharan Africa and in the Middle East, reliable data on their numbers, influence, activities, and length of stay are extremely difficult to come by (see Table 3.3).

Of greater long-range significance than direct military aid may be the GDR's program for training civilian officials. The administrative model presented by the GDR is an attractive one for authoritarian developmental regimes. The payoff for the GDR is, in part, the prospect of having influence on officials in various countries. More important from an ideological and psychological perspective is the confirmation of the historical triumph of their system that such regimes will give the GDR leaders.

It is thus hardly surprising to read that in the years between 1977 and 1982, for example, 952 Third World trade union officials studied at the FDGB academy or that another 404 persons studied at other GDR universities while a further 285 had GDR vocational training. To take another example, the GDR itself, through its controlled journalists' organizations, maintains formal ties with a number of Third World liberation organizations, including the PLO; nor was it unexpected that the GDR would support the call for a "new international information order."[38]

With respect to the Third World, the GDR has recently appeared in the role of supplicant for trade and raw materials. The emphasis given to Mexico before, during, and since Honecker's state visit undoubtedly had something to do with that nation's emergence as a major

TABLE 3.3
GDR Military Personnel in Selected Third World Countries

Country	Number of GDR Personnel
Algeria	250
Angola	450
Ethiopia	550
Guinea	125
Iraq	160
Libya	400
Mozambique	100
South Yemen	75
Syria	210
Total	2,320

Source: International Institute for Strategic Studies, The Military Balance, 1983–1984 (London: IISS, 1983), p. 22.

oil producer. GDR interest in such regimes as those of Iran under the shah or the ayatollah, or of the Philippines under Marcos, is certainly a matter of seeking markets and raw materials outside the CMEA sphere. The long-term limitation of Soviet energy deliveries, even with GDR participation and investment in their exploitation, intensifies the search for politically accessible and economically viable Third World sources. It is this need that accounts for the position of Iraq and Iran as the GDR's two leading trading partners in the Third World (see Table 3.4).

Increasingly, GDR policy in the Third World has differentiated among different sorts of countries. Some are objects of commercial interest; others are politically important. Among the latter, a further distinction can be made between revolutionary states with either a socialist or a nonsocialist orientation. The GDR's political and military involvement is greatest with the former (e.g., South Yemen or Angola), but it tries to find a common "anti-Imperialist" connection with all of them.[39]

TABLE 3.4
GDR Trade with Third World Countries in 1982 (in billions of Valuta-Mark)

Country	Amount
Iraq	1,958.6
Iran	1,733.8
Brazil	840.5
Syria	651.6
India	610.7
Algeria	308.9
Angola	255.2
Mozambique	222.7

Source: Statistisches Taschenbuch der DDR 1984 (Berlin: Staatsverlag der DDR, 1984), pp. 101–102.

GDR relations with the Western industrial nations have been largely economic. Although trade with these nations (excluding West Germany and Berlin) accounts for only 19 percent of total GDR foreign trade, it involves several key items, including imports of feed grains and specialized industrial products. Moreover, trade relations are the most readily available means for enlarging the GDR's ties to Western governments— a primary goal of foreign policy for prestige reasons, if nothing else.

Generally, however, relations other than the economic sort have not flourished. Relations with the United States have suffered from controversies over human rights violations, GDR activity in the Third World, and disagreement over restitution to Jewish victims of Hitler. Moreover, Washington has regarded the GDR from a West German perspective, taking Bonn's side in disputes on inter-German relations. Given Bonn's importance to U.S. policy, there had been little interest in the past in a more active policy toward the GDR. However, East Berlin's more active diplomacy in German affairs, particularly its continued adherence to a policy of negotiations even after the Soviet Union broke off strategic weapons talks in the fall of 1983, sparked some U.S. interest, as shown by Assistant Secretary of State Richard Burt's visit to the GDR in February 1984.[40]

A shift in trading relations toward greater emphasis on Japan, Austria, and Canada, while motivated in part by economics, has also

Honecker meets with Austrian President Kirschschlager on the occasion of the latter's visit to East Berlin. Photo courtesy of the GDR Embassy, Washington, D.C.

had political overtones. For example, Canada's Prime Minister Pierre Trudeau, as the first non-German NATO government leader to visit the GDR, received a very cordial reception there. A special effort has also been made to establish ties with France, the first Western country with which the GDR has, at some political cost, reciprocally established cultural centers.[41]

In the summer of 1984, GDR diplomacy was active in relation to Western Europe. In rapid succession, Honecker received the Swedish, Greek, and Italian prime ministers (Olof Palme, George Papandreau, and Bettino Craxi).[42] In each case, increases in trade as well as continued political dialogue to deal with strategic weapons issues were the main points on the agenda. It seems likely that, notwithstanding the consequential considerations of prestige, Honecker was hoping to smooth the way for continued inter-European dialogue, specifically with respect to his planned trip to West Germany.

Finally, the GDR's active membership in the United Nations combines several aspects of its foreign policy. GDR representatives support Soviet positions in the UN, demonstrate their support of Third World protégés, and show themselves and the public at home that the GDR is a full-fledged participant in international affairs.[43]

NOTES

1. A similar perspective emerges from official descriptions of the sources of GDR foreign policy. Thus a typical semi-official statement declares that the principles of "internationalism and peace" underlying GDR foreign policy are "the expression of [the GDR's] class character . . . and the Marxist-Leninist theory of society." The GDR's close ties to the USSR and its support of revolutionary movements are said to be logical extensions of this class character. See Institut für Internationale Beziehungen, *Aussenpolitik der DDR für Sozialismus und Frieden* (Berlin: Staatsverlag der DDR, 1974), p. 49.

2. See Anita M. Mallinckrodt, "An Aussenpolitik beteiligte Institutionen," in Eberhard Schulz, ed., *Drei Jahrzehnte Aussenpolitik der DDR* (Munich: R. Oldenbourg, 1979), pp. 134–150; see also Anita M. Mallinckrodt, *Wer Macht die Aussenpolitik der DDR?* (Düsseldorf: Droste Verlag, 1972), for a discussion of participants in the foreign policy decisionmaking process.

3. Mallinckrodt, "An Aussenpolitik beteiligte Institutionen," pp. 137–138. The current head of the Central Committee Secretariat's Department of International Relations is Günter Sieber; his predecessor, Egon Winkelmann, is now the GDR's envoy in Moscow.

4. Mallinckrodt, *Wer Macht die Aussenpolitik der DDR?* pp. 205–209; Gert-Joachim Glaessner, *Herrschaft durch Kader* (Opladen: Westdeutscher Verlag, 1978), pp. 267–278.

5. Frank Bochow, "Gewerkschaften im Kampf für Frieden und sozialen Fortschritt," *Deutsche Aussenpolitik* 27 (July 1982):6–9.

6. From a speech by Kurt Hager at the 1982 observances in East Berlin of the Soviet October Revolution, *Neues Deutschland*, 6–7 November 1982, p. 3.

7. Hermann Axen, "Die DDR und der Grundwiderspruch unserer Epoche," *Einheit* 39, nos. 9, 10 (October 1984):825.

8. For background and analysis of this relationship, see Melvin Croan, *East Germany: The Soviet Connection*, Washington Paper, no. 36 (Beverly Hills: Sage, 1976); N. Edwina Moreton, *East Germany and the Warsaw Alliance: The Politics of Détente* (Boulder, Colo.: Westview Press, 1978); Henry Krisch, "Soviet-GDR Relations in the Honecker Era," *East Central Europe* 6 (1979):152–172.

9. Oft-repeated but poorly substantiated accusations have been made to the effect that, for example, it would have been Beria's policy in 1953 to agree to dissolution of the GDR in return for a neutralized, united Germany.

10. In addition to Moreton, *East Germany*, see Gerhard Wettig, *Die Sowjetunion, die DDR und die Deutschland-Frage 1965–76* (Stuttgart: Verlag Bonn-Aktuell, 1976); and Dennis L. Bark, *Agreement on Berlin* (Washington, D.C.: American Enterprise Institute, 1974).

11. A synoptic version of the old and new constitutions can be found in *Deutschland Archiv* 7 (1974):1188–1223.

12. See the treaty text in *Neues Deutschland*, 8 October 1975, p. 1.

13. *Programm der Sozialistischen Einheitspartei Deutschlands* (Berlin: Dietz Verlag, 1976), pp. 83–85.

14. For the extensive coverage of Honecker's trip, see *Neues Deutschland*, 4–8 May 1983; the joint communique is in *Neues Deutschland*, 9 May 1983, pp. 2–3. Regarding Kotchemassov, see *Frankfurter Allgemeine Zeitung*, 14 June 1983, p. 5, and *Neues Deutschland*, 12 August 1983, p. 1.

15. A good summary of the dispute, with documentation, is Ronald D. Asmus, "East Berlin and Moscow: The Documentation of a Dispute," RFE-RL Research, *RAD Background Report/158* (August 31, 1984). See also "Warning East Berlin for Slight Lean West," *New York Times*, 12 August 1984, p. E3; "Chill in Bloc: Soviet Chides Germans," *New York Times*, 6 August 1984, p. A3; "German Détente: Soviet Quandary?" *New York Times*, 6 September 1984, p. A3.

16. *Neues Deutschland*, 26–27 November 1983, pp. 6–7.

17. Compare, for example, the statements made by Honecker and Gromyko during the latter's visit to East Berlin, when Gromyko called governments such as that of West Germany "accomplices" in a "conspiracy against peace" (*Neues Deutschland*, 18 October 1983, p. 3), or the contrasting remarks of Gromyko and Oskar Fischer (*Neues Deutschland*, 5 January 1984, p. 3).

18. "On the Wrong Track," *Pravda*, 2 August 1984, quoted in Asmus, "East Berlin and Moscow," pp. 53–54.

19. In *Neues Deutschland*, 18–19 August 1984, pp. 1–4.

20. Erich Honecker, *Rede auf der Festveranstaltung anlässlich des 35. Jahrestages der Gründung der DDR* (Dresden: Verlag Zeit im Bild, n.d.), p. 18.

21. *Statistisches Taschenbuch der DDR 1984* (Berlin: Staatsverlag der DDR, 1984), pp. 100–102.

22. In 1981, 42 percent of GDR exports to the USSR were "specialized manufactures" (*Die Wirtschaft*, no. 3 [1983], p. 9); for information regarding the Soviet shares of GDR imports, see *Successful Path of Developing an Advanced Socialist Society in the GDR* (Berlin: SED, 1981), p. 63.

23. For details on the long-range program, see *Neues Deutschland*, 6 October 1979, p. 1; for a discussion of the 1983 meeting of the Joint Soviet-GDR Intergovernmental Commission, see *Neues Deutschland*, 10 June 1983, p. 6.

24. Leonid Kostandow, "UdSSR-DDR: 35 Jahre ökonomische Zusammenarbeit," *Einheit* 39 (September-October 1984):793–794.

25. "Programm der Zusammenarbeit bis zum Jahre 2000 zwischen DDR und UdSSR in Wissenschaft, Technik und Produktion," *Neues Deutschland*, 8 October 1984, p. 9.

26. Cam Hudson, "East European Media on Their Participation in Gas Pipeline Project," RFE-RL Research, *RAD Background Report/229* (November 2, 1982); Hans-Joachim Dubrowsky, "Vollständiges Bild des 'Jahrhundertgeschäfts,'" *Die Wirtschaft*, no. 10 (1982), p. 24. For one of Honecker's many references to GDR labor participation, see *Neues Deutschland*, 18 November 1982, p. 3. For recent and typical publicity, see *Neues Deutschland*, 9–10 July 1983, p. 9, and 1–2 October 1983, p. 9.

27. Heiko Polten, "Internationale sozialistische Spezialisierung und Kooperation der Produktion—Ergebnisse, Aufgaben, Perspektiven," *Deutsche Aussenpolitik* 27 (March 1982):31–46, Heiko Polten, "RGW-Kooperation in den 80er Jahren," *Die Wirtschaft*, no. 3 (1983), p. 27.

28. See Chapter 2 of the present volume. The public portrayal of the close GDR-Soviet military relationship is exemplified by the coverage of Ustinov's visit to the GDR in *Neues Deutschland*, 6–8 April 1983. Improved GDR-Soviet logistical collaboration, to the exclusion of a possibly unreliable Poland, may be the motive underlying the project's development of a direct sea-ferry link between the two countries. For a description of this project, see *Neues Deutschland*, 22–23 January 1983, p. 9.

29. International Institute of Strategic Studies, *The Military Balance, 1983–1984* (London: IISS, 1983), pp. 21–22; Stockholm International Peace Research Institute, *World Armaments and Disarmaments: SIPRI Yearbook 1983* (New York: International Publications Service/Taylor & Francis, 1983), pp. 294–298.

30. Gerhard Brendel and Hans-Joachim Dubrowsky, "Tendenzen im Handel Zwischen den RGW-Ländern," *Deutsche Aussenpolitik* 27 (October 1982):30–46.

31. Jiri Valenta, *Soviet Intervention in Czechoslovakia, 1968* (Baltimore: Johns Hopkins University Press, 1979), especially pp. 114–116, 141.

32. Some convenient summaries of the GDR's response to the crisis in Poland are Ronald D. Asmus, "The SED Attempts to Come to Grips with the Polish Crisis," RFE-RL Research, *RAD Background Report/302* (October 31, 1981); Patrick Moore, "Poland at the East German Party Congress," RFE-RL Research, *RAD Background Report/115* (April 27, 1981); of the several roundups in *Deutschland Archiv*, see 14 (October 1981):1009–1014; and for details on Honecker's trip to Poland, see Peter Jochen Winters, "Honeckers Polen-Reise," *Deutschland Archiv* 16 (October 1983):1013–1018.

33. Michael Sodaro, "The GDR and the Third World: Supplicant and Surrogate," in Michael Radu, ed., *Eastern Europe and the Third World: East Vs. South* (New York: Praeger Publishers, 1981), pp. 106–141; Melvin Croan, "A New Afrika Korps?" *Washington Quarterly* 3 (Winter 1980):21–37.

34. See Eberhard Schulz, ed., *Drei Jahrzehnte Aussenpolitik der DDR* (Munich: R. Oldenbourg, 1979), p. 679. For information on SED-Ethiopian relations, see *Neues Deutschland*, 22–23 December 1984, p. 1.

35. In a report of October 5, 1984, to the UN General Assembly, the GDR Foreign Ministry stated that total aid to "developing countries and liberation movements" came to .79 percent of produced national income, or 1,662,400 million Mark, of which 242,500 million Mark went to least developed areas. These figures include the costs of training Third World personnel in the GDR. As of January 1984, 29,157 citizens of Third World countries were receiving training in the GDR, and 6,522 had completed such training in 1983 (according to *DDR Report* 17, no. 12 [1984]:724). In a report to the 1983 UNCTAD VI conference, GDR foreign trade minister Sölle gave the same .79 percent figure for 1979 (see *DDR Report* 16, no. 8 [1983]:442). For a qualitative listing of GDR aid projects, see Siegfried Büttner, "DDR-Hilfe für Entwicklungsländer," *Einheit* 35 (October 1980):1081–1082.

36. *Die Wirtschaft*, no. 11 (1982), p. 24.

37. Klaus-Ulrich Schloesser, "Zur Rolle der Armee in den national befreiten Staaten Asiens und Afrikas," *Deutsche Aussenpolitik* 27 (October 1982):64–75.

38. Frank Bochow, "Gewerkschaften im Kampf für Frieden und und sozialen Fortschritt," *Deutsche Aussenpolitik* 27 (July 1982):11–12; Heinz Peter Schumacher, "Die medienpolitischen Aktivitäten der DDR in Dritten Welt," *Deutschland Archiv* 15 (July 1982):739–744. For information on journalists' organizations, see "Schreiben lernen in Ost-Berlin," *Frankfurter Allgemeine Zeitung*, 25 March 1983, p. 12.

39. Christian Mährdel, "Revolutionen in Asien, Afrika, und Lateinamerika: Sozialer Dimensionen nationaker Befreiung in unserer Epoche," *Asien, Afrika, Lateinamerika* 11 (March-April 1983):197–202, abstracted in *DDR Report* 16 (July 1983):375.

40. The GDR is barred from receiving the most-favored-nation designation under the Jackson-Vanik amendment; nor does it qualify for Export-Import Bank credit. For a combination of political and commercial reasons, the GDR has

shifted the bulk of its feed grain imports from the United States to Canada (although on a recent visit to East Berlin, the U.S. assistant secretary for agriculture struck a hopeful note). See Angela Stent, "Economic Relations Between the United States and the German Democratic Republic: Politics, Trade and Future Prospects"; and Michael Sodaro, "U.S.-GDR Relations in the International Setting." Both papers were presented at a conference on U.S.-GDR relations in September 1983. For a discussion of the Burt visit, see *Neues Deutschland*, 23 February 1984, pp. 1–2.

41. The French not only successfully insisted on liberal access rules for visitors to their center but forced *Neues Deutschland* to print a statement quoting French Foreign Minister Cheysson as saying that "of course the Center will be open to all" (30 January 1984, p. 1). An Italian center is to be opened in early 1985. Coverage of Trudeau's visit began in *Neues Deutschland* on 31 January 1984, and continued for several days.

42. For extensive coverge of the leaders' visits, see *Neues Deutschland* for early July 1984, especially 1, 7–8, and 11 July. For an analysis of the significance for GDR foreign policy of such visits, see Harald Kleinschmid, "Hoffnung auf den Abbau von Mauern," *Deutschland Archiv* 17 (August 1984):787–790.

43. See, for example, Oskar Fischer, "Die DDR-Zehn Jahre Mitglied der Organisation der Vereinten Nationen," *Horizont* 16 (September 1983):3–4, which includes a list of every chairmanship (and so on) that a GDR diplomat has ever held at the UN. See also Wilhelm Bruns, "Zehn Jahre Gegeneinander und Nebeneinander in der UNO," *Deutschland Archiv* 16 (July 1983):720–728. The official ten years' commemoration of the GDR's membership in the United Nations took place at a meeting of the State Council; see *Neues Deutschland*, 19 September 1983, p. 1.

4

The GDR in Germany

In seeking to establish the GDR as a viable political entity, its leaders have defined it in contrast to the Federal Republic and German states of the past. Indeed, a concerted effort has been made to locate the GDR, both politically and psychologically, within a "socialist" bloc of peoples and states. This policy has required strenuous efforts to sunder the connections between the people of the GDR, with their familial ties to West Germany and their memory and consciousness of the common German past, and "Germany" as a political and social entity. In this perspective, the Honecker policy of *Abgrenzung* (demarcation) is but a continuation of long-standing GDR policies, its more pointed enunciation made necessary by the diminution of political distance resulting from détente and *Ostpolitik*.

This *Abgrenzung* of the GDR has encompassed every area of life. Politically, it has meant denying Bonn's claims to all-German representative legitimacy; in economic and social policy, the regime has "built socialism," no longer holding back on social transformation in the interests of facilitating future unification. Culturally, there has been a steady and increasing pressure to divorce literature and the arts in the GDR from a common "German" character. Finally, and most obviously, the GDR has oriented itself in foreign and military policy toward membership in Soviet-led international institutions and alliances.

In order to accomplish this crystallization of a new East Germany, the party and state leaders of the GDR have had to struggle on two fronts: with the larger, more populous and more prosperous West German state next door, and with the historical legacy of the German past. Although we shall discuss these two aspects of GDR policy in succession, they are actually parts of the same search for political and psychological identity.

Relations Between the Two German States

From the establishment of the two German states in 1949 to roughly 1955, the continued uncertainty as to the political future of Germany and of Soviet attitudes on the subject kept the GDR command (at least verbally) to the notion of German unification.

With the integration of the GDR into the East European alliance system in the mid-1950s, the regime's chief concern in relation to West Germany became to secure from the world, and especially from Bonn, an acceptance of the GDR's independent status.[1] Hence the common feature of all GDR initiatives in German affairs during the decade and a half prior to the inter-German Basic Treaty of 1972 was an insistence on juridical affirmation of GDR sovereignty. The long-term objective on the state level became to structure inter-German relations on the model of the "peaceful coexistence" of any two states of different social systems. At the social and personal level, the regime strove to reduce individual and group ties to the West; it even canceled some of its own political initiatives, such as the proposed exchange of speakers and articles between the SED and the West German SPD in 1966. Finally, the regime sought to redefine the "nation" so as to lessen the appeal of a common German nationalism. This reappraisal of nationality and nationhood then necessarily led to a reassessment of the German historical heritage.

The process of defining the national identity has proven a difficult and prolonged one. In recent years, there have been bold changes in the official reception of the historical heritage, and even a few intimations of common German destiny. Nevertheless, it remains firm GDR policy that any attempt to "keep open the German question" (which is Bonn's policy) is a hostile and reactionary step.

Until 1971, then, it was GDR policy to maintain a strict separation from West Germany while continuing rhetorical support for unification. It was the change in the international environment brought about by the détente between Moscow and Bonn that put the GDR onto its present path of formal separation. The change was marked by the Four-Power Agreement on Berlin (1971) negotiated by the United States, Great Britain, France, and the USSR, and by the Treaty of Basic Relations (*Grundlagenvertrag*) between the two German states.

The Four-Power Agreement on Berlin and the Basic Treaty

Prior to 1971, the symbol of and often the occasion for political discord in Germany was the isolated enclave of West Berlin. For the GDR, the most desirable political goal was the elimination of West Berlin as a separate social and political unit; it especially wanted to sever connections between West Berlin and West Germany, and it sought incorporation of East Berlin into the GDR and general international recognition of its status as the GDR's capital. (The controversial status of the former Soviet sector is epitomized by the fact that the two West German chancellors who have set foot in the GDR, Brandt in 1970 and Schmidt in 1981, carefully avoided the capital of the host state.)

The Four-Power Agreement[2] meant that the continued existence of West Berlin was expressly reaffirmed by the Soviet Union; symbolically, the USSR was allowed to open a consulate in West Berlin, which underlined West Berlin's special and separate existence. The agreement dictated that West Berlin was to "continue not to be a constituent part of the Federal Republic of Germany and not to be governed by it," but it also stipulated that ties between West Berlin and the FRG were to "be maintained and developed."

The agreement clearly put an end to the chief instrument for political pressure in German affairs open to the GDR: the deliberate harassment of transit traffic between Berlin and West Germany. It committed the four powers (and explicitly the USSR) to facilitate unimpeded passage of goods and persons between West Berlin and the FRG, as well as to expedite travel of West Berliners in the GDR. Consequently, the repeated access crises of the years from 1948 to 1971 have not recurred.[3]

The Four-Power Agreement not only regularized inter-German relations in regard to Berlin, but, by opening the way to ratification of Bonn's treaties with Poland and the USSR, it also set the stage for the negotiation of the first general treaty between the two German states, the *Grundlagenvertrag* of 1972.[4]

On one level this treaty marked a substantial improvement in the GDR's status relative to the Federal Republic. For the first time, the Bonn government recognized the GDR as a fully sovereign state within secure and accepted borders, and both sides renounced the use of force. However, the two sides "established standing representations accredited to the seat of government" in place of embassies, and excluded questions of individuals' nationality. Moreover, the treaty noted the FRG's position on the national question, which was that a single German nation continued to exist. The treaty also provided for a variety of implementation accords on such subjects as travel arrangements, telephone and postal ties, environmental preservation, and transportation (including a major highway link between Hamburg and Berlin across the GDR, which was financed by the West Germans). Two particularly important provisions were that for a joint border demarcation committee and that for special visiting rights across the border for people in frontier districts.[5]

Politically, the *Grundlagenvertrag* has allowed the GDR to maintain its demarcation from the Federal Republic, and for many years relations between the two states stagnated. The GDR was never keen about the degree of contact between the Germanies brought about by the treaty, and it took measures to limit it. These included raising transit fees, limiting access by West Germans to designated categories of "sensitive" GDR officials, and restricting activities of West German journalists in the GDR.

Freedom of movement—or rather the lack of it—for East and West Germans has been a source of constant tension in the intra-German relationship. The sealing off of the last border, that within Berlin, greatly reduced the number of those fleeing the GDR. Nonetheless, attempts

FRG Federal Chancellor Willy Brandt (left) and GDR Prime Minister Willi Stoph (right) meet in the GDR city of Erfurt, March, 1970. Photo courtesy of the German Information Center, New York.

In August, 1971, the Four Powers agreed to a settlement of the issues affecting West Berlin. Former Soviet Ambassador to the GDR Pytr Abrassimov is leaving the Allied Control Council Building in West Berlin—U.S. MPs salute at the doorway. Photo courtesy of the German Information Center, New York.

GDR's Kohl (left) and Bonn's Bahr (right) exchange ratifications of the Basic Treaty. Photo courtesy of the German Information Center, New York.

have continued and somewhat over 200,000 people have fled since 1973. But as the controls along the border become more extensive and sophisticated, the number of those able to leave without permission continues to diminish. Perhaps it is this fact that enabled the GDR, by a decision of June 1982, to "forgive" civilians who fled the GDR between January 1, 1972, and December 31, 1980, thus enabling them to visit the GDR. Some 38,000 persons are thought to have been affected by this concession, which was granted after the December 1981 Schmidt-Honecker meeting.[6]

A symbol of the state of inter-German relations is the regimen on the border of the Federal Republic—at the political dividing line between two worlds, as the GDR likes to phrase it. All along the border behind the forbidden strips at its edge runs a special zone 5 kilometers in width. Special permits are needed for entrance into this zone, and normal activities within it are strictly regulated and may be prohibited by border force commanders. These regulations are enforced through some 54,000 automatic firing devices (which were removed during 1983–1984), mine fields, and constant armed patrols; at least 186 persons had died in this special zone by 1982.[7]

The entire complex of legislation, decrees, and practice is clearly designed to prevent inhabitants of the GDR from leaving the country.

Cargoes are routinely sealed, avoiding delays in checking vehicles and maintaining "normality" on the road to Berlin. Photo courtesy of the German Information Center, New York.

With legal emigration limited to pensioners and a few unwelcome literary figures, these physical barriers to flight effectively seal in the population.

From a political and psychological perspective, this complex is an extraordinarily revealing act on the part of the GDR leadership. Although party and state leaders have continually told their people that Western society is one of "inhumane (*menschenverächtender*) coldness, loneliness and social injustice . . . where money and solely money rules,"[8] the allure of Western society is presumed to be irresistible without state measures to counteract it.

An increase in movement of persons has taken place under certain provisions of the Basic Treaty. In the first decade after its signing, some 20 million West Germans (exclusive of West Berliners) visited the GDR; opportunities for eased travel to West Berlin also emerged (see Table 4.1).

Since 1974, over 10 million GDR pensioners have at least visited West Germany; over a third of a million younger GDR citizens have also been able to go westward on family business. In 1982, the catalog of "pressing family matters" was expanded to include more various family occasions—all carefully specified by the authorities.[9]

The GDR is ambivalent about its relationship to the FRG. An effective but controversial means of choking off travel to the GDR by

TABLE 4.1
Selected Data on Inter-German Travel

1. Surface travel through the GDR to and from West Berlin (in thousands of persons)

Year	Number	Year	Number
1972	11,602	1977	18,184
1973	12,787	1978	18,526
1974	13,288	1979	18,570
1975	14,255	1980	19,410
1976	14,255	1981	19,560

2. "Pressing family matters," 1974-1981

Year	Number	Year	Number
1974	38,298	1978	48,659
1975	40,442	1979	41,470
1976	42,751	1980	40,450
1977	41,462	1981	37,000 (approximate)

3. GDR pensioners to West, 1974-1981 (in thousands of persons)

Year	Number	Year	Number
1974	1,316	1978	1,384
1975	1,330	1979	1,370
1976	1,328	1980	1,555
1977	1,323	1981	1,564

4. West German visitors to GDR (including East Berlin), 1970-1981 (in millions of persons)

Year	Number	Year	Number
1970	1.3	1976	3.1
1971	1.3	1977	2.9
1972	1.5	1978	3.3
1973	2.3	1979	3.6
1974	1.9	1980	2.7
1975	3.1	1981	2.1

Sources: For 1972-1979, see Gerhard Wettig, "Die Durchführung des Berlin-Transits nach dem Vier-mächte Abkommen, 1972-81," BOIS Studien, no. 5 (1981), p. 5. For 1980-1981, see Deutschland Archiv 15, 3 (March 1982): 237. See also successive annual reports in Deutschland Archiv 12, 2 (February 1979): 221; 14, 4 (April 1981): 352; and 14, 3 (March 1982): 237.

West Germans is to make it expensive. In 1973, the GDR doubled the amount of West German currency that would have to be exchanged and extended this obligation to pensioners. The 1974 figure for West German visitors promptly fell off in a year by almost a half-million. Following lengthy negotiations with Bonn, the largest share of this increase was rescinded; the number of visitors promptly rose again.

In October 1980, after the West German elections, the GDR raised the rates of currency exchange again—and sharply. After much West

German protest, they were lowered for children under 14 in the fall of 1983.[10]

In the wake of a second large-scale West German loan in the summer of 1984, the GDR announced a series of detailed relaxations of travel regulations, ranging from lowered exchange fees for the hand-icapped to increases in the maximum numbers of days permitted annually for visits by West Germans. Significantly, the regime included "more generous administration" of the regulations regarding importation of books, other printed matter, and records into the GDR[11] (which, as we saw in Chapter 3 of this volume, particularly aroused Soviet ire).

During 1983 and 1984, groups of East Germans tried to secure their emigration by occupying the U.S. Embassy and West German missions in East Berlin, as well as the West German Embassy in Prague. After lengthy negotiations, the GDR authorities allowed several such groups to leave the country after they first evacuated the embassies (or, in the case of Prague, after they returned to the GDR) against a promise of relief from prosecution.[12] The West German government responded to one such series of "invasions" by closing its East Berlin mission to visitors (July 1984) while rebuilding the structure so as to make such sit-ins impossible.

More startling, however, was the GDR decision (in the wake of the Madrid CSCE follow-up conference's consensus on family reunifi-cation) to allow relatively large-scale emigration from the GDR. In the first three months of 1984, some 25,000 to 30,000 citizens were allowed to leave for the West (compared with 7,729 in all of 1983). No official GDR statement regarding this decision has been forthcoming.[13] Since late spring 1984, the wave of emigration has subsided, although another sit-in in the FRG's Prague Embassy in December 1984 indicated that the problem of would-be emigrants had not been resolved.

Presumably, these GDR concessions were a quid pro quo for West German economic aid, although both sides denied that any specific accommodation had been reached. GDR liberality in this matter may have been a gesture in anticipation of Honecker's projected visit to the Federal Republic.

The GDR and West Germany

The combination of increased freedom and restriction so charac-teristic of the GDR's travel policy reflects the GDR's ambivalence over its ties to the government in Bonn. In his bitter speech at Gera in October 1980, for example, Honecker made several demands that were clearly unacceptable to Bonn; subsequently, these demands have been largely ignored in inter-German politics.[14] Schmidt's plans to visit the GDR were twice postponed in Bonn, but he received a warm welcome in the GDR in December 1981—although nothing of substance emerged as a result of the meetings.[15] In the spring of 1983, Honecker seized on a controversy over the death of an FRG citizen at a border check point to postpone a planned visit to the FRG.

Erich Honecker and Helmut Kohl meet in Moscow on the occasion of Chernenko's funeral (March, 1985). Photo courtesy of the German Information Center, New York.

The GDR clearly indicated its preference for the continuation of the SPD/FDP (Free Democratic party) cabinet in Bonn under Schmidt. When in October 1982 the Kohl/Genscher government assumed office nonetheless, the GDR response was at first very hostile; later its tone softened considerably. A similar ambivalence is evident in the GDR treatment of Franz-Josef Strauss, before and after his surprising visit to East Berlin in July 1983 and his activity on behalf of a large West German bank credit to the GDR.

In its eagerness to block deployment of new U.S. missiles in the Federal Republic, the GDR in late 1983 took a very conciliatory line toward the West Germans. Honecker met with many Bonn political figures; he repeatedly stressed the need to protect the inter-German relationship from harm, even appealing "in the name of the German people" for a "coalition of reason" to preserve peace and shelter GDR-FRG relations from "a new ice age." Much of this language and attitude seems to have survived the start of missile deployment, yet a routine reassertion of West German views on the fate of the nation aroused the GDR leadership to a bitter attack.[16]

Nevertheless, the spring of 1984 saw a rescheduling of Honecker's visit to West Germany, partly in response to Kohl's invitation at the time of Andropov's funeral. As we saw in Chapter 3, the prospect of this visit, which would have been a highly visible symbol of good West–East German relations at a time of extremely bad Soviet-U.S. relations (late September 1984), aroused increasing displeasure in Moscow—perhaps as a result of factional jockeying within the Soviet leadership. It is also possible that Bonn concessions to the GDR and (in economic and military matters) to Moscow would not have been forthcoming in sufficient measure to make the trip "worthwhile." In any event, the GDR seized on abrasive remarks by a West German political leader as well as on "arrangement difficulties" to postpone the trip.[17] It seems likely, however, that at some later time, perhaps after the commemoration of the fortieth anniversary of the defeat of Hitler's Germany, or when Soviet strategy becomes more clearly defined, Honecker will visit his old home in the Saar after all—a personal and political triumph that Honecker would surely relish.

In this situation there seem to be two constants in the GDR's approach to West Germany. One is that the GDR has a strong economic interest in the maintenance of good relations. This interest has arisen from such concessions as interest-free clearing arrangements ("the Swing"), the granting of private bank credits, and a variety of hard-currency payments ranging from unofficial "ransoms" for political prisoners to postal and highway fees.[18]

The other factor is the development, despite *Abgrenzung*, of common outlooks among Germans in both states. A growing sense of mutual security interests, signaled by parallel peace movements, the penetration of the GDR by West German electronic media and popular culture, the evidence that ordinary people favor stable inter-German ties—all these factors are reflections of the regime's judgment that it cannot completely break away from a German identity.[19] An important part of the GDR response to this understanding lies in its policy toward the heritage of the German past, to which we now turn.

THE GDR AND THE GERMAN PAST

As long as the two German states competed for the prize of a future reunited Germany, the question of national identity did not loom large for the GDR leadership. Once the GDR shifted to buttressing its own state autonomy, however, the appeal to nationalism became a source of delegitimation as well as a political liability. Unlike its East European counterparts, the GDR could not rely on nationalism either to offset Soviet pressure or to justify unpopular domestic policies. The reason is clear: in the context of peaceful coexistence with West Germany, any appeal to "German" loyalties ran the risk of generating unwanted desires for greater concessions to German unity than the regime could afford. Hence the development of normal *German interstate* relations was nec-

Improvements on the Wall are a constant undertaking. Photo courtesy of the German Information Center, New York.

essarily accompanied by increased official exertions to block the development of good *intra-German* relations.

West Germany can be regarded as a hostile state because the two Germanies, in the GDR view, no longer share one nation. Soon after then Chancellor Willy Brandt had spoken of the continued existence of two German states in one German nation, Walter Ulbricht declared that the GDR was a "socialist German national state"—a characterization that has remained a fundamental argument of the GDR leadership. Any such efforts to maintain that there is a single German nation, a single German culture, a single German responsibility for the past have all been denounced as a threat to the maintenance of peace in Europe.[20]

It was in this connection that the policy of *Abgrenzung* took on great importance and was extended to all aspects of GDR life. In 1974, for example, the 1968 constitution was amended in such a way as to remove "all-German" references: the proclamation of the GDR as a "socialist state of the German nation" was changed to "socialist state of workers and peasants." Similar changes were made in the SED program adopted in 1976 and in the names of countless public organizations (one example: the "German Academy of Sciences" was renamed the "Academy of Sciences of the GDR").

This *Abgrenzung* of any all-German characteristics has at times been extended to the field of German culture generally, and to German literature in particular. The context of such rejection is usually overtly political. Klaus Höpcke, GDR Deputy Culture Minister (and in charge of book publishing), declared that "certain forces" in West Germany are encouraged to perform anti-detente tricks in cultural affairs; at the end of the 1970s, therefore, "the contention that there existed only one German literature was revived. This was designed to shore up the thesis of a continuing existence of a unitary German culture and thus support the so-called "holding open the German question."[21]

During this period, the question of what constituted the German nation, and whether there was such a nation in the GDR or whether there might perhaps be a new GDR "national consciousness," became the subject of intense attention. These changing views not only affected policy toward Bonn, but, more important, they shaped the GDR's attitude toward the historical heritage of a common German past.

GDR theorists sought for the basis of a new socialist nation in the notion of the nation as a dynamic construct, evoked by particular socioeconomic conditions and responsive to changing circumstances. Thus the GDR is the political-institutional framework for the gradual emergence of a new "German," but socialist and progressive, nation— and one that incorporates some of the best features of the German past; West Germany, by contrast, is aggressive and decadent, and represents the infusion of undesirable foreign (i.e., U.S.) elements into German culture and life.

The development of a distinctive social order in the GDR is cited as the basis for a new nation. For example, Kurt Hager has defined the nation as the result of a lengthy historical process of social development,[22] which in turn is related to the integrative processes of the socialist community.

In practice, the attempt to redefine German nationhood in this way has foundered in the face of the obvious existence of German language, customs, and historical legacies in the GDR. By December 1974, therefore, Honecker found himself bound to admit that "the overwhelming majority" of GDR citizens were indeed German by nationality, in the sense that their customs and traditions were German. But even this ingenious redefinition of nation and national culture does not seem to have had sufficient popular appeal. Within the past several years, consequently, a revised attitude has emerged.

In a policy-setting speech at East Berlin's Museum of German History, Kurt Hager declared that

[a]s a socialist state the GDR is deeply rooted in German history, above all in the centuries of struggle by all the progressive forces of our people for freedom and social progress. . . . It [GDR] continued the tradition (Steht in der Kontinuität) of everything good . . . [in] German history.[23]

It was precisely the GDR's Marxist-Leninist outlook, Hager further declared, that allowed it to take a properly dialectical stance toward all of German history, including such controversial elements of it as Prussia. The development of a socialist nation in the GDR was a law-determined (*gesetzmässig*) event, the result of a lengthy class struggle. Only in such a socialist nation could the masses truly benefit from the great achievements of the German past, from the accomplishments of the medieval poets through Goethe, Schiller, and Heine, to the modern Communist writers.

This rediscovery of virtue in the German past has become a widespread phenomenon. Whether we point to the restoration of the statue of Frederick the Great to its former place in the middle of East Berlin, or the staging of a public celebration on Hegel's 150th birthday, or the naming of a regiment of border troops after Gneisenau, the Prussian officer of the Napoleonic era, or the expenditure of government money to rebuild the Sans Souci palace complex of Frederick the Great in Potsdam—it is clear that a major decision has been taken to appropriate as much of German history as possible, and to use it for buttressing the legitimacy of the GDR.

The new view of the German past in the GDR today is aptly characterized by the historian Ingrid Mittenzwei: "A people cannot pick out its traditions: it must confront them, and it should do so in a differentiated manner."[24] This more nuanced approach to historical events and persons can be put to political use, as shown by the treatment of the 500th birthday of Martin Luther in the fall of 1983. For many years, the GDR image of Luther had been a hostile one: he was too conservative and vituperatively hostile to the peasants; moreover, he placed his trust in princes. But all that has changed. Honecker himself stressed the positive qualities of Luther, his cultural contributions, the importance of his work in his later years, and his advocacy of social and economic reform. Honecker's remarks reflected the official theses on the Luther celebration published in the SED's theoretical monthly *Einheit.*[25]

The Luther celebrations also afforded opportunities by which the regime could demonstrate good relations with the GDR's Evangelical Church, impress foreign visitors and (as most of the important sites of Luther's career are in the present-day GDR) earn foreign currency, as well as demonstrate the depth of regime commitment to a more rounded view of the German past. How serious this commitment was may be gathered from two bits of evidence: the large sums spent renovating sites associated with Luther's career and the fact that no fewer than eight Politburo members were listed as belonging to the official Luther committee, including Honecker as chairman.

As previously noted, the rehabilitation of Luther's image was not only accompanied by a renewed appreciation of many other historical figures from the German past, including Bismarck,[26] but it was also paralleled by an extensive and successful program of landmark restoration and preservation.[27] The celebration of the GDR's thirty-fifth anniversary (October 1984) was marked by references to the general German past—

most notably by the festive reopening of the Schauspielhaus theater as a gala concert hall in the heart of East Berlin. At the same time, Honecker made a point of staging anniversary galas with veterans of the anti-Nazi struggle and early contributors to the building of the GDR.[28]

In many spheres of life, then, the regime has sought to derive political advantage from a closer identification with the German past. What successes is it likely to achieve in this way? Evidence from the late 1960s and 1970s tends to show that such "GDR patriotism" as existed was directly related to a sense of economic and social accomplishment.[29] Efforts to translate such feelings into a GDR-specific national consciousness seem to have failed, but many GDR citizens may well be content with a mixture of social and economic security combined with renewed acceptability of pride in all things German. (One is reminded of the GDR headline that emerged when an East German officer made a successful space flight: "First German in Space Is a Citizen of the GDR.")[30] Whether this policy will have any long-range effectiveness in reconciling the population of the GDR to the division of Germany remains to be seen.

NOTES

1. See Siegfried Kupper, "Politische Beziehungen zur Bundesrepublik Deutschland 1955–1977" (pp. 403–434) and Ulrich Scheuner, "Das Problem der Nation und des Verhältnis zur Bundesrepublik Deutschland" (pp. 85–108), both in Eberhard Schulz, ed., *Drei Jahrzehnte Aussenpolitik der DDR* (Munich: R. Oldenbourg, 1979).

2. The text of the agreement and supporting documents is available in Dennis L. Bark, *Agreement on Berlin* (Washington, D.C.: American Enterprise Institute, 1974), pp. 117–131. The relevant language states that "the four Governments will mutually respect their individual and joint rights and responsibilities, which remain unchanged" (Part I, paragraph 3) and "[will act] on the basis of their quadripartite rights and responsibilities . . . which are not affected" (Preamble).

3. The GDR did unilaterally change the status of East Berlin in 1979 by providing for direct election of *Volkskammer* members; hitherto, East Berlin had been represented by delegates chosen by the city's municipal assembly (as West Berlin is still represented in Bonn). For details, see Henry Krisch, "Soviet-GDR Relations in the Honecker Era," *East Central Europe* 6 (1979):168.

4. Siegfried Kupper, "Politische Beziehungen zur Bundesrepublik Deutschland," pp. 431–452, in Schulz, ed., *Drei Jahrzehnte*; the text (in German) is in *Vertrag über die Grundlagen*, published by the Press and Information Office (Bonn) in 1972.

5. Peter Jochen Winters, "Vereinbarungen und Verhandlungen mit der DDR im Gefolge des Grundlagenvertrages," *Deutschland Archiv* 15 (December 1982):1305–1312.

6. Jan Hoesch, "Ein Erfolg im Schatten. Die Teil-Amnestie für Flüchtlinge vom 21. June 1982," *Deutschland Archiv* 15 (October 1982):1017–1019.

7. Karl Wilhelm Fricke, "Altes Grenzregime mit neuen Bestimmungen," *Deutschland Archiv* 15 (June 1982):567–589. In conjunction with a state visit to

the GDR by the Austrian president, Honecker announced that the automatic firing devices would be dismantled. See *Neues Deutschland,* 6 October 1983, p. 3.

8. See Konrad Naumann, considered by some to be a notorious hardliner, in *Neues Deutschland,* 27–28 November 1982, p. 5.

9. The details of this enumeration can be found in *Deutschland Archiv* 15 (May 1982):555.

10. For the official announcement of this incident, see *Frankfurter Allgemeine Zeitung,* 29 September 1983.

11. See the detailed list in *Frankfurter Allgemeine Zeitung,* 26 July 1984, pp. 1–2.

12. See "East Berlin Lets 38 Go to the West," *New York Times,* 7 April 1984, p. 1; "Die Bundesregierung warnt vor weiteren Fluchtversuchen über Ost-Berliner Missionen," *Frankfurter Allgemeine Zeitung,* 30 January 1984, p. 4.

13. See "Joy and Awe for East German Exiles," *New York Times,* 19 May 1984, p. 4; see also the GDR comment reported in the *Frankfurter Allgemeine Zeitung,* 6 April 1984, p. 12. In an interview with the Swedish newspaper *Svenska Dagbladet,* Honecker bristled when asked about the emigrants. It was, he said, just a matter of the Helsinki agreement's procedures for family reunification—and besides, no one ever asks about those who emigrate from the Federal Republic, do they? See *Neues Deutschland,* 30 June–1 July 1984, p. 5. See also Ronald D. Asmus, "A New Wave of East German Emigration," RFE-RL Research, *RAD Background Report/45* (March 28, 1984).

14. See *Neues Deutschland,* 14 October 1980, pp. 3–5.

15. *Treffen des Generalsekretärs des ZK der SED und Vositzenden des Staatsrates der DDR, Erich Honecker, mit dem Bundeskanzler der BRD Helmut Schmidt, in der Deutschen Demokratischen Republic, 11.–13. Dezember 1981* (Berlin: Panorama, 1981).

16. The changing attitudes toward the Kohl regime are reflected in *Neues Deutschland,* 14 October 1982, p. 2, and 27–28 November 1982, p. 4; for details on Strauss's visit, see *Neues Deutschland* 25 July 1983, p. 1, and "Visit to East by Strauss Startles Bonn," *New York Times,* 27 July 1983, p. A3. For a description of the response of GDR citizens to his visit, see *Frankfurter Allgemeine Zeitung,* 28 July 1983, p. 2. Honecker's appeal was contained in his letter to Kohl, in *Neues Deutschland,* 10 October 1983, p. 1. For a discussion of the renewed attack on all the Bonn parties, see *Neues Deutschland,* 11–12 February 1984, p. 2. General assessments of this period are Peter Jochen Winters, "Ungewisser Herbst," *Deutschland Archiv* 16 (November 1983):1121–1124, and "East Germany's Moves at Border Confuse Bonn," *New York Times,* 4 October 1983, p. A3.

17. See the coverge in *Frankfurter Allgemeine Zeitung,* 5 September 1984, pp. 1–2. See also "Honecker Decides to Postpone Visit to West Germany," *New York Times,* 5 September 1984, p. 1; and "East Germans Affirm Ties to Bonn as Goal," *New York Times,* 11 September 1984, p. A11. *Neues Deutschland,* 5 September 1984, p. 2, carried a brief and laconic announcement of the postponement of Honecker's visit.

18. An accounting of all the ways in which the GDR secures hard currency from Bonn is provided in "Pauschalen, Gebühren, Forderungen," *Frankfurter Allgemeine Zeitung,* 12 August 1983, p. 4.

19. "TV Brings Western Culture to East Germany," *New York Times,* 13 February 1984, p. C19.

20. Eberhard Schneider, "Der Nationsbegriff der DDR und seine deutschlandpolitische Bedeutung," Report 33 (Cologne: Bundesinstitut für ostwissenschaftliche und internationale Studien [BOIS], 1981). As recently as the time of its Sixteenth Congress, the SED had declared that it was "firmly committed to its goal of restoring the national unity of Germany." See Hermann Weber, Kleine Geschichte der DDR (Cologne: Edition Deutschland Archiv, 1980), p. 112.

21. Klaus Höpcke, "Aktuelle Aspekte der Leninschen Theorie von den zwei Kulturen" Einheit 35 (April 1980):431.

22. Kurt Hager, "Die entwickelte sozialistische Gesellschaft," Einheit 26 (November 1971):1228–1231.

23. Kurt Hager, "Unsere sozialistische DDR ist tief in der deutschen Geschichte verwurzelt, Neues Deutschland, 22 July 1981, p. 4.

24. Ingrid Mittenzwei, "Die Zwei Gesichter Preussens," Forum, no. 19 (1978):8–9. In a recent authoritative article, Ernst Diehl stated that confronting one's history means "not detouring around complicated, contradictory" persons, events or processes but, rather, "taking a stand pro or con." See Ernst Diehl, "Der geschichtliche Boden unseres Vaterlandes," Einheit 39 (October 1984):921.

25. The official theses on Luther are in Einheit 36 (September 1981):890–903. Honecker's speeches at the first and second sessions of the official Martin Luther Committee of the GDR are in Neues Deutschland, 14–15 June 1980, p. 3, and 30–31 October 1982, pp. 1, 3–5. For a thorough survey and analysis of the celebrations, see Ronald D. Asmus, "Honecker on Luther Year Celebrations," RFE-RL Research, RAD Background Report/248 (December 2, 1983). See also the review by Detlef Urban of GDR television's miniseries on Luther, which treats his religious preoccupations fairly and squarely, in Deutschland Archiv 16 (December 1983):1253–1255. An excellent summary of the GDR's handling of the Luther anniversary is Robert F. Goeckel, "The Luther Anniversary in East Germany," World Politics 37 (October 1984):112–133.

26. See Kurt Hager's discussion of Bismarck's positive side in Neues Deutschland, 16 December 1983, pp. 3–5. See also "Luther, Bismarck, Honecker," Frankfurter Allgemeine Zeitung, 19 February 1983, p. 10.

27. The following three examples are from different spheres: restoration of the Deutsches Theater in Berlin (Neues Deutschland, 30 September 1983, p. 3); reconstruction of the Huguenot Französische Friedrichstadtkirche in Berlin (Frankfurter Allgemeine Zeitung, 18 April 1983, p. 7); and the establishment of an American Indian museum in the villa of author Karl May (Neues Deutschland, 24–25 December 1983, p. 4).

28. See the fulsome coverage of these events in Neues Deutschland, 2 October 3, and 5, 1984, pp. 1ff. A visitor to East Berlin in summer 1984 could not help but be struck by the extent of reconstruction of old historic buildings.

29. Henry Krisch, "Nation Building and Regime Stability in the GDR," East Central Europe 3, no. 1 (1976):15–29. The standard background work on this subject is Gebhard Schweigler, National Consciousness in a Divided Germany (Beverly Hills, Calif.: Sage, 1975).

30. The same headline was, in fact, reprinted on the fifth anniversary of the flight. See Neues Deutschland, 26 August 1983, p. 3.

5

The GDR:
A Socialist Industrial State

PLANNING AND INDUSTRY

The German Democratic Republic is clearly one of the world's leading industrialized nations. Two GDR authors write that "the German Democratic Republic is a highly developed industrial state, with a productive agriculture" in which, for example, some 40 percent of industrial equipment is less than five years old, and where (according to UN figures) four-tenths of a percent of the world's population produces 1.5 percent of world national income.[1] As a recent comparison indicated, the GDR ranks first in Eastern Europe in GNP per capita. On a world scale, the GDR's per capita GNP ranks it behind most Western countries but still among the twenty highest and ahead of or on a par with such countries as Italy, New Zealand, or Great Britain.[2] In labor productivity its rank is even with that of Great Britain but some 30 percent below France or West Germany.[3]

In actual production, the GDR ranks first in the world in such items as potash fertilizer and brown coal (lignite), sixth in cement, twelfth in electrical energy, sixth in synthetic fibers, and also sixth in beer.[4] In recent years, the GDR's economic planners have concentrated resources on key branches of industry in the forefront of technical and industrial progress. The result of this effort is that almost half of all industrial production is concentrated in three branches: machinery and transport vehicles (23 percent), electronics and electrical equipment (10 percent), and the chemical industry (16 percent)—in other words, "those main branches that are necessary for the economy of a modern industrial nation."[5]

Efforts to maintain the GDR's position as a modern industrial state have encountered increasing difficulties in the late 1970s and early 1980s. These difficulties involve demographic problems, resource constraints, and the effects on the GDR economy of global economic conditions. We will look in detail at these recent problems, and at the response of

TABLE 5.1
Industrial Production in the GDR, 1936 and 1975 (in percentages)

Branch	1936	1975
Machinery, transport vehicles	16.1	24.2
Food processing	28.5	16.6
Chemical industry	6.4	15.1
Light industry	13.6	11.3
Electrical and electronic equipment	2.7	11.2
Metalworking	10.5	7.9
Textiles	10.6	6.6
Energy and fuels	9.0	5.1
Construction materials	2.6	2.0

Source: Deutsches Institut für Wirtschaftsforschung, Handbuch DDR-Wirtschaft (Hamburg: Rowohlt Taschenbuch Verlag, 1977), p. 313.

the regime to them, after surveying the development and current organization of the industrial and planning system in the GDR.

Origins and Development
of a Socialist Industrial Economy

The territories that were to become the GDR were already substantially industrialized before World War II, especially in the southern Saxon and Thuringian territories. Moreover, the war damaged industries in the Soviet Zone less than those in the western zones. Industrial property damage in the Soviet Zone was less than 15 percent of prewar stock, but dismantling of industrial plants by the Soviet occupation authorities came to 26 percent of the total, such that total losses in the future GDR amounted to 41 percent.[6]

The industrial structure of the Soviet Zone was characterized by light and processing industries, with optics and chemicals the best-known products. Its dominant trade pattern was east and west across Germany, exchanging food and manufactures for fuel, raw materials, and heavy manufactured goods. A comparison of shares of production by branches of industry in 1936 and 1975 illustrates this relationship (see Table 5.1).[7]

The dominant facts of economic life in the Soviet Zone were the destruction caused by the war and the Soviet determination to obtain economic benefits from the occupation in the form of labor, property, and goods drawn from current production. In 1946–1948, reparations and dismantling absorbed a quarter of the total social product, and even in 1953, the last year of reparations, a tenth of the social product (and most industrial capacity) was devoted to these purposes.[8]

At the same time, the Soviet authorities initiated measures to destroy the power of the owners of industry. In fall 1945, the Soviet Military Administration ordered the confiscation of all German state, army, and Nazi party property; most of the heavy industry involved went to Soviet-German joint stock companies (SAGs). It also required that the KPD/SED leadership sponsor a referendum in Saxony in June 1946, leading to the confiscation of property belonging to war criminals, Nazis, and (loosely defined) "war profiteers." By spring 1948, 9,281 enterprises, including 3,843 that accounted for 40 percent of Soviet Zone industrial production at that time, had been seized.[9]

In the middle 1950s, most production levels of the pre-1945 period had been reached or surpassed, while an increasing proportion of the GDR's industrial capacity was organized in nationalized industry. Enterprises were placed under state administration and, after 1948, under the German Economic Commission, whose branches became the industrial ministries of the new GDR government. The plants themselves were designated "People's Own Enterprises" (Volkseigene Betriebe, or VEB) and were organized into associations of enterprises (VVBs) as well. (The SAGs were returned to German authority and added to the VEB total.) More than half of the property in the GDR was now state (or co-op) controlled.[10]

Economic growth in the decade after Stalin was rendered extremely difficult by the political turmoil of the de-Stalinization era (1956–1958) and the drive to complete the collectivization of agriculture (1959–1960). Above all, there was the continuing problem of refugees. The attraction of the Federal Republic for young and skilled persons was especially harmful to economic growth; by 1961, the equivalent of every fifth employed person had fled.[11]

After the Berlin Wall had stanched the outflow of people, the regime acted to improve the economic system by the proclamation in January 1963 of the "New Economic System of Planning and Leadership" (NÖSPL).[12] The reform was intended to reduce adherence to quantitative goals; "economic levers" were to give incentives for managers. Other features were price inducements for technological profitability as a main success criterion for plant management and inducements for technological innovation. In less than a decade, however, major aspects of this system were abandoned in practice, although the NÖSPL was never formally revoked. There were several reasons for this. As with similar reforms elsewhere in Eastern Europe, the new system involved substantial changes in thinking and work habits, and brought about an unavoidable degree of initial dislocation. Moreover, the regime intervened directly to foster new "structure-determining, high-technology industries"—an action that, of course, ran directly counter to the spirit of the NÖSPL.[13]

The resulting economic crisis in 1970 or so helped secure the removal of Ulbricht. The new Honecker style in economic matters was marked both by greater realism in goal setting and by a major shift toward improving production by providing material incentives—the oft-cited unity of social and economic policy designed to ensure rising living standards. At the SED Eighth Congress in June 1971, Honecker proclaimed the "main task" (*Hauptaufgabe*) of party, state, and society to be "the further raising of the material and cultural standard of living of the people on the basis of rapid development of socialist production, increasing efficiency, scientific-technical progress, and growth of productivity."[14] The economic policy of the Honecker years may be summed up by the oft-repeated slogan about "work paying off" in the GDR.

The Organization of Planning and Industry

Planning and plan implementation in the GDR economy follow the general Soviet pattern.[15] Strategic decisions as to economic policy remain the prerogative of the party leadership, in particular the Politburo and the Secretariat (see Table 5.2). Both short- and long-range plans are discussed first within the party and ratified by the Central Committee before being enacted by the *Volkskammer* and implemented by government ministries and local government bodies. The SED's discussion of economic questions is, in turn, shaped by studies generated in and data gathered by the State Planning Commission (Staatliche Plankommission, or SPK).

Under Honecker there have now been four Five-Year Plans, including the current one running to 1985. The plans themselves are broken down into annual and semiannual installments, and are subsumed under longer-term (usually fifteen-year) "perspective" plans. The actual plan figures are, of course, the result of horizontal bargaining between the ministries and the SPK, as well as of hierarchical bargaining chiefly among enterprise and combine directors and planning officials. Considerable attention is paid in the GDR to generating "counterplans" at the enterprise and branch levels, plans that, in effect, form part of the informational input for the SPK. The actual plan figures are generally regarded more as guidelines than as commands.

The industrial and agricultural ministries are the link between the central planning and directing agencies and the production units in each field under their supervision. In that capacity they may issue "product catalogs" of especially crucial items of supply, carry out quality control, and encourage formation in enterprises of housing departments and consumer goods production departments in capital goods enterprises.

At the intermediate level between ministry and enterprise, a substantial reorganization has taken place. The associations of enterprises (VVB) have been replaced by Combines (*Kombinate*). The latter are normally directly subordinated to ministries such that, in many cases,

TABLE 5.2
Political Leadership of the GDR Economy

Name	Responsibility	Politburo	Secretariat	Council of Ministers
Erich Honecker	general	member	general secretary	
Günter Mittag	industry, planning	member	secretary	
Werner Felfe	agriculture	member	secretary	
Willi Stoph	administration	member		chairman
Harry Tisch	labor	member		(heads TU organization)
Werner Jarowinsky	trade and supply	member	member	
Günther Kleiber	machinery, Middle East trade	member		deputy chairman, minister of machine building
Gerhard Schürer	planning	candidate		chairman, State Planning Commission
Wolfgang Rauchfuss	supply			deputy chairman
Gerhard Weiss	CMEA			deputy chairman, permanent CMEA delegate
Herbert Weiz	technology, Soviet economic ties			deputy chairman, minister of science and technology
Walter Halbritter	prices			head of Price Office of Council of Ministers
Horst Sölle	foreign trade			minister of foreign trade

Source: Author's reading of the GDR press.

the industrial structure of the GDR has been reduced to three levels: ministry, combine, and enterprise.

Combines now account for roughly 90 percent of industrial production, employing over 90 percent of all workers in centrally managed industry and construction. Each industrial combine employs an average 27,000 workers; about half of all the combines are concentrated in four ministries: electrical/electronics, heavy engineering, chemical industry, and light industry.[16]

What the regime hopes to achieve through formation of these units is greater efficiency in production through (1) shorter information flows, (2) improved application of research, (3) more flexible response to demands, and (4) improvements in rationalization and investment. The key element to realizing these goals is the performance of the combine director. The combine was to bring more decisionmaking to the production level, but, in fact, it has lessened the power of the plant manager at the expense of the combine director. According to Manfred Melzer, the "director can both change the functions and tasks of individual enterprises, . . . centralize activities such as research, investment, sales, market research, and accounting, . . . [and] take over . . . state functions— price setting, standardization, and tasks involved in the socialist economic integration." Although the number of combines has grown, the quantity of enterprises has decreased as their average size has increased; the number as of 1979 was less than a third of that of 1960.[17]

The GDR's Industrial Economy: Accomplishments and Problems

That the industrial power of the GDR has grown during the Honecker era is evident from the standard compilations of economic data. In addition to general economic growth, there was marked progress in supplying consumer durables, subsidizing basic costs, providing a wide variety of social services, and engaging in a massive effort to solve the housing problem by 1990.

A cursory survey of GDR industrial growth will indicate the economy's basic strength. Using 1950 = 100 as a base figure, we find that gross industrial production reached 565 by 1971 and 885 by 1979. Produced national income rose from 179 billion Mark in 1979 to 210 billion in 1983. (About 70 percent of this income came from industry.) Although planned targets for produced national income have not always been met, the resulting growth is impressive nonetheless, given that it rose as much in 1971–1980 as it had in the preceding twenty years.

How has this economic strength affected the lives of the people in the GDR? What problems does the GDR economy face in the future? To answer the first question we will look at programs relating to housing, consumer goods, and subsidies for basic items; to answer the second one, we will consider energy- and labor-supply difficulties. The housing problem had reached serious proportions by the time of Honecker's

TABLE 5.3
Housing Plans and Accomplishments

Years	New Apartments	Modernized Apartments	Total
1966-1970	364,000	---	364,000
1971-1975	399,586	209,080	608,666
1976-1980	599,387	253,740	813,127
1980	120,206 (71%)*	49,017	169,223
1981	125,731 (68%)*	59,619	182,350
1982	122,417 (65%)*	64,636	187,053
1983	122,636 (62%)*	74,585	197,221
1984 (first half)	---	---	101,438
1981-1985 (plan)	600,000	330,000-350,000	930,000-950,000

*Figure in parentheses represents new housing as percentage of the whole.

Sources: Die Wirtschaft, no. 19 (1981), p. 10; Neues Deutschland, 4-5
December 1982, p. 4, 19 January 1984, p. 4, and 14-15 July 1984, p. 3;
Statistisches Taschenbuch der DDR 1984 (Berlin: Staatsverlag der DDR, 1984),
p. 60.

assumption of the party leadership in 1971.[18] Although the pre-1945 territory of the GDR had been relatively well provided with housing per inhabitant, the economic priorities of the new regime barred meaningful investment in renewal of housing stock. As a consequence, even as late as 1978, almost half of all existing apartments in the GDR had been built before 1919.

A "comprehensive census" of housing in the GDR disclosed the "alarming state" of housing. As part of the stress on social policy at the Eighth SED Congress (June 1971), housing became the centerpiece of GDR social policy. In the words of the party program: "The program of building housing is the very core of the social policy of the [SED]. It is designed to solve the housing question by 1990."[19] The regime has steadfastly put this policy into practice. By 1975, some 600,000 apartments had been built or modernized; in the next Five-Year Plan period, the total was increased by about a third; and by 1990, between 2.8 and 3.5 million apartments are projected to have been made available (see Table 5.3). By providing financial aid and technical services, the regime has also encouraged housing cooperatives and even private individuals to build homes.

Emphasis in the early phase of the housing program was on industrial construction methods; the "Apartment Series 70" was used for two-thirds of GDR apartment construction. Such methods, involving transportation of massive amounts of prefabricated materials to large building sites for use by large machinery, made it necessary to build large residential complexes, often far from city centers. Complexes intended for 100,000 or more people, such as the Berlin-Marzahn, a much-heralded "new borough" on the edges of East Berlin, Leipzig-Grünau, and others, have arisen as a result.

Recent years have witnessed a change of policy favoring restoration and conservation of existing housing stock in central cities; permission for demolition of housing must now be granted by the Housing Ministry. Aside from aesthetic considerations, it is hoped that this policy will save fuel and commuting time and lessen the need to construct new social amenities. Moreover, whereas each newly built apartment requires that eighty tons of material be produced, transported, and used in construction, the amount of material needed for restoration is far less.[20] Housing construction is subject to the same pressures for greater efficiency, especially in the use of fuel and raw materials, as in other sectors; it is a particularly pressing question in housing because rents charged bear no relation to construction or financing costs. New apartments rent for about 1 Mark per square meter, with converted old buildings renting more cheaply still. Honecker has reiterated, however, that rent will continue to be subsidized.

The Honecker commitment to social welfare has had an ambivalent tone. Although extensive benefits were provided for various social groups,[21] a general subsidy for necessities was made available, and the expansion of a consumerist life-style went forward vigorously, there was also an increase in privileged access to certain of these goods.

As Honecker had pledged in 1981 that increases in the cost of industrial goods would not affect the cost of basic items, such services are all heavily subsidized. In recent years, these subsidies have amounted to roughly one-third of total state expenditures and have been especially important in the context of food, rents, and commuter fares (see Table 5.4). The resulting strain on the state's budget has led to lower subsidies in the most recent years, particularly as the rate of increase in these subsidies has actually exceeded the increase in produced national income.

An offsetting factor has been the series of disguised price increases in the form of higher prices for "new and improved" products. Moreover, many desirable but not strictly necessary items are available chiefly in special, high-price "Delikat" or "Equisit" shops, or in exchange for hard foreign currency in "Intershops." (In 1981, the number of Delikat shops increased within six months from 540 to 800!) The Intershops have been especially troublesome socially and ideologically in that GDR citizens are legally permitted to own West German currency (given to them by relatives from the Federal Republic, for instance), thereby

TABLE 5.4
State Subsidies of Basic Goods and Services, 1979-1982 (in billions of Mark)

Year	Total Subsidy/% Increase over Previous Year	Food / % Increase	Rent / % Increase	Fares / % Increase
1979	49.2	7.7	6.5	2.7
1980	52.7 / 7%	7.8 / 1%	7.0 / 8%	2.9 / 7%
1981	58.3 / 10.5%	11.2 / 44%	8.2 / 17%	2.9 / 0%
1982	61.4 / 5%	11.7 / 4.3%	8.8 / 7%	3.0 / 3.5%
1983	62.6%	12.1 / 3.3%	9.3 / 5.3%	3.1 / 3.2%

Sources: Statistisches Taschenbuch der DDR 1984 (Berlin: Staatsverlag der DDR, 1984), pp. 105-106; Neues Deutschland, 19 January 1984, p. 3.

providing random members of the GDR population special access to scarce consumer goods. The regime weathered a crisis in public morale in 1977-1978 by introducing restrictions on access to these facilities.[22]

It is noteworthy in this connection that although the GDR has built a society of wide access to opportunities, it has not become egalitarian in its rewards. An estimate of relative monthly earnings as of 1981 shows the great discrepancies that continue to exist (see Table 5.5). Nonetheless, the material rewards of consumption have become widely distributed, as most GDR households are equipped with the standard amenities of modern industrial societies (see Table 5.6).

Among the serious problems faced by the GDR economy is providing for an assured energy supply at a stable and affordable price. In the early 1970s, the regime counted on expanding use of oil, almost all of it imported from the USSR.[23] As a consequence of the first oil price rise, growth in energy consumption as well as imports of Soviet oil began to decline; by the decade's end, the GDR had to adjust to even sharper cutbacks in Soviet deliveries. First, it turned to domestic brown coal (lignite) as the primary energy source for generating electricity. Second, it undertook a substantial program of nuclear power development. Third, it pressed on all sectors of society, both industry and consumers, the importance of energy conservation and secondary energy recovery.

Finally, the availability of imported oil became more problematical as Soviet deliveries shrank;[24] in 1981 and 1982 they averaged only 18 million tons annually after reaching a high of over 19 million tons in 1980. Moreover, to secure future deliveries, the GDR had to participate with both labor and investment capital in the development of Soviet

TABLE 5.5
Monthly Earnings in Selected Occupations (1981)

Category	Monthly Wage (GDR Mark)
Politburo member	6,000–8,000
Kombinat director	4,000–6,000
Professor	2,000–3,000
Factory foreman	2,000–3,000
Doctor	1,500–2,500
Schoolteacher	1,000–1,500
Worker (general)	1,000–1,200
Worker, metal fabricating	1,113
Worker, textiles	887
Collective farmer	1,000–1,200
Sales clerk	800
Retiree	340

Source: Eugene K. Keefe, ed., East Germany: A Country Study, 2d ed. (Washington, D.C.: Department of the Army, 1982), pp. 132–133.

extractive industries. With Soviet oil now amounting to only slightly over 80 percent of imports, the GDR had to conserve or buy expensive OPEC oil. Consequently, the GDR has moved to replace oil as a heating fuel and turned more to the use of lignite and nuclear energy.

The GDR is the world's largest producer of lignite (over a quarter of the world's production total in 1980), and in 1983 brown-coal generators accounted for 81 percent of its electric-power generation. Unfortunately, much of this coal is strip mined, which brings with it problems of waste ("overburden") disposal and water in the pits. For example, a 16 percent increase in coal production would involve a 36 percent overburden increase and the removal of 100 percent more water.[25]

The utilization of coal for energy is regarded as a "bridge to the nuclear age" in the GDR.[26] In 1973, the first of three 440-megawatt reactors came on line (two others followed in 1975 and 1978). By 1977, the amount of power from nuclear reactors was almost 4.5 times that

TABLE 5.6
Consumer Durables per 100 Households

Item	1970	1975	1979	1981	1983
Passenger cars	15.6	26.2	34.1	39	44
Television sets*	69.1	81.6	86.5	89	114
Refrigerators	56.4	84.7	98.6	99	125
Washing machines	53.6	73.0	80.0	83	94

*The percentage of households with color television receivers rose from
 2 percent in 1975 to 18.6 percent in 1980.

Sources: Doris Cornelsen,"The GDR in a Period of Foreign Trade Difficulties:
Developments and Prospects for the 1980s," in U.S. Congress, Joint Economic
Committee, East European Economic Assessment. Part 1--Country Studies, 1980
(97th Cong., 1st sess., 1981), p. 311; Neues Deutschland, 15 April 1981, p. 8,
and 19 January 1984, p. 5; Frankfurter Allgemeine Zeitung, 15 April 1982;
Neues Deutschland, 12 December 1982, p. 4; Hannjorg F. Buck and Johannes
Kuppe, "SED-Bericht 'zur Lage,'" Deutschland Archiv 15 (April 1982): 40; and
Statistisches Taschenbuch der DDR 1984 (Berlin: Staatsverlag der DDR, 1984),
p. 115.

from hydropower sources, and in 1980, 12 percent of all electricity was
generated from nuclear plants (see Table 5.7).

All GDR nuclear power plants are of Soviet design and manufacture
(through the CMEA joint enterprise *Interatommash*). GDR proponents
of the nuclear power program are confident that nuclear power will be
an important GDR energy source. Fears about safety and waste disposal
in the West are, in their view, nurtured by the oil lobby and justified
only because capitalists cannot be trusted to handle this energy source
with care.

Since 1979, there has been a persistent attempt by the regime to
foster energy conservation. Some measures taken were aimed at individual
efforts (e.g., slower driving), but more important were measures pushed
in industry and transportation. Among these were a shift of freight
from trucks to railways and barges, an increase in the utilization of
"secondary energy" (i.e., waste heat resulting from industrial processes),
and a reduction in the use of raw materials.[27]

A final problem is that of labor supply and productivity. Both
ideologically and constitutionally the GDR is committed to a policy of
providing jobs for all, just as its citizens are obliged to perform socially
approved work—a policy that leads to "full employment," or what an
East Berlin newspaper called "too many unproductive jobs." The result
is a drive for increased labor productivity; although 1982 and 1983 saw

TABLE 5.7
GDR Energy Sources

I. Consumption by Fuel Source (percentages of total)*

Year	Brown Coal	Oil	Natural Gas	Hydro†	Nuclear†
1975	68	18	7	1.5	3.2
1978	64	21	7	---	---
1980	65	18	10	1.7	11.8
1981	67	17	10	1.7	11.6

*Figures do not add up to 100 percent due to omission of imports and minor
fuel sources (e.g., hard coal, between 3 percent and 6 percent).

†Figure represents percentage of electricity generated.

II. Projected GDR Nuclear Capacity, in megawatts (1971-1990)

Time Period	Added Capacity	Total Capacity
1971-1975	800	880
1976-1980	440	1,320
1981-1985	1,320	2,640
1986-1990	1,880	4,520

Sources: I: Wolfgang Stinglwagern, "Genügend Energie für die Zukunft?"
Deutschland Archiv 16, 3 (March 1983): 263-64. II: William G. Davey,
Nuclear Power in the Soviet Bloc, Policy Research Series No. 4, LA-9039
(Los Alamos, N.M.: Los Alamos National Laboratory, 1982), p. 23.

increases of over 4 percent and 5 percent in productivity, the GDR still
lags behind such countries as France and West Germany. More labor
is not available to be added to the work force. Over 8 million people
are employed in the GDR (a 6 percent increase since 1970); over three-
fourths of the working-age population, including about 80 percent of
working-age women, are on the job (see Table 5.8). One consequence
of this is the call for introduction of ever-higher numbers of robots into
industry (Honecker spoke of 45,000 robots by 1985; as of fall 1984, the
number had reached 35,000). Each of these robots was to replace 2.5
"laborers" (Arbeitskräfte).[28]

TABLE 5.8
Composition of the GDR Labor Force by Gender and Branch (as of 1982)

I.   Total labor force: 8,445,300
      Percentage of population in labor force: 50%; 78.3% of population of
      labor-force age

      By selected branches:

      Industry   37.9%

      Services ("Nonproducing")   20.7

      Agriculture/forestry   10.7

      Trade   10.1

II.   Women as portion of labor force: 49.5%
      Women in labor force as proportion of women of labor-force age: 79.1%

      Women as proportion of total in each branch:

      Industry   42.2%

      Services   73.1

      Agriculture/forestry   39.9

      Trade   73.0

      Each branch as proportion of women in labor force:

      Industry   32.3%

      Services   30.6

      Agriculture/forestry   8.6

      Trade   15.0

Source: Statistisches Taschenbuch der DDR .1984 (Berlin: Staatsverlag der
DDR, 1984), pp. 33-37.

To see the GDR economy through a period of global recession, the leadership is turning to emphasis on qualitative improvements: higher productivity, new technology, and a shift in investment from new capital projects to more efficient use of existing plants. This has been coupled with an all-out effort to achieve a favorable balance of payments with the West, in part to maintain eligibility for those Western credits that finance purchases of goods needed for the economy and for consumption. A sharp reduction in imports has weakened both of these stimuli for higher performance. Despite these difficulties, the leadership in East Berlin remains committed to the notion that "stable economic growth is indispensable for socialism, and that little or no growth is incompatible with the fundamental economic principle of socialism—the unity of economic and social policy."[29]

It is clear that this program will require substantial efforts by GDR workers and managers. Günter Mittag has declared that "growth in labor productivity was, is and will remain the core and key" for implementing the welfare policies of the Honecker era. Labor productivity, in turn, is a crucial element in industrial "intensification . . . [and] the only path to further economic growth, without which there will be no social progress."[30]

As we have seen, however, GDR economic policy is committed to providing material incentives for the population. Accordingly, in the midst of efforts to increase labor efficiency, the regime has also announced improved social benefits for families with three or more children, as well as improvements in pension benefits.[31]

AGRICULTURE

GDR agriculture, like Soviet agriculture, is organized into collective farms and subject to centrally directed planning; unlike its Soviet counterpart, however, GDR agriculture is not a drain on the economy, and it can generally feed the GDR population at adequate levels.

Agriculture in the GDR occupies a place of growing political importance, which stems from two factors: the increasing political importance of an assured supply of high-quality foodstuffs and the rising costs of inputs into agriculture, particularly oil and feed grains that need to be imported for hard currency.

Honecker has commented on both of these developments. In the spring of 1981, he remarked that "it is well known that food supplies play a growing role in the international class confrontation between Socialism and Imperialism." Several months later he declared, "Today the urgency of the grain problem is quite comparable to that of the oil problem."[32] This latter declaration is emblematic of a continuing and largely successful campaign to conserve fuel and energy in the farming sector.[33]

During the period covered by the Five-Year Plan ending in 1981, GDR investment in agriculture amounted to 25.4 billion Mark (during 1981, over half of that was for agricultural construction). In that same period, 239 million tons of foodstuffs were produced. In 1982, agriculture accounted for almost 8 percent of produced national income and under 11 percent of the labor force.

The Physical Basis

Agriculture is quite feasibly carried out over most areas of the GDR. The total amount of agricultural land in the GDR is slightly more than 6 million hectares (or about 15.5 million acres). The amount of

TABLE 5.9
Land Use in GDR (in thousand hectares)

	1983	1982	1981	1978
Agricultural area	6,250.4	6,258.5	6,273.8	6,286.4
Under cultivation	4,733.5	4,730.8	4,741.4	4,618.4
Arable land in LPG	5,358.2	5,348.2	5,291.8	5,392.5

Sources: Statistisches Taschenbuch der DDR 1984 (Berlin: Staatsverlag der
DDR, 1984), pp. 67–69; Neues Deutschland, 2 March and 3–4 July, 1982.

NOTE: 1 hectare = 2.6 acres

land available to agriculture has actually declined in recent years, as a
result of rapid expansion of urbanization and industrialization.

The incorporation of small or marginal parcels of land in the area
sown with grain or used as pasture land is being pushed. A factor
specific to the GDR is the extensive practice of strip-mining lignite;
although efforts at land reclamation have recently been stepped up, it
remains difficult to rescue arable agricultural land from competing uses
(see Table 5.9).

A closely related problem concerns soil quality—a crucial consideration given the GDR's plan to increase agricultural productivity,
especially in fodder grains. Consequently, GDR farmers have been
exhorted through official statements to take better care of the soil. The
party's chief agricultural spokesman, Werner Felfe, described the soil as
"one of the most precious of natural resources," and called for greater
accountability of collective farms in this regard.[34]

The problem lies partly in the large-scale and widespread use of
both chemical fertilizers and agricultural machinery. Heavy use of
chemicals is due in part to the current organization of agriculture, which
involves separating animal from plant production, and thus manure from
field. Between 1967 and 1977, the average distance over which fertilizer,
feed, and manure were transported in agricultural enterprises doubled,
from 4 to 8 kilometers. These trends make intelligible the observation
of a cattle raiser: "[With the organization of agriculture] by strict categories
of product and technology, I often ask myself, who is actually in charge
of the soil? In a group of specialists, one can always shift responsibility
to someone else."[35] Indeed, in its effort to promote good soil-conservation
practices, the regime has remembered and recommended the virtues of
traditional peasant wisdom![36]

Recently, new measures of soil and water protection have been
announced. A land-use law of 1981 instituted differentiated user fees

for various categories of land, and a new water-use law was put into effect in early 1982. Although the total water supply per capita is adequate for foreseeable needs, there is little margin for drought or a major increase in water use, given that about 90 percent of all water supplies are already in use. The irrigation program continues to have official backing; in the first ten months of 1984, some 279,000 hectares of land were irrigated.[37]

The Organizational Basis: Origin and Development

Before 1945, the territories forming the GDR were noted for large landholdings; these areas (particularly those in the northern regions) were dominated politically and socially by a landholding class. Thus the question of landholding assumed a political aspect for the new authorities, and whatever the economic costs might be, the revolutionary transformation of East German society could not be implemented without a radical break with past landholding patterns.

In the Soviet Zone of Occupation, private landholdings in excess of 100 hectares accounted for almost a third of the total agricultural area in 1945. Such properties, together with holdings of the state and of persons judged to be Nazis, were expropriated without compensation; the amount of land thus made available for redistribution came to about 3.25 million hectares (from over 13,000 separate properties).[38]

The land was then redistributed to landless rural laborers, farmers with minimal holdings, and refugees from the lost eastern territories. Each eligible family received up to 5—and in special circumstances up to 10—hectares. Such land could not be sold, leased, or mortgaged. Some 209,000 new farms were formed, with an average size of 8 hectares.

This land reform was pushed through in the summer and fall of 1945, and was a priority political measure for the Soviet authorities and Communists. Although the actual work of redistribution was carried out by "land commissions" composed of landless or land-poor peasants in each community, the driving force was clearly the Soviet occupation administration. In 1952, a slow collectivization of agriculture got under way with three types of agricultural production cooperatives (Landwirtschaftliche Produktions-Genossenschaften, or LPG) of differing degrees of amalgamation, with Type-III LPGs, the loosest kind, the most frequently chosen. Each member-family was allowed a half-hectare (maximum) "private plot."

In the spring of 1960, the GDR leadership decided to achieve full collectivization of agriculture. Although it had taken over seven years to collectivize about half the arable land of the GDR, the authorities now forced through a further collectivization of another 40 percent of land area to over 80 percent of the total and raised the number of collective farms from 10,465 to 19,345—all within five months' time.[39]

The campaign was accompanied by massive propaganda and political efforts to persuade GDR farmers to enter the collectives—despite what Ulbricht himself described as the surrounding atmosphere of "doubt and distrust." Public pressure on recalcitrant peasants, including nonstop "agitational" efforts by urban and party volunteers backed up by the efforts of the security services, had its desired effect.

The collectivization of agriculture (with over 80 percent of the arable land worked in Type-III LPGs) was not the final reorganization of the agricultural system. In the 1970s, the GDR leadership decided to introduce an "industrialized (*industriemässiges*) agricultural system." This system was designed to improve productivity through specialization and economies of scale. Thus in 1970 there were 9,009 LPGs, but by 1979 there were 1,448 crop-producing farms and 3,568 farms specializing in livestock. The process has been carried further in the most recent period such that, by early 1982, the number of special crop collectives stood at 1,065, and of animal husbandry, at 2,819. There was further specialization through LPGs for horticulture, interenterprise cooperatives for animal husbandry, and thirty-odd animal-fattening stations. Examples of these mammoth agricultural units include a station for 24,000 cattle, a pig-rearing enterprise for 80,000 swine, and a half-million-crate egg-producing unit.[40]

In one rural district near Schwerin, for example, aside from collective and state farms, there are various agrochemical centers, two joint construction units, two units for irrigation and land improvement, and one drainage unit. These enterprises perform irrigation, fertilization, construction, and other technical services for all the collective and state farms in three adjoining rural districts; they also employ 796 workers, of whom 25 have university training, 60 have vocational certification, and 44 are skilled workers (*Meister*).[41]

There are tendencies in the GDR toward unit autonomy and the danger that resources concentrated in these special institutions could be (and, indeed, have been) used for nonagricultural purposes. The party has had to intervene repeatedly to make it clear to the managers of these enterprises that their primary task was to help in agricultural production and not to "fulfill" the plan through profitable moonlighting.

The party's response to the problems of overspecialization has been to encourage the creation of cooperation councils (*Kooperationsräte*), in which the specialization of agricultural tasks will be overcome. The increasing size of agricultural units has also caused concern among peasants with respect to the future status of their villages. Possibly to assuage such fears, an SED spokesman mentioned the need for "territorial production units" (i.e., the old villages) in which peasants would be able to follow the entire "production process." He also called for "closer ties to the village," which must be made a more pleasant place in which to live.[42]

While maintaining the juridical independence of the LPGs—and thus their leaders' formal responsibility for performance—the leadership has decided to increase the role of the cooperation councils. In November

1984, Honecker revealed that more binding financial and planning arrangements among cooperating LPGs had been tried out in eighty-eight councils, and that the resulting system would be extended throughout the GDR in 1985–1986. A sign that these *Kooperationsräte* are to become the main administrative units in agriculture is Honecker's further remark that councils of party secretaries of the GOs in the respective LPGs would be strengthened and put under direct and close supervision of the district (*Kreis*) party leaderships.[43]

In 1984, the GDR instituted a new fiscal policy regarding the LPGs. Official procurement prices were raised in the hope of stimulating production through profit incentives. Simultaneously, the hitherto existing subsidies to the agricultural sector for machinery, fuels, and chemicals were abolished. It was hoped that by this means the LPGs and VEGs would be induced to be more sparing in their use of these now more expensive inputs.[44]

Agricultural Production and Consumption

Agricultural production in the GDR is concentrated in the collective farm sector, which is consequently the major source for state procurements of agricultural commodities: 95 percent of all crops, 76 percent of animal products, 91.6 percent of grain, 94.1 percent of sugar beets, 90 percent of potatoes, and 92.8 percent of milk. The produce from private plots of land is an important supplement to collectively produced goods. Although the area devoted to such plots dropped from 733,000 hectares in 1960 to 227,300 in 1974, the regime has since recognized their importance by allowing employees of LPGs, and urban persons generally, to work their half-hectares. Moreover, the regime now officially encourages that traditional institution, the allotment garden; in 1980 there were almost 8,000 such gardens covering 45,000 hectares.

These various sources supply significant amounts of fresh produce, eggs, and limited amounts of meat to the state purchasing organizations, and often, through local governments, directly to schools, old age homes, and similar institutions. Although the animal holdings of the private plots and allotment gardens have significantly declined over the past two decades, the role of these plots in the general agricultural picture remains an important one. In the first half of 1984, these sources accounted for more than 15 percent of all animals delivered for slaughter as well as over 40 percent of the eggs and wool brought to market.[45]

General trends in food production showed a steady rise. On the basis of 1957–1961 = 100, an index of total food production in 1978 was 142. Production of grain is an especially important factor for ensuring the supply of both bread and animal feed. Over half the arable land of the GDR is sown with grain and half of that with feed grains. From this sown area have come yields of over 10 million tons annually, with a per-hectare yield of close to 45 decitons.[46] The commitment to secure feed grains so as to ensure a meat supply has led the GDR into foreign

TABLE 5.10
Per Capita Consumption of Selected Foodstuffs in the GDR (1970-1983)

Year	Milk (liters)	Butter (Kg)	Meat (Kg)	Vegetables (Kg)	Sugar (Kg)
1970	98.5	14.6	66.0	84.8	34.4
1975	100.8	14.7	77.8	90.0	36.8
1980	98.7	15.2	89.4	93.8	40.6
1983	105.4	15.7	92.1*	90.7	39.2

Sources: Allen A. Terhaar and Thomas A. Vankai, "The East European Feed-Livestock Economy, 1966-85: Performance and Prospects," in U.S. Congress, Joint Economic Committee, East European Economic Assessment. Part 2--Regional Assessments (97th Cong., 1st sess., 1981), p. 563; Helmut Semmelmann, "Worin besteht das Getreideproblem?" Neuer Weg 37, 5 (1982): 203-205.

*Of which pork accounts for 57.7 kg

trade difficulties. Whether changes in agricultural methods, increased use of pasture feeding, and a planned expansion of sown acreage by 1985 of 120,000 hectares will allow the GDR to cut grain imports by the planned amount remains to be seen.[47]

What has this production record meant to GDR consumers, especially consumers of food? In recent years, they have had a steadily rising amount of food available. In 1982, some shortages appeared, especially of meat and butter, and particularly in small towns. These shortages have been attributed to distribution difficulties, as well as to the channeling of meat supplies into the export market. The regime took them seriously enough for Honecker to stress that overcoming these difficulties would be a priority matter.[48] The GDR, along with Hungary and Czechoslovakia, has the highest proportion of animal products in total caloric intake (41 percent in 1965) of the CMEA countries.[49]

This high consumption of butter and meat (three-fifths of all meat consumed is pork), which from one perspective is a great triumph for the GDR's socialist agriculture, has also become a cause for concern for GDR health professionals (see Table 5.10). With an average daily intake of over 3,000 calories, a third of the population was regarded in 1970 as overweight. Indeed, GDR economists calculated that economic losses due to obesity in the population came to 3 billion Mark.[50] It is unclear what the long-range health effects of such a diet will be.

THE GDR IN THE WORLD ECONOMY

Foreign trade is an important aspect of the GDR's economic life, accounting for about 15 percent of national income (see Table 5.11). A

TABLE 5.11
Patterns of GDR Foreign Trade

I.   Volume of Trade with Particular Countries, Regions (in millions of
     Valuta-Mark)

Year	Amount / Percentage		Country / Region
1970	39.6	100	Total
	15.5	39.0	USSR
	11.2	28.0	Other CMEA countries
	9.7	24.5	Industrial West
	1.6	4.0	LDCs
1980	120.1	100	Total
	42.6	35.5	USSR
	32.7	27.0	Other CMEA countries
	33.0	27.5	Industrial West
	7.3	6.0	LDCs
1981	133.0	100	Total
	43.9	37.5	USSR
	34.5	26.0	Other CMEA countries
	37.9	28.6	Industrial West
	6.5	5.0	LDCs
1982	145.1	100	Total
	55.2	37.9	USSR
	36.3	25.0	Other CMEA countries
	40.8	28.0	Industrial West
	8.4	6.0	LDCs
1983	160.4	100	Total
	60.8	37.9	USSR
	39.5	24.6	Other CMEA countries
	47.1	29.3	Industrial West
	8.6	5.3	LDCs

II. Five Leading Trading Partners: USSR, West Germany (with West Berlin),[*]
     Czechoslovakia, Hungary, and Poland

     *Counted separately in GDR statistics.

Sources: Statistisches Taschenbuch der DDR 1984 (Berlin: Staatsverlag der
DDR, 1984), pp. 100-102; Statistisches Jahrbuch der DDR 1983 (Berlin:
Staatsverlag der DDR, 1983), pp. 235-238; Maria Haendke-Hoppe,
"Konsolidierung in der DDR-Aussenwirtschaft," Deutschland Archiv 17, 10
(October 1984): 1060-1068.

small country with a limited resource base, it is dependent on external sources of raw materials, which it pays for with industrial products. At the same time, it is an importer of high-technology equipment and consumer goods, and it pays for these in large part with borrowed funds. The former contingency describes GDR trade with the Soviet Union, Eastern Europe, and the Third World; the latter describes its trade with the industrial nations of the West.

Prior to its achievement of general international recognition in the early 1970s, GDR foreign trade policy was largely dictated by political considerations—specifically, by its attempts to secure diplomatic gains through economic relations.[51] In subsequent years, trade policy came to be dominated by economic factors. Thus GDR trade with the West aimed at securing new technology, choice consumer goods, and hard-currency reserves; trade with the Third World was focused on securing specific resources; trade with the Soviet Union was designed to ensure deliveries of Soviet raw materials while enhancing the GDR's standing through the supply of choice industrial goods.

As this last point demonstrates, foreign trade, although carried on for economic reasons, cannot escape political ramifications. Much of foreign trade policy is designed to maintain the country's living standards—an objective of primary political importance. The GDR's role as a supplier of important technical goods to the USSR has obvious implications for the GDR's political standing within the East European bloc. These considerations help explain the continuing stress placed on trade policy by the GDR's leadership.

The GDR's leading trade partner is the Soviet Union, which in recent years has accounted for over a third of total GDR foreign trade (the GDR, with its 9-percent share of Soviet foreign trade, is in turn the leading trade partner of the USSR). The position of the Soviet Union in GDR trade, already dominant through its provision of essential elements of industrial life, is likely to grow in the future. During the Five-Year Plans of the 1970s GDR-Soviet trade grew by 78 percent, and current plans call for a further increase of 55 percent by 1985.[52]

GDR trade with the Soviet Union is increasingly focused on GDR exports of specialized manufactures, such as marine diesel engines; the GDR supplied the Soviet Union with 60 percent of its imports of this item. Certain whole branches of the GDR economy exist for exports to the Soviet Union; the chief example is shipbuilding—there are some 3,000 "GDR ships" in the Soviet merchant marine.

These goods must pay for essential Soviet deliveries, but the exchange is occurring with increased difficulty. The increased volume of goods traded buys smaller increments of scarce Soviet raw materials, despite the commitment of GDR labor and capital investments in the Soviet extractive industry. Nevertheless, the GDR exports to the Soviet Union needed to finance oil imports more than tripled in the decade of the 1970s.[53]

The city of Rostock is a busy port on the Baltic coast. Photo courtesy of the GDR Embassy, Washington, D.C.

As a result, the GDR accumulated debts of over 3 billion transfer rubles in 1980–1982 in its trade with the USSR. Accordingly, in 1983 and early 1984, the GDR made special efforts to attain a positive balance of trade with the USSR. In 1983, GDR imports from the Soviet Union grew by a modest 5.9 percent, and exports rose by 14 percent. This positive trade balance was achieved despite the fact that the price paid by the GDR for Soviet oil in 1983 reached world-market levels.[54]

GDR trade with the West has consisted principally of the importation of consumer goods (ranging from Volkswagens to jeans) and technology.[55] As a response to Western political pressures, much of the trade with the West was shifted to Japan, France, and Austria in 1982–1983.

East Berlin took very seriously indeed the sharp rise in GDR indebtedness to the West. In 1982, the regime proudly announced a positive trade balance with the "nonsocialist" countries; in 1983, it announced a "substantial" surplus—results that were due to drastically curtailed imports (some 30 percent) and a 10 percent rise in exports. Prompt payment of interest (the equivalent of $1 billion in 1982) and charges, together with reduction of the principal, improved the GDR credit rating.[56] Even so, the GDR was over $8 billion in debt to the West at the close of 1983. The political and psychological damage of defaulting was avoided, however, with the help of the West Germans (as discussed later in this chapter). By late 1984, GDR hard-currency reserves were at an all-time high.

Reducing the GDR indebtedness to the West by curtailing imports has serious limitations. The items imported are the very things needed for social stability and efficient production of exports. Thus the GDR will continue to depend on the reluctance of both its Soviet and Western creditors to allow a GDR default.[57]

The GDR's import difficulties are exemplified by two vital commodities: feed grains and oil. For the past twenty-five years, the GDR has imported between a quarter and a third of its grain supply; this imported grain (as feed grain) became a crucial increment for securing adequate supplies of meat. Furthermore, given Soviet agricultural problems, the imported grain has meant hard-currency imports. After U.S.-GDR relations were established, the United States became a leading supplier of such grain; from 1975 through 1979, U.S. grain accounted for between 40 and 60 percent of all grain imports—and in 1980, the United States supplied no less than 82.5 percent of the GDR's imported grain. Subsequently, the GDR made a pronounced effort both to increase domestic supplies (the 1983 harvest exceeded 10 million tons of grain)[58] and to diversify the origins of grain imports, contracting in 1983 to buy 1 million tons of feed grains from Canada.[59]

We may recall that the GDR is wholly dependent on external sources for its oil, and that in the latter half of the 1970s, Soviet deliveries accounted for between 86 and 90 percent of these imports. Under the "Bucharest formula" for pricing Soviet oil deliveries (an average of world prices for the preceding five years), the GDR felt the 1973–1974 "oil shock" after 1980 and can expect the impact of the 1979 oil supply crisis in the mid-1980s. At the same time, Soviet delivery quotas have leveled off to the point reached in 1977–1978—that is, about 17 million tons. Consequently, the GDR has found it necessary both to institute serious conservation measures and to buy oil for hard currency. In 1980, the GDR supplied 13 percent of its oil imports from these sources, and this trend has continued: in 1982, some 4 million tons (out of a total of 21.7 million tons) came from non-Soviet, presumably Third World sources. In 1983, GDR trade with its presumed leading OPEC suppliers (Iraq and Iran) accounted for 43 percent of all GDR trade with the Third World.[60]

A nearly unique element in GDR-West trade relations is the GDR's favored position in trading with the Federal Republic.[61] First, there is the GDR's special status under the 1957 Rome treaties that established the Common Market, by which its trade with the FRG is regarded as domestic trade. This means that GDR exports to West Germany and West Berlin are free of Common Market tariffs, and are not subject to taxes levied on imported goods. For the GDR, such trade is of substantial significance: West Germany is its second- or third-largest trading partner, well ahead of any other industrialized Western country, and it accounts for 6.5 percent of total GDR foreign trade.

A second unusual feature of inter-German trade is the extension of a credit "swing" to the GDR.[62] Under this arrangement, which goes back to 1950 agreements on interzonal trade, the GDR has an extension of nonpenalty time for the repayment of its trade deficit until an annual clearing of accounts takes place; the GDR therefore receives the equivalent of an interest-free loan until year's end. The amount of this swing is fixed by an arrangement between the two German states and has been set at varying levels, sometimes on a shifting scale; in 1976, it was fixed for five years at 850 million units (Verrechnungseinheiten, or VE). In December 1981, Schmidt and Honecker extended the agreement for another six months (it would otherwise have fallen back to 200 million VE). In June 1982, the two German states announced a three-year agreement that had the effect of lowering the swing by slow steps: to 770 million in 1983, 690 million in 1984, and 600 million in 1985.

This agreement resulted from the conjunction of political and economic pressures. For the FRG, the maintenance of a special status for inter-German trade emphasizes the "special" nature of the German situation. For the GDR, maintenance of trade with the FRG on an easy basis is of economic advantage, but it does not occur at a political price that the GDR would deem exorbitant; East Berlin was unwilling to link the swing to an overtly political counteroffer, although the GDR did ease access somewhat between East and West Berlin at the same time that the agreement was announced. The 600-million VE level is economically acceptable to the GDR because in recent years it has not made full use of the amount available, using 740 VE million in 1980 and 670 VE in 1981.[63]

In the summer of 1983, this special relationship was further strengthened when a West German banking consortium, with official Bonn backing, granted the GDR a 1 billion Deutsche Mark (DM) credit. In 1984, a second guaranteed bank loan of 950 million DM was arranged. These moves allow the GDR to continue its policy of financing needed imports on the basis of West German willingness to grant economic benefits. The Bonn government does so in pursuit of its own, noneconomic goals of maintaining special ties to the Germans of the GDR; it has clearly developed a commitment to at least minimal East German prosperity.[64]

The trade that is financed in this way has risen steadily over the past decade and a half, amounting in 1982 to about one-fourth of the GDR's non-CMEA trade (see Table 5.12).

To what extent the GDR leadership will continue to pursue its recent strategy of expanding inter-German trade more quickly than general trade with the West is hard to foretell.[65] Politically, the GDR cannot be interested in giving Bonn too powerful a lever over GDR policy in inter-German matters. The GDR's political preferences, however, may be outweighed by global economic conditions. In recent years, the GDR has managed to continue on its economic course despite increasingly adverse international influences. Whether it can continue to do so will have an important bearing on the domestic legitimacy of the regime.

TABLE 5.12
Inter-German Trade (1980-1984)

Year	Amount*	Change**	GDR Amount†
1980	10.8	17.0	7,305
1981	11.6	7.0	8,004
1982	13.0	12.0	9,358
1983	13.8	6.1	10,206
1984††	6.9	-4.7	---

Sources: Re amount and change: Maria Haendcke-Hoppe, "Konsolidierung in der DDR-Aussenwirtschaft," Deutschland Archiv 17, 10 (October 1984): 1065; re GDR amount: Statistisches Taschenbuch der DDR 1984 (Berlin: Staatsverlag der DDR, 1984), p. 101.

* in billions of VE (DM equivalents)

**January-June

† percentage over previous year

††in millions of Valuta-Mark (excludes West Berlin)

NOTES

1. Eugen Faude and Gerhard Grote, "Die DDR in der Weltwirtschaft," *Die Wirtschaft*, no. 2 (1981), pp. 14–15.
2. Paul Marer, "Economic Performance and Prospects in Eastern Europe," in *East European Economic Assessment, Part 2: Regional Assessments* [cited hereafter as EEEA, Part 2] (Washington, D.C.: Government Printing Office, for U.S. Congress, Joint Economic Committee, 1981), pp. 19–95. See also World Bank, *World Development Report 1982* (New York: Oxford University Press, 1982), p. 111.
3. Erich Honecker, in *Neues Deutschland*, 27–28 November 1982.
4. Faude and Grote, "Die DDR," pp. 14–15.
5. Günter Mittag, in *Neues Deutschland*, 4–5 December 1982, p. 5.
6. Deutsches Institut für Wirtschaftsforschung Berlin, *Handbuch DDR-Wirtschaft* [cited hereafter as *Handbuch*] (Hamburg: Rowohlt Taschenbuch Verlag, 1977), p. 19.
7. Ibid., p. 20; Doris Cornelsen, "Die Industriepolitik der DDR. Veränderungen von 1945 bis 1980," *Der X. Parteitag der SED/35 Jahre SED Politik, Versuch einer Bilanz* (Cologne: Edition Deutschland Archiv, 1981), pp. 46–48.
8. Ibid. Cornelson, "Die Industriepolitik der DDR."
9. Hermann Weber, *Kleine Geschichte der DDR* (Cologne: Edition Deutschland Archiv, 1980), pp. 29–31; Gregory Sandford, *From Hitler to Ulbricht: The*

Communist Reconstruction of East Germany, 1945-46 (Princeton, N.J.: Princeton University Press, 1983), ch. 5.

10. *Handbuch*, pp. 57–59; Weber, *Kleine Geschichte*, pp. 61–62.

11. Cornelsen, "Die Industriepolitik der DDR," pp. 50–51.

12. This and the following paragraphs are based on ibid., pp. 53–55; on *Handbuch*, pp. 57–61; and on Michael Keren, "The Rise and Fall of the New Economic System in the GDR," in Lyman H. Legters, ed., *The German Democratic Republic: A Developed Socialist Society* (Boulder, Colo.: Westview Press, 1978), pp. 61–84. See also Manfred Melzer, "The GDR: Economic Policy Caught Between Pressure for Efficiency and Lack of Ideas," in Alec Nove, Hans-Hermann Höhmann, and Gertraud Seidenstecher, eds., *East European Economies in the 1970s* (London: Butterworths, 1982), pp. 48–52.

13. For a good discussion of the problems created by these reforms, see Jürgen Strassburger, "Economic System and Economic Policy: The Challenge of the 1970s," in Klaus von Beyme and Hartmut Zimmerman, eds., *Policymaking in the German Democratic Republic* (New York: St. Martin's Press, 1984), ch. 2.

14. "Direktive des VIII. Parteitages der Sozialistischen Einheitspartei Deutschlands zum Fünfjahrplan für die Entwicklung der Volkswirtschaft der Deutschen Demokratischen Republik," *Documente der Sozialistischen Einheitspartei Deutschlands*, vol. 13 (Berlin: Dietz, 1974), p. 183.

15. This entire section is based on *Handbuch*, pp. 61–74; see also Melzer, "The GDR," pp. 54–61.

16. Manfred Melzer, "Combine Formation in the GDR," *Soviet Studies* 33 (January 1981):88–106. The number of VVBs dropped from 85 in 1967 to 13 in 1979, whereas the number of *Kombinate* rose from 37 in 1973 to 132 centrally directed and 93 locally controlled combines in 1983. See Melzer, "Combine Formation," p. 55; *Neues Deutschland*, 24 June 1982, p. 6; *Statistisches Taschenbuch der DDR 1984* (Berlin: Staatsverlag der DDR, 1984), p. 49; Eugene K. Keefe, ed., *East Germany: A Country Study* (Washington, D.C.: Government Printing Office, 1982, pp. 112–113).

17. Melzer, "The GDR," p. 79; Keefe, *East Germany*, p. 113. For an excellent profile of a successful forty-one-year-old combine director, see "Er sagt: 'Als ich damals das Kombinat gebildet habe . . .,'" *Frankfurter Allgemeine Zeitung*, 8 August 1983, p. 8.

18. *Handbuch*, pp. 140–166; SED, Central Committee, *Successful Path of Developing an Advanced Socialist Society in the GDR: Facts and Figures* (Berlin: n.p., 1981), pp. 19–22; *Die Wirtschaft*, no. 10 (1981), p. 19 (graphics); Wolfgang Pehnt, "Rückkehr in die Stadt," *Frankfurter Allgemeine Zeitung*, 23 April 1983; Cornelsen, "Die Industriepolitik der DDR," pp. 303–304; "Unser Wohnungsbauprogramm zeigt, was der reale Sozialismus leisten kann," *Die Wirtschaft*, no. 7 (1980), p. 4; *Statistisches Taschenbuch der DDR 1983*, p. 60.

19. *Programm der Sozialistischen Einheitspartei Deutschlands* (Berlin: Dietz, 1976), p. 30.

20. "Erfolgreiche Bilanz 1980 im Wohnungsbau der Republik," *Neues Deutschland*, 24 December 1980, p. 3; Günter Mittag, in *Neues Deutschland*, 4–5 December 1982, p. 5; Karl Schmiechen, "Innerstädtisches Bauen," *Die Wirtschaft*, no. 3 (1983), p. 4; Wolfgang Junker, "Qualitativ neue Aufgaben in Bauwesen," *Die Wirtschaft*, no. 6 (1982), pp. 5–6. The old apartments of the GDR are a refuge for semilegal squatters, mostly young and single persons who have dropped out of the intensely competitive public life of their country. For an amusing first-hand report, see "Die Szene vom Prenzlauer Berg," in Peter

Wensierski, Lothar Reese, and Norbert Haase eds., *VED Nachwuchs* (Hamburg: Rowohlt, 1983), pp. 197–211.

21. Especially as announced in a party-state decree immediately following the Ninth SED Congress in 1976, these programs include improved maternity benefits, raised incomes for low-paid workers, increases in old-age pensions and disability benefits, and a reduction of weekly working hours for shift workers, benefits for newly formed households, and increased student aid. See Cornelsen, "Die Industriepolitik der DDR," pp. 302–303.

22. See Erich Honecker, in *Neues Deutschland*, 13 February 1981, p. 4. See also the discussion in *Osteuropa-Wirtschaft* 21 (1982):55; and in Keefe, *East Germany*, pp. 118–119.

23. Central Intelligence Agency, National Foreign Assessment Center, *Energy Supplies in Eastern Europe: A Statistical Compilation*, ER 79-10624 (December 1979), pp. 40, 42; John M. Kramer, "The Policy Dilemmas of East Europe's Gap," in *EEEA, Part 2*, pp. 459–475; Robin Watson, "The Linkage Between Energy and Growth Prospects in Dilemmas Confronting the GDR," RFE-RL Research *RAD Background Report/48* (March 11, 1983); Wolfgang Stinglwagner, "Genügend Energie für die Zukunft," *Deutschland Archiv* 16 (March 1983):262–272. The annual percentage increase in total energy consumption dropped steadily throughout the late 1970s, but only once (in 1980) was there actually a *decrease*. The increases for 1976 through 1979 ranged from 3.9 percent down to 1.4 percent; the decrease for 1980 was 1.2 percent; and the increase for 1981 was a meager 0.3 percent (see Stinglwagner, "Genügend Energie," pp. 253–254).

24. Maria Haendcke-Hoppe, "DDR-Aussenwirtschaft unter neuen Vorzeichen," *Deutschland Archiv* 16 (April 1983):382; Maria Haendcke-Hoppe, "DDR-Aussenhandel im Zeichen schrumpfender Exporte," *Deutschland Archiv* 16 (October 1983):1069–1970.

25. CIA, *Energy Supplies in East Europe*, p. 42; Willi Stoph, in *Neues Deutschland*, 4-5 December 1982, p. 3; Diethelm Müller, "Internationale Tendenzen bei der Braunkohlenförderung," *Die Wirtschaft*, no. 12 (1982), p. 15. (Strip mining also requires replacement of some 2,750 hectares of arable land annually.) See also Günter Mittag, "Oekonomische Strategie der Partei dient der weiteren Verwirklichung des Kurses der Hauptaufgabe," *Einheit* 39, nos. 9,10 (September–October 1984):807.

26. SED, *Successful Path*," p. 48; William G. Davey, "Nuclear Power in the Soviet Bloc," Policy Research Paper No. 4 (New Mexico: Los Alamos National Laboratory, March 1982); Stinglwagner, "Genügend Energie," pp. 268–269; S. Collatz, "Die Kernenergetik—eine entscheidende Primärenergiequelle," *Die Wirtschaft*, no. 8 (1981), p. 26; Olaf Dahms, "Zum Aufbau der Kernenergetik in einigen RGW-Ländern," *Die Wirtschaft*, no. 12 (1982), p. 28.

27. See the articles in *Neues Deutschland*, 21 September 1979, p. 2, and 17–18 November 1982, p. 14; Klaus Steinitz and Joachim Wartenberg, "Zur Sicherung der Energie-Rohstoffversorgung," *Die Wirtschaft*, no. 1 (1983), p. 15; Günter Kertscher, "Die Herausforderung der 80. Jahre," *Neues Deutschland*, 16-17 May 1981, p. 9. Between 1977 and 1983, the percentage of secondary energy recovered rose by 21 percent. See Helmut Rieck and Manfred Jäger, "Energiereserven, die sich rasch und kostengünstig erschliessen lassen," *Neues Deutschland*, 21 October 1982, p. 3.

28. For one of the numerous references to the installation of robots, see *Neues Deutschland*, 24 June 1982, p. 5; Werner Gruhn and Günter Lauterbach,

"Das Roboterprogramm der DDR," *Deutschland Archiv* 16 (April 1983):408–415. On labor, see *Frankfurter Allgemeine Zeitung*, 27 March 1982, p. 8; Ronald D. Asmus, "Microelectronics, Robots and Socialism in the GDR," RFE-RL Research, *RAD Background Report/340* (December 9, 1981); *Statistisches Taschenbuch der DDR 1983*, pp. 33–37. For the 1983 figures on robots, see *Neues Deutschland*, 16–17 July 1983, p. 3. Günter Mittag declared industrial robots to be "not just an enhancement of existing technology, but rather a catalyst" of an all-encompassing modernization of GDR industry. The 35,000 robots of 1984 were said to be four times as numerous as the number of 1980. See Mittag, "Oekonomische Strategie," p. 806.

29. Doris Cornelsen, "Die Wirtschaft der DDR in den achtziger Jahren," *Die DDR vor den Herausforderungen der achtziger Jahre. Sechzente Tagung . . . 24. bis 27. Mai 1983* (Cologne: Edition Deutschland Archiv, 1983), p. 39.

30. Mittag, "Oekonomische Strategie," pp. 805–806.

31. *Neues Deutschland*, 23 May 1984, p. 1, and 29 May 1984, p. 3.

32. *Neues Deutschland*, 14 April 1981, and 20 November 1981, respectively.

33. Honecker was cited, for example, by Werner Felfe, "35 Jahre erfolgreiche Agar—und Bündnispolitik der SED," *Einheit* 39 (September-October 1984):814–816.

34. *Neues Deutschland*, 5–6 February 1983, p. 9; Werner Felfe, "Die sozialistische Land- , Forst- und Nahrungsgüterwirtschaft im Schrittmass der 80er Jahre," *Einheit* 27 (February 1982):133; *Neues Deutschland*, 3–4 July 1982, p. 4.

35. Hans-Bernhard Nordhoff, "Industriemässige Agrarproduktion in der Sackgasse," *Deutschland Archiv* 15 (May 1982):487–491; for information on the case of manure to field, see Karl Hohmann, "Zur Entwicklung der DDR-Landwirtschaft im Fünfjahrplan 1976–1980," *Deutschland Archiv* 14 (May 1981):473–482; concerning the "cattle raiser," see *Frankfurter Allgemeine Zeitung*, 21 July 1982, p. 9.

36. *Neues Deutschland*, 4 May 1981.

37. Hans Reichelt, "Das neue Wassergesetz und seine höheren Anforderungen an alle Bereiche der Wolkswirtschaft," *Die Wirtschaft*, no. 8 (1982), p. 3; an interview with Reichelt is in *Neues Deutschland*, 5 October 1981, p. 3. See also Honecker's speech to the Ninth CC Plenum in *Neues Deutschland*, 23 November 1984, p. 5.

38. Sandford, *From Hitler to Ulbricht*, pp. 82–83, 98–101; Weber, *Kleine Geschichte*, p. 28; Hans Immler, *Agrarpolitik in der DDR* (Cologne: Verlag Wissenschaft und Politik, 1971), pp. 29–49.

39. Weber, *Kleine Geschichte*, p. 100.

40. Felfe, "Die Sozialistische," p. 132; Organization for Economic Cooperation and Development, *Prospects for Agricultural Production and Trade in Eastern Europe: Poland, German Democratic Republic, Hungary*, vol. 1 [hereafter cited as OECD 1981] (Paris: OECD 1981), pp. 103–104. Slightly different totals for the numbers of agricultural units are given in *Neuer Weg* 37 (1982):24–25.

41. See the article by a district SED secretary, Eva Hempel, entitled "Kooperative Einrichtungen und genossenschaftliche Demokratie," *Einheit* 37 (February 1982):150–153.

42. Felfe, "Die Sozialistische," p. 136.

43. Erich Honecker, speech to the Ninth CC Plenum, in *Neues Deutschland*, 23 November 1984, p. 6.

118 THE GDR: A SOCIALIST INDUSTRIAL STATE

44. Felfe, "35 Jahre," p. 816; B. V. Flow, "German Democratic Republic," in RFE-RL Research, *RAD Background Report/224* (December 28, 1984).
45. Karl Eckart, "Die Bedeutung der privaten Anbauflächen für die Versorgung der Bevölkerung in der DDR," *Deutschland Archiv* 16 (April 1983):415–420. For recent figures, see *Neues Deutschland*, 14–15 July 1984, p. 4.
46. *OECD 1981*, p. 140; *Neuer Weg* 37 (1982):24–25; Felfe, "35 Jahre," pp. 814–815; Honecker speech to the Ninth CC Plenum, *Neues Deutschland*, 23 November 1984, p. 5.
47. Ronald D. Asmus, "The Grain Problem in the GDR," RFE-RL Research *RAD Background Report/112* (May 13, 1982); Helmut Semmelmann, "Worin besteht das Getreideproblem?" *Neuer Weg* 37 (1982):204–205.
48. *Frankfurter Allgemeine Zeitung*, 1 July 1982, p. 5; for Honecker's remarks, see *Neues Deutschland*, 2 November 1982.
49. *Neuer Weg* 37 (1982):25; *OECD 1981*, p. 108.
50. *OECD 1981*, p. 108.
51. Hanns-Dieter Jacobsen, "Die Aussenwirtschaftspolitik der DDR gegenüber dem Westen zu Beginn der achtziger Jahre," *Die DDR vor den Herausforderungen der achtziger Jahre . . . Mai 1983* (Cologne: Edition Deutschland Archiv, 1983), pp. 66–78. (In English: "Foreign Trade Relations of the GDR," in Klaus von Beyme and Harmut Zimmerman, eds., *Policymaking in the German Democratic Republic* [New York: St. Martin's Press, 1984], ch. 3.)
52. *Neuer Weg* 37 (1982):64. In the first half of 1984, trade with the CMEA countries rose by 14 percent and that with the USSR, by 18 percent. See *Neues Deutschland*, 14–15 July 1984, p. 5.
53. Maria Haendcke-Hoppe, "DDR-Aussenwirtschaft unter neuen Vorzeichen," *Deutschland Archiv* 16 (April 1983):381–384; Doris Cornelsen, "The GDR in a Period of Foreign Trade Difficulties: Developments and Prospects for the 1980s," *East European Economic Assessment, Part 1: Country Studies* (Washington, D.C.: Government Printing Office, for U.S. Congress, Joint Economic Committee, 1981), pp. 313–314. According to Günter Mittag (in *Neues Deutschland*, 8 November 1983, pp. 2–4), the GDR in 1982 supplied the following shares of important Soviet machinery imports: (a) oil refining equipment: 33 percent, (b) agricultural machinery: 44 percent, (c) printing equipment: 43 percent, (d) air conditioning units: 49 percent, and (e) machine tools: 33 percent.
54. Maria Haendcke-Hoppe, "DDR-Aussenhandel im Zeichen Schrumpfender Westimporte," *Deutschland Archiv* 16 (October 1983):1068–1069; Maria Haendcke-Hoppe, "Konsolidierung in der DDR-Aussenwirtschaft," *Deutschland Archiv* 17 (October 1984):1061–1062; *Neues Deutschland*, 19 January 1984, p. 5.
55. Jacobsen, "Die Aussenwirtschaftspolitik"; Haendcke-Hoppe, "Konsolidierung" and "DDR-Aussenhandel." An even greater level of intra-German involvement in consumer goods supplies is marked by the announcement that Volkswagen (VW) is planning to build an engine plant in the GDR; some of the output of this plant will go to VW in payment, and some will be used to power the GDR's weak, hitherto two-cylinder "Trabant." See German Information Center, "This Week in Germany" 15 (February 17, 1984):3.
56. Haendcke-Hoppe, "DDR-Aussenhandel," p. 1069; Haendcke-Hoppe, "Konsolidierung," pp. 1067–1068; *Neues Deutschland*, 19 January 1984, p. 5; *Business Week*, 20 February 1984, p. 46. For debt figures, see also *New York Times*, 26 May 1982, p. D1, and 17 June 1983, p. D1, both of which show a near doubling of the GDR's hard-currency debt between 1975 and 1982.
57. Jacobsen, "Die Aussenwirtschaftspolitik," pp. 77–78.

58. At the Tenth SED Congress in 1981, Honecker called for a 1-million-ton reduction of grain imports by 1985. Subsequently, party sources demanded a faster rate of reduction—"at least" a million tons in 1982 and "more than two million by 1985." See Ronald D. Asmus, "The Grain Problem in the GDR," RFE-RL Research, *RAD Background Report/112*, (May 13, 1982); see also Semmelmann, "Worin besteht das Getreideproblem?"

59. For 1975 through 1979: *OECD 1981*, p. 167. For 1980 and 1981: Haendcke-Hoppe, "Konsolidierung," p. 381; Haendcke-Hoppe, "DDR-Aussenhandel," pp. 1070–1071; *Neues Deutschland*, 19 January 1984, p. 4.

60. Haendcke-Hoppe, "DDR-Aussenhandel," p. 1069; Haendcke-Hoppe, "Konsolidierung," p. 1066; *Statistisches Jahrbuch der DDR 1983* (Berlin: Staatsverlag, 1983), pp. 239, 251; *Statistisches Taschenbuch der DDR 1984*, pp. 100–101.

61. *Handbuch*, pp. 268–271; Eberhard Schulz, ed., *Drei Jahrzehnte Aussenpolitik der DDR* (Munich: R. Oldenbourg, 1979), pp. 458–462.

62. *Handbuch*, p. 266; Ronald D. Asmus, "New Inter-German Agreement on 'Swing' Credit Announced," RFE-RL Research, *RAD Background Report/141* (June 28, 1982); *Frankfurter Allgemeine Zeitung*, 5 December 1981, p. 3.

63. *Neues Deutschland*, 19–20 June 1982, p. 2; Asmus, "New Inter-German Agreement on 'Swing' Credit Announced." A story in the *Frankfurter Allgemeine Zeitung* (21 June 1982, p. 3) stated that GDR use of the swing had "rarely exceeded 600 million mark" in recent times. As previously noted, the swing is calculated in bookkeeping units called "Verrechnungseinheiten" (VE).

64. *New York Times*, 28 February 1984, p. A3; *Frankfurter Allgemeine Zeitung*, 26 July 1984, pp. 1–2; Ronald D. Asmus, "A Second Credit for the GDR," RFE-RL Research, *RAD Background Report/142* (August 3, 1984).

65. Jacobsen, "Die Aussenwirtschaftspolitik," pp. 68, 73–74.

6

Managing a Modern Society

REGIME AND SOCIETY

With the domestic and international stabilization of the GDR's political system in the early 1970s, the focus of GDR policies has moved from ensuring the basic legitimation and maintenance of the regime to other less fundamental but more complex and equally important tasks. These may be summed up as implementation of the regime's economic and social policies, and regulation of its relationship to "society" (i.e., to those social groups whose affirmative participation in GDR life is important for the fulfillment of the former objective). In this chapter and the next, accordingly, we will survey GDR policies in a wide variety of fields: cultural life, education, youth and sports, the role of women, church-state relations, and problems of dissent.

One fundamental aspect of this set of problems is the regime's own attitude toward what may be termed "social control." As Thomas Baylis has pointed out, the regime's self-awareness is closely linked to the idea of ideologically correct regulation of social processes. The conscious and deliberate participation of the masses in social and political life "can be developed only by the party on the basis of its 'close ties' with the masses, its sophisticated evaluation and generalization of their experiences, and its utilization of scientifically educated, professional theorists."[1] In addition to issuing extensive ideological formulas for culture, scholarship, and social life in general, the regime seeks to understand the social forces it hopes to guide. This effort cannot be understood in the categories so often used by Western observers—namely, those of "liberalization" or its opposite—but, rather, is a function of modern "enlightened" authoritarianism. In practice, this takes two chief forms: a limited toleration of social autonomy and of discussion, and the measurement of public attitudes.

In common with the Soviet Union and the other East European regimes, the GDR has developed survey research on a large scale as a means of improving the efficacy and legitimacy of governance by giving party and state more accurate information about mass attitudes than deductive ideological assumptions can provide. In the words of Peter

Ludz, "as a policy tool, survey research has three major functions: to inform the policy makers; to control, manipulate and mobilize the people; and to help the ruling party govern more effectively."[2] Of course, the knowledge acquired in this way is also a factor in making the ruling elite more aware of the depth and complexity of social developments; at both the manipulative level and the responsive level, the use of survey research is a learning experience for the political leadership.

To be sure, survey research is a matter of scholarly interest as well as an adjunct to public policy. Although the development of empirical social research cannot be detailed here, we may note a policy consequence of this scholarly trend. The idea that social phenomena are too complex and long lived to be subject to "simple" solutions through administrative fiat leads to a more nuanced social policy, one less prone to directed social transformations. Examples of the policy consequences proceeding from such deeper understanding include demographic policy (population trends, fertility, abortion), the regime's ambivalent cultural policy, and its attitude toward organized religious life in the GDR.[3] It must be remembered that the regime continues to rely on more direct, and quite severe, methods of social control through courts, police, and social pressure, as recent restrictive legislation demonstrates. Hence we may set the foregoing discussion into a realistic perspective by quoting Erich Honecker's remarks of June 1982: "The ever-growing movement for order, discipline and security in factories and residential districts . . . [should be encouraged]. More than ever we must foster initiatives, as well as intolerance against damaging public property and disturbing public order."[4]

Nonetheless, although the continuing political dominance of the SED as a ruling party and the omnipresence of the security forces in GDR life are beyond dispute, there are indications (at least in theoretical discussions) that the party and state leaderships are aware that social differentiation will be a fact of GDR life for the middle-range future, if not longer.[5] Both effective economic growth and implementation of social policy will require a more differentiated administrative and political approach to social groups. In the differentiated treatment of particular groups (materially as well as otherwise) lies the opportunity to harness the energies of those groups for the regime's purposes.

Of course, such a perspective runs counter to the inherited ideology with its egalitarian stress on the future assimilation of social classes and of mental and manual labor. Moreover, a focus on differential accomplishment in the key fields of science and technology raises doubts about the ideologically founded primacy of the proletariat. As Dietrich Staritz has pointed out, a prominent feature of Honecker's assumption of power in 1971 was the reassertion of the social role (and privileges, as in access to education) of the proletariat. If the party then enjoins social scientists to conduct their researches "without prejudices or wishful thinking," one must wonder both to what extent this will be allowed and what its effect on the political stability of the GDR might be.[6]

CHURCH AND STATE

In the territories that became the GDR, the Communist regime inherited a religious tradition of politically subservient Lutheran Protestantism and a numerically weak Catholicism. In the early postwar years of radical sociopolitical transformation, church-state relations were marked by ideological and material pressure on the churches by the political authorities. In Communist eyes, the "believing" community represented an obsolete social and ideological order that had to be opposed militantly in order to build the new society. Yet the religious life of GDR citizens is currently marked by intensity of conviction, growing engagement with social and political problems, and a public expression of religious belief that has become an important social force. Indeed, aside from the unique position of the Catholic Church in Poland, the Christian religious institutions of the GDR have become, politically, the most important such institutions in Eastern Europe.[7] Moreover, the latitude allowed the churches for expression of their views and for organized public activities marks a degree of social autonomy unusual in Communist countries as well as a distinct political risk for centralized direction of political and social life in the GDR.

The Evangelical Community

The GDR is unusual among Communist countries (except for Estonia and Latvia) in that the religious background of its population is overwhelmingly Protestant. Historically, most German Catholics have lived in the western and southern areas of the Reich; the division of Germany resulted in an almost entirely Protestant country. The Protestant, or Evangelical, community is now organized into two loosely related parts of almost equal size. Reformed (i.e., Calvinist) and (some) Lutheran congregations are organized in the Evangelical Church of the Union (Evangelische Kirche der Union, or EKU); this church and the strictly Lutheran United Evangelical Lutheran Church (Vereinigte Evangelisch-Lutherische Kirche, or VELK) are coordinated through a League of Evangelical Churches in the GDR (Bund Evangelischer Kirchen in der DDR), which is led by an elected Conference of Church Leaderships. The chairman of this *Konferenz* is, de facto, the "head" of GDR Protestantism; the current (1984) incumbent is the former Saxony VELK leader, Bishop Johannes Hempel. The Evangelical churches of the GDR were pressured by the regime into breaking ties with West German churches by 1972. Nevertheless, the EKU statutes state that it would collaborate with its West German brethren whenever, in its judgment, the common interests of Evangelical Christians in both German states required it. (Efforts to form a unified Evangelical Church in the GDR after a hopeful start stalled in 1981.)[8]

The social presence of the Evangelical churches in the GDR is made manifest through some 4,000 clergy in over 7,000 parishes. The churches are a major force in health and social service work. There are over 50 church-run hospitals, 89 institutions for the physically handicapped, and numerous other similar institutions. The churches, in fact, constitute a major "private" employer. They also publish newsletters, hold "church days" (*Kirchentage*), which constitute important occasions for unofficial expressions of opinion on social issues, and have opened their liturgy and services to experimental forms (jazz and blues services) and controversial participants (e.g., the balladeer Wolf Biermann).

A sign of the churches' vitality is their spread into new "socialist" towns. The most striking example of this was the establishment of the new Evangelical Church in Eisenhüttenstadt, the iron and steel center on the Oder River once known as Stalinstadt. In this town there is an Evangelical community that, five years after receiving official permission to do so, completed construction of the "first newly built" community center in a GDR development area. The minister of this church has spoken of the unfilled spiritual needs in the center of a materially successful life in the GDR.[9]

The social space accorded to the Evangelical churches is a considerable departure from past policy in such matters. Up to the late 1950s, the regime followed a "classic" Communist policy of seeking to drive organized religion out of public life and to propagate atheist values among the people. Meaningful public positions were reserved for nonbelievers; atheist propaganda was widely disseminated; and the times and places for religious instruction and nonliturgical activities of churches were restricted. A specific challenge to church practice was the establishment of a coming-of-age ceremony for fourteen-year-olds—namely, the explicitly socialist and atheist *Jugendweihe* ("youth consecration") ceremony meant to compete with confirmation. For all Christians, participation in the *Jugendweihe* is barred in a formal sense; many sincere believers allow their children to participate in it, however, because avoidance of same would hamper the young persons' academic and professional advancement. Thus church leaders encourage their parishioners not to participate, but accept those who do; party officials denounce but cannot prevent participation of FDJ members at church confirmations. When, as in 1977, an extraordinary 97.3 percent of all eighth graders opted for the *Jugendweihe*, we must assume that some did so for reasons of opportunity and not purely out of conviction.[10]

After 1961, the focus of state policy shifted from combating the domestic influence of the churches to sundering their ties with West Germany and its "NATO Churches." The setting up of separate GDR church organizations met a largely positive response, as the churches bowed to political imperatives. The new church attitude was exemplified by the oft-quoted statement by the then conference chairman Bishop Schönherr, "We do not want to be a church against, or alongside, but in socialism."[11]

This statement of 1971 marks, on the church side, the beginning of a new era of cautious cooperation with the state. Although the SED leadership also gradually accepted the churches as a social institution, the practical consequences of improved relations were slow in coming.

To put church-state affairs on a more cooperative footing, Honecker met with Schönherr and other state, party, and church officials on March 6, 1978. The results of this meeting have served as the official benchmark for church-state relations ever since.[12] The churches obtained a series of concessions, such as guaranteed broadcast and telecast time for church services, and promised aid for church building and charitable work. Honecker also upheld the principles (enshrined in the GDR constitution)[13] of freedom to practice religion, the internal autonomy of the churches, and the equal status of all citizens regardless of belief. Schönherr's response, pointedly printed in the party daily, was that "the relationship between State and Church is good to just the extent that the individual Christian citizen experiences it to be so in his daily social life."[14]

From the regime's standpoint, a church "in socialism" was a good legitimating device for the GDR population, the West Germans, and the world community, as the Luther celebrations indicate. There have been a number of other public gestures in recent years designed to show the regime's hospitable attitude toward the churches; even in times of public disagreement, as over the peace issue, SED ideological spokesman Kurt Hager declared that the common views of party and churches were more important than their differences.[15]

Nevertheless, differences have arisen between the regime and the Evangelical community. The issues include equal treatment for believers in education and employment, conscientious objection to military service and paramilitary training in secondary schools, opportunities for the churches to perform their social tasks, and the churches' hospitality in opening their services to nonbelievers and cultural experimentaton. These issues have not been resolved to the satisfaction of either party, nor have the churches been stopped from speaking out on all of these questions. Within the framework of GDR politics, the churches have been able to organize autonomous social activities, publicize the views of clergy and laity, and intercede for GDR citizens in confrontation with public authorities.

At a church festival in Dresden in July 1983, for example, over half a million persons attended workshops and cultural events, prayed and heard sermons, and took part in discussions—all this in a gathering organized and supervised by church authorities, without prior censorship of leaflets, and with candid discussion of complaints against the civil authorities.[16] The churches have become secular as well as religious refuges, providing opportunities to discuss environmental as well as security issues.[17] The "Church in Socialism" has proven to be a hardy and needed institution indeed.[18]

Other Religious Communities

Until recently, Roman Catholicism in the GDR had been characterized by withdrawal from political and social engagement. The chief points at issue between the regime and the roughly one-third of a million practicing Catholics and their church have been participation in the *Jugendweihe*, abortion (in 1972 CDU deputies in the *Volkskammer* voted against legislation liberalizing rules for abortion—the only vote of its kind in an East European Communist state), and the GDR's desire to require that East German church areas sever their administrative ties to West German dioceses. In practice, many church units technically still straddle the border (the Bishopric of Berlin still includes parts of both the GDR and West Berlin), but since 1972–1973, "Apostolic Administrations" have given the churches in the GDR de facto separation from the churches in the Federal Republic.[19]

Almost all Catholic clergymen in the GDR are trained at the theological seminary in Erfurt; admission to this institution is apparently under church control. Leadership of the Roman Catholic Church in the GDR lies with the bishop of Berlin, currently Joachim Meissner, a clergyman raised in the GDR. Meissner was installed in Berlin in April 1980 and named a cardinal by Pope John Paul II in 1983. His elevation coincides with a change in the GDR Catholic Church from being a "ghetto church," concentrating on charitable and pastoral work, to making its voice heard on social issues.

In October 1981, Erfurt Bishop Joachim Wanke declared the role of the churches to be that of providing an alternative to a secular, materialist environment, a world of wants (*Habenwollen*) where the "very notion of transcendence might as well be uttered in Chinese" for all the sense that frantically busy but conformist and uninspired citizens are able to make of it. Finally, in 1983, the Berlin Bishops Conference issued a pastoral letter on war and armaments that took stands parallel to those of the Evangelical churches and the unofficial peace movement in the GDR.[20]

The once-flourishing Jewish community of the East German cities has now shrunk to about six hundred professing Jews and several thousand persons of Jewish origins. The GDR has cooperated in the maintenance of several Jewish cemeteries, particularly the cemetery in East Berlin. Although bitterly anti-Israel in foreign policy, the regime in recent years has been scrupulous in its acknowledgement of the specifically anti-Jewish dimension of Nazi crimes, explicitly including the 6 million Jewish victims of Hitler.[21]

THE PEACE MOVEMENT

One of the most astonishing and self-revealing aspects of recent GDR history is the emergence of a politically autonomous peace movement. This development touches upon many aspects of life in the GDR: the response of citizens to the often and publicly proclaimed dangers of nuclear war, the analogous development of peace movements in both German states, the stubborn insistence of some elements of the GDR population on pursuing social-political initiatives apart from regime direction, and the relationship of these efforts to the role of the churches in providing logistical support and an organizational umbrella for this movement.[22] The involvement of the churches stems from their own prior concern with questions of military service and paramilitary education, going back to the early 1960s.

The problem of an alternative to the universal (male) military service arose with the introduction of conscription in 1962. There must have been considerable opposition to this, especially from church sources, for after negotiation between state and church, a decree of the National Defense Council permitting modified alternative service was issued as early as 1964. This decree provided for the creation of construction units (*Baueinheiten*) within the NVA, to which inductees, upon petition, could be assigned. By the mid-1970s, some three to five thousand young men entered such units, which continue to exist in the NVA. From the beginning, but with mounting intensity since 1978, there has been dissatisfaction with this alternative. Participants in the construction units essentially performed military service without weapons. For the most part, these units build military installations and thus directly support the GDR defense effort. Demands for a truly alternative service were raised at Evangelical youth meetings in Dresden in 1981. Under the label of "social peace service" (*sozialer Friedensdienst*), it foresaw two years of work in social services together with "political" training in such topics as peaceful conflict resolution.[23]

The reaction of the regime to this proposal of a social peace service was swift and hostile. Politburo member Werner Walde snapped that, after all, the GDR was itself one gigantic peace service. The regime's spokesman for church affairs, Klaus Gysi, rejected such a service on various grounds, among others that it defamed GDR soldiers by suggesting that service in the NVA was "unsocial war service."[24] The continuing drumfire of propaganda in favor of voluntary enlistment suggests that reluctance to serve has not been overcome. Defense Minister Hoffmann summed up the regime's viewpoint: GDR military service is "the most effective way of serving peace."[25]

Soldiers who serve in the construction battalions (and those who refuse all service, or reservists who wish to switch to noncombatant reserve duty) face problems upon their return to civilian life. Church leaders have repeatedly taken up with authorities problems of professional and educational discrimination against such men. The churches' concern is largely due to the fact that about three-fourths of those individuals who served in these units are communicants of the Evangelical churches.

Similar conflicts have characterized the dispute over paramilitary education (*Wehrkunde*) in secondary schools. First made a compulsory subject in 1978, it has now been extended to both of the last two years of school. Efforts by church authorities to reduce or eliminate the class, or at least to make it optional, have been rebuffed; teacher enthusiasm,

Anti-nuclear rallies are be-
coming more frequent in the
GDR. Photo courtesy of the
GDR Embassy, Washington,
D.C.

judging by official comments in pedagogical periodicals, seems also to
have been moderate.[26]

Paramilitary education is seen by both church and laity in the
GDR as but one symptom of a wider militarization of society, characterized
by the proliferation of games and toys with military themes, school
class trips to military exercises, hostile attitudes toward the West being
propagated, and denunciations of pacifism. Thus, while the authorities
have repeatedly denounced pacifism as an ideology irrelevant to and
unacceptable in the GDR, Bishop Hempel declared at the *Kirchentag* in
July 1983 that, given prospects of a nuclear war in Europe, "we cannot
support the doctrine of a just war."[27]

It is out of such concerns that a more general peace movement
has emerged. Beginning in 1981, this movement produced a series of
programs for peace action, including the 1983 demand for unilateral
GDR and Soviet sacrifices for peace, as well as a popular movement
of public engagement and affirmation, the wearing of a "peace badge"
with the motto "Swords into Ploughshares" and the slogan "Create
Peace Without Weapons."[28]

An early and typical example of this public movement is the
Dresden Peace Forum of February 13, 1982. Organized by an unofficial
group of young people, it was given official church sponsorship to
forestall official prohibition. Scheduled for the anniversary of the de-

structive Allied bombing of Dresden in 1945, it was attended by four to five thousand persons, and it included a candlelight march to a war-damaged church. A highlight of the forum was a frank question-and-answer session between church officials and members of the audience. All of the themes that we have just covered were raised and discussed. Church leaders reminded the audience of the limits to the churches' influence and urged their listeners not to rush to political martyrdom.[29]

An example of the peace movement spreading from its church basis to wider circles was presented at the Dresden Peace Forum. This was the "Berlin Appeal" of January 25, 1982. Modeled on similar petitions circulated in West Germany, it was initiated by Reiner Eppelmann, an East Berlin Evangelical clergyman involved in pastoral work with young people. Among its more than two hundred signatories were writers, workers, clergy, and the since-deceased dissident Communist physicist, Robert Havemann. As was typical for the GDR peace movement, it was addressed equally to East and West, it supported alternatives to the "balance of terror," and it upheld the propriety of unofficial peace protests. It also directed five specific questions to the GDR public and to the authorities: Should we not renounce the production, sale, and import of war toys? Should we not replace military instruction in our schools with peace education? Should we not introduce a *sozialer Friedensdienst*? Should we not desist from military displays on public occasions? Should we not abandon civil defense, as it is really a variant of psychological war preparation?[30]

The further spread of this movement was shown by the exceptional permission granted in December 1981 to the GDR novelist Stephan Hermlin to hold an international writers' and scientists' meeting on peace in East Berlin. Not only was this an officially tolerated "private" meeting, but among those invited were several writers who had been more or less forced out of the GDR and were living in the west. Although many of the speeches at this meeting followed the official line, the very fact that some of the participants criticized GDR policy—including remarks against the imposition of martial law in Poland—and that even the orthodox president of the Writers' Union, Hermann Kant, declared that one must understand even unjustified fears (i.e., of Soviet missiles) gave the meeting its special flavor. Typically, the protocol was printed in only a few hundred copies, which subsequently circulated in the GDR as a semiofficial publication.[31]

The response of the authorities to this unanticipated, undesired, but insistent input into the political process has been to temporize. From the spring and summer of 1982 on, there has been a large-scale propaganda campaign against the unofficial peace movement—which, given the context of Communist politics, is already a signal achievement. But the authors of the agitation—at least the more prominent ones—have not been persecuted. Thus Eppelmann was called in for questioning, held for two days, and then, after official church protests, released.[32]

Not all peace activists have been so fortunate. The regime has been especially harsh in its treatment of a group of young persons in the Thuringian town of Jena. Their activities, which involved dissent on issues other than peace, resulted first in a wave of arrests (whereupon some of the activists were released after church intervention) and later in the forcible expatriation of one of the leading figures of the Jena "peace scene," Roland Jahn.[33]

The touchiness of the authorities was further demonstrated by the explicit, albeit unpublished, prohibition against wearing the "peace badge," including instances of police action to force removal of the badges in public and a ban on their being worn in school. Today the badge survives in less public ways, as does the spirit behind it.[34] The peace movement has not stopped the GDR either from continuing the militarization of the life of society or from accepting the stationing of new Soviet missile units in the GDR in late 1983. It has, however, accustomed much of a generation of young GDR citizens to speak out, independent of official guidance, on issues they deem crucial to their future.[35]

EXPRESSION AND SUPPRESSION OF DISSENT

In the GDR, as in other Communist countries, there is centralized and ideologically justified political control over the expression of ideas, as to both form and content; there is also an administrative mechanism, centered in the security services, for enforcing this political control. It should be remembered that dissent is in large part created by the regime, not by the dissenters. It is the monopolization of expression by the systems of censorship, by the criminalization of disagreement and criticism, and by ambiguous policies as to what may be said in the way of constructive criticism and what may not that transform some ideas into "dissenting" ones.[36]

A classic example of this ambiguity, and of how it allows the regime to retain the political and psychological initiative in relation to social forces, is Honecker's oft-cited statement on the absence of cultural taboos: "In my opinion, if one proceeds from a firm socialist position, there can be no tabus in literature and art. That applies to questions of content as well as of style: in short, questions of what one refers to as artistic mastery."[37] This has been taken as his signal for a freer, more varied cultural life. Although his expectation has often been borne out, Honecker has not prevented some writers from being subjected to political pressures and others from being subjected to "criminal" proceedings, and he has not stopped recurrent attacks on various "undesirable" artistic practices, precisely in the areas of "content as well as of style," from taking place.

There is a unique qualification to the GDR's control of expression, and that is the relationship to West Germany. It is possible to receive information from West Germany, either from visitors or via West German television; it is also possible for some GDR authors to publish in West Germany certain materials not publishable in the GDR. These contacts generally take place in the absence of language barriers or culture shock—such that even emigration or expatriation is not the wrenching experience it often can be for citizens of other East European countries. All of these contacts help defuse nationalist dissent—a process furthered by the regime's policy of pressing unwanted writers to emigrate and, in some cases, granting permission for extended stays in the FRG.

We may distinguish two main varieties of dissent in the GDR.[38] There is a long tradition of Marxist opposition, based in part on older social democratic traditions and in part on critical responses to the "consumer socialism" that has developed especially since the late 1960s. Another strain of dissident thought is that associated with creative artists in theater and literature, and directed at a lessening of restrictions on the expression of unorthodox ideas and use of innovative form in the arts.

The "Marxist" Dissenters

Wolfgang Harich, Robert Havemann, and Rudolf Bahro are three representative figures for this Marxist-derived opposition to GDR orthodoxy. Their ideas and personal fate are illustrative of the regime's attitude and responses to this phenomenon.

Wolfgang Harich was an editor at the leading GDR philosophy journal in the 1950s and, along with others of the "Harich Group," wished to pursue de-Stalinization further than the party thought desirable. The Harich Group's platform called for "a break with Stalinism but not with Marxism-Leninism," a "German road to Socialism," and all-German political cooperation between the SPD in the West and a de-Stalinized SED.[39] The response of the regime was to sentence Harich and others in his group to lengthy prison terms.

Robert Havemann was a Communist and physicist. Under the Nazis, the latter talent saved him from the death penalty he had earned in the former capacity. After a politically unexceptional career in scientific research, Havemann attracted public notice at East Berlin's Humboldt University in 1963–1964 with a series of lectures that were halted by party decree. In his books and statements, Havemann defended the notion of a socialism that would combine economic planning with political democracy. He vigorously opposed restrictive, politically administered dogmas, ridiculing them as products of the "Chief Administration for Eternal Truths." A vigorous supporter of the Prague Spring, he came to favor a neutralized and reunited Germany and to attack GDR-style socialism as overly consumerist and ecologically harmful. The authorities gradually eliminated him from all public positions, finally subjecting him to several years of virtual house arrest prior to his death in 1982.[40]

Rudolf Bahro was a GDR economist, youth league official, and economic administrator.[41] He broke with the regime by publishing (in the West) "The Alternative," his lengthy critical analysis of the socio-political system of the USSR and GDR. Bahro linked Soviet (and Soviet-style) systems with the historical heritage of Russian backwardness, stressed the oppressive and alienating character of the state, called for a democratized party ("League of Communists"), and advocated rational planning of economic life by societal interests, with due concern for the environment. For Bahro, the GDR was simply not as efficient, not as innovative, as it could (and as a "socialist" state should) have been. For his pains, he was sentenced to a prison term, from which he was freed by amnesty in 1979. He now lives in the Federal Republic, where he is an active campaigner for the Green party.

What is significant for the legitimacy and continuity of the GDR is that this school of dissidents relies on a reformed Marxism, embodied in institutions of political and intellectual freedom to realize an acceptable social order in the GDR. As a result both of German left-wing traditions and of the emergence of the GDR as a relatively stable society, there apparently exists a large social stratum of well-educated, technically proficient, more-or-less Marxist people for whom the GDR is both insufficiently modern and effective, and at the same time far too materialistic, consumerist—and, in that limited sense, "too Western" as well.

Literary and Artistic Dissent

Cultural life in the GDR has suffered from the regime's wavering policies toward its creative intelligentsia. Although after the war a substantial number of creative intellectuals settled in the GDR as the preferred "socialist" German state, many were subsequently disenchanted with the GDR (both in the late 1940s and after the ebb of de-Stalinization in 1957) and left for the Federal Republic. The early period following construction of the Wall, with the introduction of economic reforms in 1962–1963, seemed to promise a period of cultural thaw. At the Eleventh SED Central Committee Plenum in December 1965, however, a virulent attack on "harmful tendencies" in the arts was launched by none other than Erich Honecker, who denounced "boundless philistine scepticism" in some members of the intelligentsia. The balladeer Wolf Biermann (who had emigrated *to* the GDR in 1953), the novelist Stefan Heym, and Havemann were singled out for criticism.[42]

After Honecker's accession to power in 1971, however, a more liberal line on the arts set in. Expectations that the international recognition of the GDR after 1971 would help to produce a more liberal ideological atmosphere ran afoul of the requirements of *Abgrenzung* from the West. In 1976, a crisis, whose consequences are still with us, overtook GDR cultural policy. It began with the regime's actions against Wolf Biermann, who had been banned from public performances in the GDR since 1965. The regime allowed him to appear at a cultural festival in the Federal Republic. While Biermann was in Cologne (November 1976), it was announced in East Berlin that permission to reside in the GDR had been withdrawn from Biermann, who was thus effectively expatriated.

A striking and unusual response from GDR intellectuals ensued. A dozen of the best-known literary personages in the GDR sent an Open Letter of protest to the party leadership. Within a week, it had been signed by more than a hundred other intellectuals from various disciplines, and it had the backing of an extraordinary gathering of the country's most distinguished artistic figures—but all to no avail as far as Biermann was concerned.[43]

A few years after the Biermann controversy, a new confrontation took place.[44] Eight prominent writers were expelled from (or lost offices in) the Berlin branch of the Writers' Union; they had protested against harassment of Stefan Heym, who in turn had supported Havemann. Both Heym and Havemann had violated certain new restrictions placed on public contacts with West German news media and on publishing in the West. More writers were denounced, expelled, or induced to leave the GDR. The emigration of such intellectuals went on aside from the times of crisis; the 1977 exit of the poet Rainer Kunze is a case in point. It some instances, writers were allowed to live in the West on extended visas.

In recent years, a demand for literature that would be more "useful" politically has again been heard. The new line was laid out by Honecker, by the Berlin SED chief, Konrad Naumann, who emerged as a hard-line spokesman on cultural matters, and by FDJ officials. In November 1982, Erhard Aurich, then FDJ Second Secretary, called for more "real heroes" (such as construction brigadeers) and denounced both the tendency to "disseminate pessimistic views about our [i.e., GDR] life and future" and the use of "black and gray" as the fashionable colors for depicting GDR reality.

Worthy of note is the shrill tone of abuse against certain writers for allegedly pandering to Western desires for defamation of the GDR's "actual socialism"; one FDJ official even asked whether certain writers had not "long since crossed the line between socialism and capitalism."[45]

At the 1978 GDR writer's congress, the newly elected head of that organization, Hermann Kant, declared (with reference to dissenters):

> Don't be led astray, speak up in your association so that you are heard
> . . . [and] argue, but do it here, in this association, in this country. And
> when you argue, do it with logic, sense and *Parteilichkeit*. If your arguments
> are any good, then you will succeed—yes, God knows, sometimes later
> rather than sooner, but succeed you will. . . . That is what this association
> is for. . . . It is a socialist association in a socialist land; that defines its
> potential as well as its responsibilities.[46]

By the time of the 1983 Writers' Congress, Kant could say that "the grass has grown over many an affair that had enraged us," and that both dissenters and the writers' organization might have been more skillful in their relationships; only those writers who have moved away both geographically *and* philosophically were written off as enemies. Generally, Kant focused on his organization's work for peace and pledged it to be a "clearly political organization, a socialist part of a socialist society."[47] Indeed, the open dissent and expulsion of writers that marked the late 1970s seems to have died down in the opening years of this decade; the regime insists that artists "support socialism in unity with the working class," but it also allows some prominent dissenters (such as Stefan Heym) to remain in the GDR and publish abroad as before.[48]

Writers' and other artists' organizations, however, are more properly understood as part of the regime's apparatus for setting general cultural policy (and will be discussed as such later in this chapter). The main instrument for suppressing dissent that cannot be dealt with ideologically and politically is the Ministry for State Security.

The Organization of State Security

As in the USSR and other Communist states, the GDR, from its inception, has had a political police establishment whose purpose is to prevent, halt, or at least be aware of actions—including speech and writing—that seem to threaten the political and social order of "real socialism." These are the functions of the Ministry for State Security (Ministerium für Staatssicherheit, or MfS), which was separated out from the Ministry of the Interior; the latter continues to supervise the "ordinary" People's Police (*Volkspolizei*).[49]

After a period of administrative and political turmoil in the early 1950s, the MfS's State Security Services (SSD, or *Stasis* in GDR vernacular) have settled down to a long period of efficient stability under their current head, Erich Mielke. Mielke, who has been the minister for State Security since 1957 and now enjoys the military rank of full general, is a veteran Communist militant from the Weimar period. Following his flight to the USSR (and his military service in Spain), he returned to Germany and to police work in 1946. In 1976, at the SED Ninth Congress, he became a full member of the Politburo (having been a candidate since 1971). Mielke's long service has become typical of his chief subordinates and of the higher echelons of the security services generally.[50]

The MfS has some seventeen thousand full-time staff members, of whom about eight thousand are uniformed officers;[51] it is also said to use approximately one hundred thousand informers, whose contributions enrich the dossiers (from the schoolchild's *Schulerbogen* to the employee's *Kaderakte*) that accompany GDR citizens through life. Mielke has declared the work of informers to be essential to his ministry's successes, which would have been "unthinkable without the active help and support of our citizens, . . . close collaboration with whom is being deepened and extended." Inasmuch as informing presumably lacks great social appeal, Mielke (and he has cited Honecker on this point, as well) makes it clear that such collaboration with the security organs is a civic duty, declaring that "our party regards safeguarding the state security of the GDR not just the obligation of specially designated organizations, but rather as the civic and social concern . . . of every citizen."[52]

The domestic role of the security services in controlling expression of politically untoward views has not diminished in the relatively relaxed international atmosphere of the détente era. The influx of foreign visitors and Western media representatives, as well as the growth of the autonomous social forces connected with the peace and environmental movements, has meant an increased state effort at monitoring and controlling events ranging from dissidents' interviews with West German television to unauthorized punk rock concerts.

From Mielke's perspective,[53] the GDR is a prime target for efforts directed at ideological subversion, especially by Western media. Freedom, Mielke has declared, is not a "license for anarchy, criminality, and anti-socialist plotting." Unfortunately, Western governments "abuse the million-fold contacts in transit, travel and visits for diversionary activity, espionage, assaults on the people's economy, [and] hostile traffic in people."

These efforts to interfere with the peaceful building of socialism in the GDR sometimes find willing helpers among the GDR population itself. There are apparently "politically wavering citizens who have been misused for anti-socialist purposes," or who have weakened under the "massive ideological" campaign of the enemy and, although brought up in the GDR, fall under enemy influences.

As in other Communist countries, the definition of political actions is left to the regime itself.[54] What is "slander hostile to the state" (staatsfeindliche Hetze)? Which conversation with a Western journalist is "treasonous passing on" of information? Moreover, the criminalization of "innocent" activity is common; in the GDR, it most notoriously takes the form of Republikflucht (unauthorized "flight from the German Democratic Republic"). In short, any individual who survives an unsuccessful attempted crossing of the GDR border, with all its attendant perils, will be jailed for having tried to leave the GDR.

How many people are jailed for political crimes in the GDR? Exact figures are obviously hard to come by. For the period 1945–1968, counting only GDR courts, and excluding Soviet occupation tribunals, Fricke estimates that there were some 45,000 convictions for political crimes in the GDR.[55] Current but unofficial estimates range from 3,000 to 7,000. One indicator may be the total number of people amnestied at various intervals (not all of whom, of course, are political prisoners). If we accept West Berlin estimates that about 1,500 of the almost 22,000 persons released in 1979 were political prisoners, then, given the total of 92,000 amnestied between 1951 and 1979, a proportional figure would be roughly 5,000 political prisoners. Honecker declared in October

1979, after the last amnesty, that there were "no more political prisoners in his country"; he did not define what had constituted such derelictions in the past, and clearly there could be different definitions in the future.[56]

Since 1963, the West German government has "purchased" political prisoners through two lawyers, one in the GDR and one in the Federal Republic. In 1979 alone, Bonn allegedly paid 50 million DM for 700 prisoners, and in 1983 a like sum freed about 1,000. Press reports said that over a seventeen-year period, the FRG had paid the equivalent of $500 million, which would mean between 20,000 and 25,000 prisoners freed. (The present rate is said to average 1,250 annually.) The effect of recent incidents of refuge seeking in U.S. or West German embassies as a means of escaping from the GDR on the two-decades-old arrangement for ransoming prisoners remains to be seen.[57]

In recent years, the GDR regime and dissenting forces have settled into an uneasy relationship, one in which the regime's security forces monitor all intellectual and social trends and, when the leadership deems it necessary, intervene forcefully. On the other hand, peace and environmental activists continue their activities, and creative artists continue to create in ways not to the liking of the authorities. The regime clearly has decided to permit some activity of this sort, perhaps as a social safety valve, perhaps as a legitimating tactic both at home and abroad. Thus far, especially when compared to the security situation in the Poland of the 1970s, for example, the regime's security needs seem to have been effectively served.

CULTURAL LIFE

Cultural life in the GDR is characterized by continuous creativity; GDR culture is one of ample quantity and, indeed, quality. Despite the political control and occasional crises, one must credit GDR cultural life with substantial accomplishments.[58]

Control of GDR Culture

The control of GDR culture is justified by ideology. All artistic work must be informed by *Parteilichkeit* ("party-mindedness") and must contribute to the "struggles of our times" (to quote the theme of the 1978 writers' congress). For literature, the theater, and similar work, the principle of socialist realism, as adapted from Soviet practice, has been obligatory since 1951. In practice, *Parteilichkeit* and socialist realism mean what is allowed by political authorities and what is gained through pressure, negotiation, and bold expression.[59] Cultural policy, therefore, is neither an administrative deduction from ideological principles nor just the result of struggle between intellectuals and politicians. It is the outcome of an often-confused, ill-defined process with many participants, in which the authorities seek ideological justification and intellectual support, while artists and writers seek opportunities for creative expres-

The restored Schauspielhaus is an impressive hall in East Berlin. Photo courtesy of the GDR Embassy, Washington, D.C.

sion. In many cases, moreover, the restraints on cultural activity, while enunciated in the name of intellectual orthodoxy, may in fact be instruments of careerism and opportunism by artists and writers themselves.

The control of cultural life is centered in the SED Politburo and Secretariat. Aside from Honecker, the leading political supervisor of cultural matters is Kurt Hager, who has had a lengthy career in ideological work and generally sets forth the party's views on intellectual questions. Joachim Hermann has also been active in this area. Hager and Hermann, as members of the Secretariat, supervise the departments for science, education, and culture, as well as those for agitation and propaganda. Other Politburo members engaged in setting cultural policy include, from time to time, the hard-line Berlin SED first-secretary, Konrad Naumann, and Defense Minister Heinz Hoffmann, whose views on patriotism and attitudes toward the military have important cultural ramifications. FDJ leaders may also expound cultural policy, especially in youth-related areas. Of lesser importance is the minister of culture, Hans-Joachim Hoffman.

Cultural policy is mediated between the leadership and cultural practitioners by "social organizations"—that is, monopoly associations in the various cultural fields. It is worth noting that the regime has tried to have respected figures in arts and letters serve as their heads. The writers' association was headed for many years (1952–1978) by the noted Communist novelist Anna Seghers; since then it has been led by the respected and politically well-connected novelist Hermann Kant. Presiding over the Academy of Fine Arts have been such well-known figures as the novelist Arnold Zweig (1950–1952), Communist poet Johannes R. Becher (to 1956), and, from 1965 until his death in 1982, the very talented film director Konrad Wolf. The current head is a theater director and one-time Brecht pupil, Manfred Wekwerth.[60]

Phases of Cultural Policy

The early postwar phase of GDR cultural policy may be called the "antifascist" stage. Great stress was placed on the dissemination of non-Nazi and anti-Nazi works. In vogue were Gotthold Lessing's plays, novels by Communist and left-wing authors, and the many works that had been banned by the Nazis. (The endless renditions of Beethoven's Ninth Symphony as a kind of "peaceloving" anthem—particularly the "Ode to Joy" chorale in the last movement—dates from this period.) Many prominent authors and other artists went to the Soviet Zone, later becoming luminaries of the GDR cultural scene. Among the most famous of these were the playwright Bertolt Brecht, the novelist Anna Seghers, the philosopher Ernst Bloch, and the opera director Walter Felsenstein.

Under the impress of late-Stalinist cultural repression, the GDR entered a phase of "struggle against formalism in art and literature, and for a progressive German culture." The Central Committee resolution with this title led to a campaign for socialist realism and against specific "modernist" works, among them the books of Brecht and Zweig and the sculptures of Ernst Barlach.[61]

Following the de-Stalinizing "thaw" in the cultural life of the Soviet Union, a free cultural atmosphere was proclaimed; but in the aftermath of the Hungarian uprising, and with the victory of Ulbricht in the SED's interparty struggles, the limits of cultural expression were again drawn more tightly. The later years of Ulbricht's regime were marked by the proclamation of a "Bitterfeld Path" in culture, which attempted to bring a closer union between cultural life and the working masses (who were themselves encouraged to become cultural practitioners). Following the construction of the Berlin Wall, however, a new wave of critical artists emerged; the emblematic figures were the balladeer Wolf Biermann and the novelist Christa Wolf. This phase ended at the

Eleventh Central Committee Plenum (December 1965) with severe official criticism of a number of writers.[62]

The SED Eighth Congress (1971) brought about an amelioration of cultural policy. Writers and artists were encouraged to engage in "creative controversies" and to seek new themes and new forms of expression. Honecker set the seal on this policy with his statement that there are no taboos for those working within a socialist orientation. The cultural policy of the Honecker decade, while not living up to this promise of broad latitude, has never gone back to the most repressive periods of the past. Often books and plays are published or produced only after many years' delay, but they sometimes do appear. There are periodic crackdowns, too, but many of the writers attacked are allowed to go on working and are occasionally still published, or allowed to publish, in the Federal Republic; some are given extended visas for residence abroad.

The party leadership has not backed away from its programmatic declaration that commits it to "support all efforts at fostering a socialist realist art." Such art is characterized in the SED's *Programm* as "resting on a deep inner identification with the reality of socialism and the life of the people . . . for peace, democracy and socialism," but there is no command as to esthetic performance.[63] Administratively, as noted, the regime has wavered between repression and toleration.

If there is a dominant theme in contemporary cultural policy, it is the renewed stress on the instrumental character of literature and the arts. The notion of "culture" is expanded to include efforts to improve productivity. The most important cultural task of the 1980s is, for example, said to be that of overcoming "physically burdensome, health threatening, and monotonous work." Literature and fine arts, in particular, are assigned tasks of depicting the life of (especially young) workers, of struggles with new technology, and, in general, the role of the "working class in the formation of our socialist present and future."[64]

How readily such an instrumental view of culture can serve to narrow the permitted range of artistic activity was demonstrated by Honecker himself. Speaking to a convocation of heads of cultural associations on the occasion of the thirty-fifth anniversary of the GDR, he declared that the times demanded works of art that would "strengthen socialism, make us aware of the grandeur and beauty of what has been achieved, under often difficult conditions . . . in whose center there would be an active, history-making hero, the working class and its representatives."[65] Such art cannot be produced by "mere observers and critics" of GDR life but only by "committed advocates."

Cultural Achievements

The assigning of values to cultural products is always, in more than one sense, a critical affair; however, there is general agreement that cultural life in the GDR has shown many substantial accomplishments, especially in literature and cinema and in the artistic treatment of the problems of women.

GDR literature had its beginnings in the work of returned émigrés, but with the passage of time there emerged writers shaped by life in the GDR itself and able to concentrate on GDR-specific themes. Preeminent among them is Christa Wolf, whose novels, such as *The Divided Sky, The Quest for Christa T,* and *A Model Childhood,* deal with such themes as the division of Germany, the place of the individual in a socialist society, and the experience of childhood under the Nazis, and are always adorned by interesting experiments in narrative technique.

Hermann Kant, in his novels *Die Aula* and *Das Impressum,* has written effectively of social mobility and professional life in the GDR. Stefan Heym has used the historical novel, especially *Queen v. Defoe, The King David Report,* and *Collin,* to attack state control of arts and the effects of Stalinist dictatorship on the moral climate of socialism. Gunther de Bryun, Erwin Strittmatter, Erich Loest, and others have also focused on the everyday life in and dilemmas of the GDR; Strittmatter, in particular, has written of the transformation of the countryside.[66] The problems of an advanced socialist society, particularly the achievement of a planned qualitative improvement in social life, has been the subject of Heiner Müller's increasingly pessimistic dramas. The sharp pen of social commentary has been wielded by the poet Rainer Kunze (whose close ties to the intellectuals of the Prague Spring are highlighted in his "The Wonderful Years").

A vivid talent concerned with the problems of youth in the contemporary GDR is that of Ulrich Plenzdorf, whose tales of youth subculture and social conflict in the GDR, with their emphasis on youth jargon and styles, have made him widely known in both Germanies. So intense was the reaction of young people in the GDR to his stories that special discussion sessions were set up to allow young readers and audiences an officially sanctioned outlet for their feelings. Plenzdorf's best-known works are *The New Sorrows of Young W* and *The Legend of Paul and Paula.*

An important aspect of contemporary GDR literature is the attention paid to women and their problems, often by women writers. Aside from Christa Wolf, even a very brief survey must include Brigitte Reimann's novel *Franziska Linkerhand,* Irmtraud Morgner's *Trobadora Beatriz,* and the semidocumentary anthologies of women's experiences, Sarah Kirsch's *The Panther Woman* and Maxie Wander's *Good Morning, Beautiful.*

GDR cinema has also had a noteworthy efflorescence. The leading GDR director was undoubtedly Konrad Wolf; his semiautobiographical films *I Was Nineteen* and *Mama, I'm Alive* are powerful, rather than merely conventional, statements against Nazism and war; of his other films, *Solo Sunny* is a vivid look at contemporary life and at women's perspectives.

Other outstanding GDR directors include Heiner Carow, Hermann Zschochek, Frank Beyer, and Lothar Warneke. Among the outstanding films of recent years, in addition to those of Wolf, have been *Our Short Life, Apprehension, May I Call You Petruchka?, On Probation, The Seventh Year, Jacob the Liar, The Stop-Over,* and many more. Again, one characteristic of many of these films is the focus on the problems that women face in everyday GDR life—a focus that, in part, reflects the high proportion of GDR women who work. A characteristic theme of GDR art—that of the decent and well-motivated individual in the face of social pressures—is sharpened by the addition of women as protagonists.

An area of GDR cultural activity marked by careful but not merely mechanical preservation of traditions is music. The maintenance and embellishment of such traditional institutions as the Leipzig Gewandhaus Orchestra (now in its attractive new home), the Bach Thomanerchor, and the East Berlin Comic Opera of Felsenstein are all a testimonial to the faithful care given a rich musical tradition.

A special feature is the acceptance and sought-after assimilation of once-scorned popular genres, including jazz and rock, and some of their typical settings, such as the disco. Indeed, the FDJ official Hartmut König declared in October 1982 that "German Rock had its birthplace in the GDR," and that better discotheques would be developed from among the over six thousand amateur discos. GDR jazz, folk, and rock combos are encouraged to participate in political rallies; at least one GDR group, "Die Puhdys," has been awarded official decorations.

Given the fact that "in the media age we [i.e., the GDR] are subject to influences against which we can only put up our own accomplishments,"[67] the regime has little choice but to allow light entertainment and popular culture while seeking to shape it into acceptable forms. The establishment of a formal light entertainment organization for the more than nine thousand entertainers at work in the GDR is an outward sign of this trend.

NOTES

1. Thomas A. Baylis, "Agitprop as a Vocation: The Ideological Elite in the DDR," paper delivered at the Fifth Annual Conference of the Western Association for German Studies (October 9–10, 1981).

2. Peter C. Ludz, "German Democratic Republic," in William A. Walsh, ed., *Survey Research and Public Attitudes in Eastern Europe and the Soviet Union* (New York: Pergamon Press, 1981), pp. 247–248.

3. Peter C. Ludz, *Mechanismen der Herrschaftssicherung* (Munich: Carl Hanser Verlag, 1980), especially Part IV.

4. *Neues Deutschland,* 18–19 June 1982, p. 3.

5. The discussion in this paragraph and the following one is based largely on Dietrich Staritz, "DDR: Herausforderungen der achtziger Jahre," *Die DDR vor den Herausforderungen der achtziger Jahre . . . Mai 1983* (Cologne: Edition Deutschland Archiv, 1983), pp. 21–32.

6. Ibid., p. 25.

7. There are about eight million Protestants and one million Catholics in the GDR. For general background data, see Peter C. Ludz et al., *DDR Handbuch,*

2d ed. (Cologne: Verlag Wissenschaft und Politik, 1979), pp. 586–596; George A. Glass, "Church-State Relations in East Germany: Expanding Dimensions of an Unresolved Problem," *East Central Europe* 6, no. 2 (1979):232–249; Robert F. Goeckel, "Zehn Jahre Kirchenpolitik unter Honecker," *Deutschland Archiv* 14 (September 1981):940–946; Sharon L. Kegerreis, "A Church Within Socialism: Religion in the GDR Today," RFE-RL Research, *RAD Background Report/240* (October 8, 1980); Ronald D. Asmus, "The Evangelical Church in East Germany," RFE-RL Research, *RAD Background Report/334* (December 1, 1981). For data in German, see Horst Dähn, *Konfrontation oder Kooperation: Das Verhältnis von Staat und Kirche in der SBZ/DDR 1945–1980* (Opladen: Westdeutscher Verlag, 1982).

8. For a discussion of the joint celebration of the Augsburg Confession anniversary, see *Frankfurter Allgemeine Zeitung*, 23 June 1980, p. 7, and 20 May 1980, p. 6. The interchurch negotiations were recessed without agreement in late 1984.

9. *Frankfurter Allgemeine Zeitung*, 30 May 1981.

10. Kegerreis, "A Church Within Socialism," p. 7.

11. Ibid., p. 4.

12. For example, at the ceremonies marking restoration of Luther's hideaway on the Wartburg, Honecker held a private meeting with Bishop Leich (head of the church's Luther committee) at which he explicitly reaffirmed the validity of the 1978 agreements. See "Honecker dankt der Kirche für Friedensarbeit, *Neues Deutschland*, 23 April 1983, p. 6.

13. *Verfassung der Deutschen Demokratischen Republik* (Berlin: Staatsverlag der DDR, 1975), pp. 24, 34. Article 20 grants to every citizen equal rights regardless of profession of religion and specifically guarantees "freedom of belief." Article 39 further allows each believer to practice religion and requires that "the Churches and other religious communities order their internal affairs and carry on their activities in conformity with the Constitution and laws" of the GDR.

14. Goeckel, "Zehn Jahre Kirchenpolitik," p. 944.

15. See the citation of Hager's speech in *Frankfurter Allgemeine Zeitung*, 5 July 1982, p. 3.

16. For an account of this meeting—which was not an exceptional event in the GDR—see "Im Gegner das Geschöpf Gottes sehen," *Frankfurter Allgemeine Zeitung*, 11 July 1983, p. 4.

17. In a recent collection of GDR writings on questions of the environment and economic growth, most of the material was generated by individuals or groups connected with the Evangelical churches. See Peter Wensierski and Wolfgang Büscher, eds., *Beton ist Beton. Zivilisationskritik aus der DDR* (Hattingen: Scandica Verlag, 1981).

18. For a recent survey of the Evangelical churches' situation and details on their relationship to various "alternative" movements, see Wolfgang Büscher, "Die evangelischen Kirchen in der DDR—Raum für alternatives Denken und Handeln?" *Die DDR vor den Herausforderungen*, pp. 158–166.

19. *Frankfurter Allgemeine Zeitung*, 13 May 1980, p. 12; Klemens Richter, "Berliner Bischofskonferenz und Bistum Berlin," *Deutschland Archiv* 13 (July 1980):687–692.

20. Klemens Richter, "Zu einer Standortbestimmung der katholischen Kirche in der DDR," *Deutschland Archiv* 15 (August 1982):800–803; and "Veränderte Haltung der DDR Katholiken," *Deutschland Archiv* 16 (May 1983):454–458.

21. November 9, the anniversary of the 1938 "Crystal Night" attacks on Jews, has become an occasion for marking officially the disaster that befell German Jews. For a typical example, see "Blutnacht war Schritt auf dem Weg zum Krieg," *Neues Deutschland*, 9 November 1983, p. 4.

22. The unofficial peace movement has spawned a voluminous literature in recent years. Two useful collections of basic documents and commentary are Klaus Ehring and Martin Dallwitz, eds., *Schwerter zu Pflugscharen. Friedensbewegung in der DDR* (Hamburg: Rowohlt, 1982); and Wolfgang Büscher et al., eds., *Friedensbewegung in der DDR. Texte 1978-1982* (Hattingen: Scandica, 1982). A good recent summary in English is Ronald D. Asmus, "Is There a Peace Movement in the GDR?" *Orbis* 27 (Summer 1983):301-341. Two recent discussions by American authors are Pedro Ramet, "Church and Peace in the GDR," *Problems of Communism* 33 (July-August 1984):44-57; and Joyce Marie Mushaben, "Swords into Plowshares: The Church, the State and the East German Peace Movement," *Studies in Comparative Communism* 17 (Summer 1984):123-136.

23. See Studiengruppe Militärpolitik, *Die Nationale Volksarmee* (Hamburg: Rowohlt, 1976), pp. 55-61; and Buscher et al., *Friedensbewegung*, pp. 169-171; see also texts reprinted in *Deutschland Archiv* 14 (October 1981):1111-1113; and *Frankfurter Allgemeine Zeitung*, 19 October 1981, p. 1. The form chosen for public dissemination of the decree on alternative service—publication only in the official register of laws—indicates the regime's reluctance in granting it.

24. See Buscher et al., *Friedensbewegung*, pp. 174-175, 230. See also Ronald D. Asmus, "East German Official Rejects an Alternative 'Social Peace Service,'"RFE-RL Research, *RAD Background Report 273* (September 23, 1981).

25. *Neues Deutschland*, 26 March 1982, p. 3.

26. See the documentation in Buscher et al., *Friedensbewegung*, pp. 64-68; and Ehring and Dallwitz, *Schwerter zu Pflugscharen*, pp. 156-181; see also Karl Wilhelm Fricke, "Forcierte Militarisierung im Erziehungswesen der DDR," *Deutschland Archiv* 15 (October 1982):1109-1111. For a representative sample of GDR views favoring this development, see the articles abstracted in *DDR Report* 16 (May-June 1983):324-325, 327-328.

27. Hempel is quoted in *Frankfurter Allgemeine Zeitung*, 11 July 1983, p. 4. See also "In Militaristic East Germany, Pacifists Mobilize," *New York Times*, 28 November 1983, p. A2. The official view is that while a nuclear war may not be prudent, it would be, on the part of Communist states waging a (necessarily) defensive struggle, "a horrible, presumably final, but nonetheless just war." Cited in *DDR Report* 17 (January 1984):30. The development of ever more sophisticated and horrible technology is said not to rob war of its nature as a continuation of politics (*DDR Report* 17 [January 1984], p. 48).

28. For discussion of the 1983 demand, see *Neues Deutschland*, 22-23 October 1983, p. 2; and Ronald D. Asmus, "*Neues Deutschland* Prints Dissenting Views on Arms Control," RFE-RL Research, *RAD Background Report/254* (October 31, 1983). The "peace badge" depicts a statue of a man beating a sword into a plowshare; it is the statue given to the United Nations headquarters by the USSR!

29. See the documentation in *Deutschland Archiv* 15 (May 1982):533-541, 547-549, 552-554; *New York Times*, 15 February 1982, p. A3; and Marlies Menges's eyewitness account in *Die Zeit*, 22 February 1982, p. 2. See also the detailed account in Ehring and Dallwitz, *Schwerter zu Pflugscharen*, pp. 68-87.

30. For the text of and supplementary documents relating to the "Berlin Appeal," see Ehring and Dallwitz, *Schwerter zu Pflugscharen*, pp. 205-230.

31. Documentation of this protocol can be found in *Deutschland Archiv* 15 (March 1982):313–326; "Ich habe mir einen Traum erfüllt," *Die Zeit*, 31 December 1981, pp. 15–16; for a similar gathering as part of an all-European writers' meeting in The Hague in May 1982, see *Frankfurter Allgemeine Zeitung*, 28 May 1982, p. 25; documentation in *Deutschland Archiv* 15 (July 1982):772–780.

32. An example of the regime's response is the FDJ's staging of mass rallies with the slogans "Peace must be armed" and "Make peace against NATO weapons." See *Neues Deutschland*, 28 May 1983, p. 3. A similarly motivated meeting between FDJ officials and proregime young Christians was covered in *Neues Deutschland*, 17 February 1983, p. 3.

33. See the extensive coverage in *Frankfurter Allgemeine Zeitung*, 9 November 1982, p. 1; 17 February 1983, p. 3; 21 February 1983, p. 3; and 9 August 1983, pp. 1–2.

34. The ban was communicated verbally to church authorities by Klaus Gysi. See Buscher et al., *Friedensbewegung*, pp. 290–292.

35. Such broader concerns include environmental actions such as tree-planting and bicycle-riding campaigns, as well as discussions on armaments. The 1984 *Friedensdekade* (Ten Days of Peace), held from November 11 to 21, dealt with such issues as hunger in Africa and education barriers for believers. Peace was still a prominent concern, however; a physicians' group, during a panel discussion, called for unilateral WTO disarmament gestures as a way of ending the arms race. See B. V. Flow, "Debate Within the East German Protestant Church Widens," RFE-RL Research, *RAD Background Report/225* (December 29, 1984).

36. For an interesting discussion of this issue from a very different standpoint, see Pedro Ramet, "Disaffection and Dissent in East Germany," *World Politics* 37 (October 1984):85–111.

37. *Neues Deutschland*, 18 December 1971.

38. Karl H. Kahrs, "The Theoretical Position of the Intra-Marxist Opposition in the GDR," *East Central Europe* 6, no. 2 (1979):250–265; Werner Volkmer, "East Germany: Dissenting Views During the Last Decade," in R. L. Tökes, ed., *Opposition in Eastern Europe* (Baltimore: Johns Hopkins University Press, 1979); Henry Krisch, "Political Legitimation in the German Democratic Republic," in T. H. Rigby and Ferenc Feher, eds., *Political Legitimation in Communist States* (London: Macmillan, 1982); M. Donald Hancock, "Intellectuals and System Change," in Lyman H. Legters, ed., *The German Democratic Republic: A Developed Socialist Society* (Boulder, Colo.: Westview Press, 1978); "Schere im Kopf" (special report), *Die Zeit*, 1 June 1979, pp. 8–11.

39. Weber, *Kleine Geschichte*, p. 92; Hermann Weber, ed., *Der deutsche kommunismus* (Cologne: Verlag Wissenschaft und Politik, 1963), pp. 492ff.

40. Ronald D. Asmus, "East German Dissident Thinker Robert Havemann Dies," RFE-RL Research, *RAD Background Report/96* (April 22, 1982). *Frankfurter Allgemeine Zeitung*, 13 April 1982, p. 6; Robert Havemann, *Dialektik ohne Dogma: Naturwissenschaft und Weltanschauung* (Hamburg: Rowohlt, 1964); Robert Havemann, *Fragen, Antworten, Fragen* (Hamburg: Rowohlt, 1972); Robert Havemann, *Morgen: Die Industriegesellschaft am Scheideweg* (Munich: Piper, 1980).

41. Rudolf Bahro, *Die Alternative. Zur Kritik des real existierenden Sozialismus* (Cologne: Europäische Verlags-Anstalt, 1977); Jeffrey Lee Canfield, "Bahro's Communist Alternative," RFE-RL Research, *RAD Background Report/272* (December 11, 1979). A considerable scholarly literature, in both English and German, has grown up around Bahro's theses.

42. Weber, *Kleine Geschichte,* pp. 126–127.

43. The text of this letter, with accompanying articles, is in *Die Zeit,* 10 December 1976, pp. 15–16; see also Joachim Nawrocki, "Es knistert im Gebalk der GDR," *Die Zeit,* 3 December 1976, p. 8, and Dieter E. Zimmer, "Ausgestossen in Deutschland," *Die Zeit,* pp. 7–9. The signatories were Sarah Kirsch, Christa Wolf, Volker Braun, Franz Fühmann, Stephen Hermlin, Stefan Heym, Günter Kunert, Heiner Müller, Rolf Schneider, Gerhard Wolf, Jurek Becker, Erich Arendt. Christa and Gerhard Wolf are husband and wife. Four of the twelve signers (Sarah Kirsch, Günter Kunert, Jurek Becker, Franz Fühmann) were subsequently pressured into leaving the GDR. Kirsch, Becker, and Gerhard Wolf were expelled from the SED, and others were removed from positions in, or also expelled from membership in, the Writers' Union.

44. Martin McCauley, "East Germany: The Dilemmas of Division," *Conflict Studies,* no. 119 (June 1980):9–10; Ronald Asmus, "A New Life for Dissident Writers in the GDR?" RFE-RL Research, *RAD Background Report/210* (August 19, 1980). The writers expelled were Kurt Bartsch, Adolf Endler, Stefan Heym, Karl-Heinz Jakobs, Klaus Poche, Klaus Schlesinger, Rolf Schneider, Dieter Schubert, and Joachim Seypel. Details regarding the resolution of expulsion and its accompanying rationale—that the eight had used publication or interviews abroad to defame the GDR—are in *Neues Deutschland,* 9 June 1979, p. 4. For a description of an especially vicious personal attack on the expelled writers, together with exaggerated protestations of loyalty to the regime, see the open letter from the writer Dieter Noll to Honecker, *Neues Deutschland,* 22 May 1979, p. 4.

45. *Neues Deutschland,* 22 October 1982, p. 5, and 27–28 November 1982, p. 11.

46. *Neues Deutschland,* 30 May 1978, pp. 3–4.

47. *Neues Deutschland,* 1 June 1983, p. 4.

48. From a speech by Kurt Hager, cited in Ronald D. Asmus, "Writers' Congress in the GDR," RFE-RL Research, *RAD Background Report/133* (June 10, 1983). For the current situation of Stefan Heym, see "An East German Writer and the Wall of Silence," *New York Times,* 7 September 1983, p. C16.

49. The standard source for material on the SSD is the recently published Karl Wilhelm Fricke, *Die DDR-Staatssicherheit. Entwicklung, Strukturen, Aktionsfelder* (Cologne: Verlag Wissenschaft und Politik, 1982). See also Fricke, *Politik und Justiz in der DDR* (Cologne: Verlag Wissenschaft und Politik, 1979); Michael Naumann, "Spitzel, Stasi und Spione," *Die Zeit,* 23 February 1979, pp. 8–10; Michael Naumann, "Partei und Staatssicherheit. Die SED und der Apparat des MfS," *Deutschland Archiv* 13 (April 1980):373–377.

50. Michael Naumann, "MfS-Führungsspitze aufgewertet und verstärkt," *Deutschland Archiv* 14 (January 1981):9–11. Mielke's recently deceased First Deputy Minister Bruno Beater has held a high MfS position since 1955. The deputy minister in charge of counterintelligence, the Soviet-trained Markus (Mischa) Wolf (brother of the GDR film director Konrad Wolf), has been in full-time security work since 1953.

51. Fricke, *Die DDR-Staatssicherheit,* pp. 49–54, 61–62, 139–41.

52. See ibid., pp. 99–101; see also Erich Mielke, "Verantwortungsbewusst für die Gewährleistung der staatlichen Sicherheit," *Einheit* 35 (February 1980):156, and Mielke's speech in *Neues Deutschland,* 7 November 1978, pp. 3–4.

53. The material in the next two paragraphs is from Mielke, "Verantwortungsbewusst," pp. 155ff.

54. Amnesty International (AI) began a campaign against political repression in the GDR in early 1981 (see, for example, the AIUSA newsletter *Matchbox* for February 1981); it was consequently attacked by Honecker, in an interview with the British publisher of his memoirs, Robert Maxwell; see *Neues Deutschland,* 13 March 1981, p. 4. AI has continued to monitor GDR human rights practices; for a detailed survey of human rights abuses, especially those connected with the application of articles of the criminal code. See "Restrictions on the Right to Freedom of Expression in the German Democratic Republic," Amnesty International Briefing (New York: AIUSA, n.d.).

55. Fricke, *Politik und Justiz in der DDR,* pp. 551, 564.

56. Karl Wilhelm Fricke, "Bilanz der DDR-Amnestie 1979," *Deutschland Archiv* 13 (February 1980):127–130; *New York Times,* 16 March 1980, p. 8. In the interview mentioned in Note 54 of this chapter, Honecker said cryptically that there were "no more" [?!] political prisoners in the GDR.

57. *Frankfurter Allgemeine Zeitung,* 16 June 1981, p. 4; the GDR lawyer involved is Wolfgang Vogel, who also helped to arrange the Gary Powers–Rudolf Abel exchange. For a roundup of West German press accounts of recent developments in the ransoming of prisoners, see the *German Tribune,* no. 1119, 5 February 1984, p. 3.

58. A good recent overview of GDR culture is "Kultur und Gesellschaft in der DDR," in the special issue (*Sonderheft*) of *Deutschland Archiv* (1977). See also Irma Hanke, "Continuity and Change: Cultural Policy in the German Democratic Republic Since the VIIIth SED Party Congress in 1971," in Klaus von Beyme and Hartmut Zimmerman, eds., *Policymaking in the German Democratic Republic* (New York: St. Martin's Press, 1984), ch. 6.

59. An extremely perceptive analysis of the social and psychological dynamics of this process is provided by Irene Böhme, *Die Da Drüben. Sieben Kapitel DDR* (Berlin: Rotbuch Verlag, 1983), pp. 116–126.

60. See the report by Manfred Jäger in *Deutschland Archiv* 15 (August 1982):804–805.

61. Ludz et al., *DDR Handbuch,* pp. 630–636; *Neues Deutschland,* 13–14 December 1981. When Schmidt visited the GDR in 1981, a highlight of the trip was his visit to the Barlach museum in Güstrow.

62. Weber, *Kleine Geschichte,* pp. 126–127. A good collection of documents on SED cultural policy before 1971 is Elimar Schube, ed., *Dokumente zur kunst-, Literatur- und Kulturpolitik der SED* (Stuttgart: Seewald Verlag, 1972). Materials from the Eleventh Plenum of December 1965 are on pp. 1076–1116.

63. *Programm der Sozialistischen Einheitspartei Deutschlands* (Berlin: Dietz Verlag, 1976), pp. 70–71.

64. Ursula Ragwitz, "Der X. Parteitag über die Kulturpolitik der SED," *Die Wirtschaft,* no. 3 (1982), p. 19; Hartmut König, at the FDJ cultural conference, *Neues Deutschland,* 22 October 1982.

65. Erich Honecker, "Reiche Kultur—vom Volke für das Volk geschaffen," *Neues Deutschland,* 21 September 1984, pp. 3–4. See also B. V. Flow, "A Tighter Grip on Cultural Policy in the GDR?" RFE-RL Research, *RAD Background Report/184* (September 28, 1984).

66. See Stefan Heym, *New York Times,* 2 January 1971, op-ed page; Gunther de Bryun, Uwe Wittstock in the supplement of *Frankfurter Allgemeine Zeitung,* 7 December 1982.

67. Gesela Steineckert, "Unterhaltung—das hat viel mit Haltung zu tun," *Neues Deutschland,* 21 September 1984, p. 3.

7

Social Policy in the GDR

WOMEN AND SOCIAL POLICY

In this chaper, we will consider certain aspects of social policy, selected on the basis that they represent crucial policy targets for a regime mindful of its need for legitimacy. Women and youth are significant social groups in this regard. The GDR's claim for positive loyalty is based in part on its policies toward women. Young people are a target for regime policies in every state: the socialization of youth so as to garner their support for the legitimacy of the regime is an especially important process for a "revolutionary" regime. In its recruitment of young people, the GDR relies heavily on policies in two areas: education and sports.

Consideration of the topics just mentioned, taken together, will provide a picture of the place of social policy in the public life of the GDR. Other policies, such as those regarding the elderly, the handicapped, and the environment, have their own importance; but the policies we will consider here are sufficient to exemplify the regime's contention that the GDR's "social planned economy" would enable the party and state leadership to "continue its policy of assuring and expanding people's material and cultural level of life."[1]

The special significance of women as a social group arises in part from the general growth of feminist sentiment, particularly in the industrialized countries.[2] In the GDR in particular, it derives also from the high proportion of women in the labor force and from the demographic problems of the society.

The part played by women in GDR society is reflected in the attention paid to their problems in literature and cinema and in the relatively (for Eastern Europe) pronounced place they occupy in party and state hierarchies. Nevertheless, the issues facing women in advanced industrialized countries are certainly also present in the GDR. They range from problems relating to inherited male attitudes, to the problems of combining career and family, to the problems involved in attaining important positions in the economic and political hierarchies that dominate all aspects of life in Communist countries.

146

GDR Policy Toward Women and the Family

Policy in the GDR is clearly directed at fostering the full participation of women in the country's life without neglect of the family. Article 20 of the GDR constitution declares that "men and women have equal rights and the same legal standing in all areas of social, state and personal life. Advancement of women, especially in professional qualification, is a task for state and society." Article 38 asserts that "marriage, family and maternity receive the special protection of the state." It goes on to speak of "equal standing of man and woman in marriage and the family." Special measures are to be taken in support of single parents and of families with many children. Parents, in turn, have both a right and a duty to raise "healthy, joyful, industrious, cultivated and public-minded [staatsbewusst]" children.[3]

Legislation in this field includes provisions for paid days off for working women who are also responsible for households, and special supplementary payments for children. Financial support is available for wives of military personnel, students, and the disabled, as well as leave time for parents (but usually mothers) of sick children under fourteen years of age and up to thirteen weeks off with pay for mothers of five or more children.[4]

Special attention is paid to securing good pre- and postnatal care for mother and child—a matter of particular importance, of course, given the GDR's demographic situation; but beyond that, such care is also a major source of legitimacy and genuine pride among the populace. The increasing birth rate (see Table 7.1) is pointed to in the GDR as evidence that it is a "state friendly to children."

Women may receive prenatal and postnatal leaves of twenty-six weeks while drawing their net average earnings, plus a 1,000-Mark payment for each childbirth. With the second and any subsequent child, there is also a payment of 65 percent of full wages from the end of the postnatal leave until the child is a year old. Beginning in 1975, the GDR has provided a "Baby Year" off with pay (at the mother's request for the first child, and automatically for all subsequent children). By early 1982, 371,000 women had taken advantage of this opportunity.[5]

Since 1972, the GDR has had a liberalized abortion law, one that grants each woman the right to make her own decisions regarding her pregnancy and its outcome. Up to the twelfth week, abortion is available at medical facilities, on demand and without cost, with the sole requirement that the doctor explain the "medical significance" of the procedure and advise on future contraceptive methods. Abortions later in the pregnancy can be performed only when there is a "danger to the life of the women" or for other grave reasons; permission for an abortion under such circumstances must be obtained from a physicians' commission. Aside from exceptional cases, no abortion may be performed in less than six months after a previous one.[6]

148   SOCIAL POLICY IN THE GDR

TABLE 7.1
Annual Births in the GDR and Infant Mortality Rate (1978-1982)

Year	Number of Births	Births per 1,000 Population
1978	232,151	13.9
1979	235,233	14.0
1980	245,132	14.6
1981	237,543	14.2
1982	240,102	14.4
1983	233,756	14.0

Year	Number of Infant Deaths in First Year	Number of Infant Deaths in First Year per 1,000 Live Births
1978	3,044	13.1
1979	3,039	12.9
1980	2,958	12.1
1981	2,923	12.3
1982	2,742	11.4
1983	2,506	10.7

Sources: Statistisches Taschenbuch der DDR 1984 (Berlin: Staatsverlag der DDR, 1984), p. 145; Neues Deutschland, 5 March 1982, p. 3.

A major motive for passage of this abortion legislation was to reduce the number of illegal abortions and to avoid the need for trips to Poland or Czechoslovakia for legal ones. A decade's experience has shown that, after an initial rise in the number of abortions done, there has actually been a steady decrease from 1972 (115,000 abortions) to 1976 (83,000). According to one Leipzig gynecologist, the chief reason given in 1972 for not wanting a child was the shortage of housing and financial strain, whereas today's motives are primarily these:

1. Family size: A two-child or, in some fewer cases, a three-child family is desired.
2. Age: The woman is either too young (perhaps still a student) or too old.
3. Family reasons: These frequently involve plans for further study or training.

4. Spacing of children: Some mothers are reluctant to have another child too long after the preceding one.

Abortions are viewed as a serious matter of late, if not last, resort, with distribution of contraception information and improved "sexual-ethical" education as preferred alternatives. Finally, the study cited here, which was based on a survey of women patients at gynecological clinics, suggested a "responsible" attitude of GDR women toward abortion, as shown in the following survey of women having abortions: their average age is 28.3 years, with only 10 percent under 18; more than 70 percent are already married; and more than half already have children.[7]

In coping with questions of marriage, parenthood, childbirth, and household roles, the GDR has also had to deal with people's attitudes and practices in these personal realms. The sociologist Herta Kuhrig writes that the GDR faces the task of deciding which traditions and past values regarding marriage and the family are to be preserved, and that there were "many questions—but certainly there were not always scientifically well-grounded answers for all of them."[8] According to Kuhrig, about one-third of all GDR marriages end in divorce, one GDR child in four is born out of wedlock, and (some) persons "live in a long-term relationship [Lebensgemeinschaft] without marrying." From Kuhrig's standpoint, these facts point to the removal of material or censorious restrictions on the free choice of marriage partner and on the termination of marriages. The high rate of illegitimacy, for example, is related to the provision of material benefits to the single mother, but also to the fading of prejudices against such mothers and their children.

Similarly, the divorce rate is undoubtedly due in part to the increasing tendency to base marriages purely on the principle of mutual attraction. With the "inner ruin" (Zerrüttung) of a marriage as the legal grounds for divorce (there are no automatic grounds, and counseling is required), a great deal does in fact depend on a correct choice of marriage partners and their mutual development for many years thereafter.

Marriages based on mutual respect and affection must be defended against the effects of the traditional views of that institution. The notions that the woman has primary responsibility for the care of young children, that a standard of household care suitable for a full-time housewife should also be expected of a working woman, and, especially, that men cannot be expected to do an equal share of such chores—these belong, in Kuhrig's words, "to those traditions that are apparently difficult to overcome."[9]

Young people in the GDR seem to share the same expectations of a marriage partner regardless of gender, but later experience does not always bear this out. If both partners are professional people (as is commonly the case in the GDR), these problems are exacerbated by demanding professional and work schedules. Marilyn Rueschemeyer has written that although "women's employment is not only accepted [in the GDR] but expected and firmly institutionalized . . . that does not mean socialist societies have solved the 'women's problem.' The participation of women in the work force does not insure their equality in the family."[10] There is often an unavoidable choice to be made involving sacrifice of professional or vocational obligations, and women are more likely to make such sacrifices than are men.[11]

Women in Public Life

The role of women in the leading political institutions of the GDR is a limited one. The presence of women in hierarchies of power is generally inversely proportional to the authority of the position: "Where power is, women are not," as one analyst has put it.[12] In the SED, for example, women constitute about a third of the party membership (among women over eighteen years of age, 10 percent are party members, compared to 45 percent of men of the same age), but only 20 of the 156 are full members of the Central Committee elected at the Tenth Party Congress.

In the most powerful party organizations, the Politburo and the Secretariat, women are hardly represented at all; there are no women among the Politburo's eighteen full members, although two of the eight candidate members are women. Of the ten secretaries of the Central Committee, Inge Lange (one of the two Politburo candidate members) is the party's specialist for women's affairs as head of the women's affairs department and chairman of the Politburo Commission for Women's Affairs (*Frauenkommission*). Her Politburo colleague, Margarete Müller, holds positions in agricultural administration.

Although, in keeping with Communist practice, no complete list of the heads of Central Committee Secretariat departments (*Abteilungen*) is published, we do know that women serve as staff members and deputy directors in some of these departments and that at least one, the cultural department, has a woman as director. At the regional and district party levels, the number of women in important positions is higher but still below a level proportionate to their party membership. Approximately one-tenth of the secretaries at the regional (*Bezirk*) level are women; none of them are first- or second-secretaries. At the district (*Kreis*) level, although 35 percent of the *Kreisleitungen* members are women, this is true of only 9 of the 261 heads of *Kreise*.[13]

Moreover, the total number of women in politically important leadership positions outside the party remains small. In part this is the result of inherited prejudices of both women and men. An important additional factor is that women's political behavior diverges significantly from that of men when both are in their twenties. For example, the proportion of women in administrative positions in industry ranges (depending on the branch) from negligible to over 35 percent, with 20 percent as an average. But of those persons filling economic leadership positions who are younger than twenty-five, an astonishing 68 percent are women. The consequences of this phenomenon in the GDR are quite striking insofar as appointment to important positions in every walk of life requires party confirmation (through the *Nomenklatur* system) and, in most cases, party membership. By dropping out of intraparty career advancement, and by being underrepresented in the party apparatus compared to their numbers in the population, women are effectively barred from many high-ranking positions for lack of this essential political qualification.

In the state apparatus, five of the twenty-five members of the State Council are women.[14] Only one woman, Margot Honecker, the wife of Erich Honecker, is currently a member of the Council of Ministers; she has been the minister for education since 1963 and is widely regarded as a competent professional in her own right. A handful of other women have attained cabinet rank, including Hilde Benjamin, who was minister of justice from 1953 until 1967.

In the primarily symbolic and representative units of the political system, the presence of women is more marked. In the current *Volkskammer*, 162 of 500 members (32.4 percent) are women. At the regional, district, and local levels, the official data from 1977 show that the proportion of women in representative bodies at each level accounted for 37.5 percent (regional), 39.7 percent (district), and 32.6 percent (local), respectively.

The representation of women, both as members and in official capacities, is markedly greater in the mass organizations, such as the FDJ and the trade union organization FDGB. In keeping with Communist practice, there is also a single mass organization just for women, the Demokratischer Frauenbund Deutschlands (DFD), whose just under one and a half million members constitute almost 16 percent of the female population of the GDR. Organized hierarchically down to the neighborhood or work-place level, its main function is to draw women into active participation in economic and social life. This includes efforts directed especially at women who are at home in residential neighborhoods, and who must be reached with educational, neighborhood improvement, and similar campaigns. The DFD also provides thirty-five seats in the *Volkskammer*, all of which are occupied by women.[15]

The participation of women in social and economic life, however, is considerably broader.[16] As we have seen, approximately half the labor force is female, with about 80 percent of working-age women employed. The integration of women into economic life has become an accepted aspect of GDR society, as both survey research and the attention paid the problems of working women in literature and cinema attest.

Nevertheless, women tend to be concentrated in "women's" occupations—trade, services, elementary education—and to be underrepresented in leading positions, even in those fields in which they form the bulk of the work force. (Light industry is an exception to this; some 37 percent of all leading personnel in this field are women.) Given the underrepresentation of women in training programs, any change in the distribution of women among occupations seems unlikely. As a percentage of trainees for skilled positions, women in 1977 constituted over 90 percent of those training to be typists and stenographers, textile workers, hairdressers, and sales personnel but fewer than 10 percent of those training to be bricklayers, automobile mechanics, carpenters, electricians, and painters.

Two professional activities in which women are well represented are medicine (especially in the general practice of an Ärtzin) and elementary and secondary-school teaching. As of 1977, 49 percent of physicians were women, and the proportion of women among teachers in the ten-year general secondary schools had reached 65.8 percent. About one-fourth of all school directors were women.[17]

Since 1971, the proportion of women students in higher education has risen from 37 percent to half of the total in 1983. Women account for a quarter of students in engineering; somewhat over half of those studying mathematics, science, and medicine; and three-quarters of students enrolled in teacher training. These figures reflect an increase compared to the situation of one or two decades ago, but this increase has not yet produced major effects in the composition of university faculties. Indeed, few deans or heads of departments are women.[18]

Despite these varied problems, the regime continues to support fuller integration of women into fields of activity hitherto regarded as male preserves. The image it wants to present is exemplified by the women who are spotlighted at official and ceremonial occasions.

In connection with International Woman's Day 1983, for example, the readers of Neues Deutschland were told about Gudrun Schlager, bricklayer, expert in power plant construction, and currently department head for organization and data processing at the Boxberg power plant complex in the northern part of the GDR. Schlager is a wife and mother, not a party member, and she has been successful in situations requiring that she compete with men. She is also active in technical innovation. At a "women's forum" dealing with the official "women's advancement plan" (Frauenföderungsplan), she raised some questions for the women in her audience: Are some of us reluctant to accept as much responsibility as we are offered? Could we not free ourselves from the "false vanity" of wishing to be "perfect housewives"? Why don't we allow men to exercise their "equal rights" to do some housework? Such is the model of a modern GDR woman.[19]

The progress made by women in the GDR is real, but so are the problems remaining in the way of satisfactory mastery of professional and personal goals. The regime itself has demonstrated its concern with social and economic advancement for women, but it does not permit the existence of an independent feminist movement.

A typical statement on this subject was Erich Honecker's toast at the official celebration of International Woman's Day in 1983. The life of our republic has shown, he declared, "that everything we have achieved is also the achievement of our women. . . . Everything we still wish to achieve will need the energy of our women, their initiative and courage."[20] At the same time, however, he made it clear that all of this womanly energy and courage was to be devoted to fulfillment of the party's goals; that is how women will advance, rather than by pursuing specifically feminist causes.

YOUTH AND SOCIAL POLICY

How would the party leadership like to see the youth of the GDR? A party expert recently wrote: "A meaningful life can be found effectively today in doing something useful for society, for the welfare of all and thereby also for one's own happiness, and in committing one's whole personality in the struggle for peace and for socialism."[21] This opportunity to "help form the developed socialist society and in fraternal solidarity with the Soviet Union to further the integration of the socialist community" is youth's "basic right and basic duty."[22]

In order to ensure the acceptance by GDR youth of this prescribed rule, the regime relies on a judicious mixture of incentives, sanctions, controls, and openings. The incentives relate chiefly to educational, vocational, and sports opportunities; the sanctions range from restrictions on vocational choice to application of the law; the controls are exercised through a variety of organizations, chiefly the Free German Youth (Freie Deutsche Jugend, or FDJ); and the openings take the form of allowing youthful taste in music and entertainment to find expression and in adapting the regime's requirements to the predilections of youth (as in the encouragement of commitments to Third World causes to satisfy youthful desires for the exotic).

As would be the case in any functioning society, the regime has obtained the acquiescence of the great majority of young people: they take their places in the life of the country, advance in their work, serve in the armed forces, and establish families. Before the building of the Wall, the loss of young people was a particularly severe aspect of the general refugee problem. Since 1961, the GDR has had to find satisfactory "life chances" for its youth: the emphasis on economic growth, technological advance, and social welfare are all aspects of a policy designed to ensure that the youth of the GDR will remain supportive.

Nevertheless, a number of problems remain. Of particular concern to the regime is asocial behavior,[23] which may range from "excessive" concentration on private pursuits to violent breaches of public order. There is a worrisome increase in excessive drinking of alcohol; alcohol abuse also extends to soldiers in active service.[24] An ominous increase in violent street crimes and acts of vandalism perpetrated by young people is a source of public concern. Destruction of public amenities and assaults on passersby have reached proportions sufficient to warrant mention in the press.[25]

More difficult to evaluate with respect to political significance is the rise of an apolitical countercultural "scene," similar to that in West Germany. Unofficial punk rock bands and groups of young people sharing squatters' quarters in old apartment houses in Leipzig or East Berlin are not politically menacing as such, but such phenomena do lessen the regime's ability to mobilize young people for public purposes.

Organization and Activities of the FDJ

There are two organizations of GDR youth: the FDJ and the "Pioneers." The latter, the Pioneer organization "Ernst Thälmann," organizes young people from six to fourteen years of age into two groups: the Young Pioneers (*Jungpioniere*) for children in grades one to three, and the *Thälmannpioniere*[26] for grades four through seven. The total membership of the two groups in 1982 was 1.3 million.[27] The chief functions of this organization are elementary political socialization and socially approved leisure-time activity.

The FDJ, which organizes young people between the ages of fourteen and twenty-five, was founded in 1946 as a unitary, nonpartisan organization, in contrast to the sectarian and partisan youth organizations of the pre-Hitler period. Although a great deal of stress was placed on maintaining an image of "antifascist unity" in the FDJ, it was from the start controlled by Communists. During the years of the GDR's Stalinization, the FDJ became a typical Communist youth organization and has remained such ever since. Its official role is that of "helper and reserve" for the SED. As the membership of the FDJ has steadily grown to reach the 1981 figure of 2.3 million members, the proportion of the targeted age group (fourteen to twenty-five) enrolled in it has also risen—to 75 percent in 1981.[28]

The role of the FDJ as a training and recruiting ground for the party and for those professions for which party membership is a prerequisite is indicated by the social composition of the organization. Although the persons in training for skilled positions constitute a relatively small part of the membership, they form a large proportion of their respective social strata. Of the FDJ membership, 44 percent are pupils (attending a primary or secondary school) or students (attending a college or university) and 22 and 19 percent, respectively, are apprentices and workers, but only 7 percent are in the army or police. Yet FDJ members account for 80 percent of all students, NVA officers, and long-term NVA enlisted personnel, 50 percent of all skilled workers, 40 percent of unskilled workers, and 20 percent of young farm personnel.[29]

In organization, the FDJ has been structured much like the party, with local organizations in schools, factories, and military units especially. Above the local level, the FDJ organization corresponds to the GDR's administrative levels, with a "parliament" (the most recent, the eleventh, was held in 1981), a central council (*Zentralrat*), and a bureau with a first-secretary and other Secretariat members.

A special feature of the FDJ is the existence of Public Order Groups (*Ordnungsgruppen*), which are used to uphold public discipline and to police youth activities, and serve as a paramilitary training force. As of November 1980, there were "more than" 37,000 members organized into "more than" 3,600 such groups.[30]

Since the late 1940s, the youth organization has been led by a first-secretary who has also been a member of the higher party leadership, and who exercises his or her power through a network of secretaries down to the district level. The leaders of the FDJ are men and women in their thirties and forties, which means that they have all made their careers since the founding of the GDR. Egon Krenz was first-secretary from 1974 to 1983, which climaxed a long career in party and youth work. He has since been promoted to full Politburo membership, a place on the Secretariat, and important ideological and international responsibilities. In this respect he resembles most of his predecessors, only one of whom has not used the FDJ position as a stepping-stone to a higher job. Of perhaps forthcoming political importance are Krenz's successor, Erhard Aurich, the FDJ's "ideological" secretary Hartmut König, and Helga Labs, who heads the Pioneers. As long as Honecker influences the promotion of cadres to replace older SED leaders, he is likely to continue to favor these younger officials who started their careers in his old organization—in many cases, while he still headed it.

Each year, approximately 200,000 fourteen year olds (previously members of the Pioneers) become FDJ members (i.e., approximately 75 percent of all young people of that age). The FDJ strives to influence these young people, at a critical time in their development, to decide about career, military service, family, and marriage in directions acceptable to the regime. The most "politically aware prepare themselves for entry into the party of Communists." All such decisions require careful preparation, since "even under socialist conditions, no one is born as a revolutionary."[31]

Among the rituals of control and socialization, the most important is the *Jugendweihe*. Since 1954, over 6 million eighth graders have participated in this ceremony; in the 1983–1984 school year, 223,800 boys and girls (over 95 percent of all fourteen-year-olds) took part in it. The authorities strive to make the ceremony an ever more public event rather than a private family affair. For example, appropriate *Jugendweihe* presents, often in the form of ideologically approved books, are prepared annually. In the ceremonies, themes of patriotism and solidarity with the Soviet Union are interwoven with those of civic virtue. Although many families in the GDR treat the ceremony as an occasion for feasting and conspicuous consumption, for many it is undoubtedly an effectively impressive ritual.[32]

The increasingly widespread and controversial process of paramilitary education is another instrument for mobilizing young people.[33]

The FDJ has now taken it upon itself to "develop class-based defense themes." Above all, the essential thing is to convince all young persons of the necessity of defending their socialist fatherland and of developing their abilities in this regard through organized paramilitary education. In the past several years, there has been an intensive campaign of political education in FDJ meetings (a whole series was devoted to the theme that "peace must be defended—peace must be armed"); these meetings have had the active participation of party speakers, military and state security officers, and reservists.

Because defending the GDR may involve "some unpleasantness and also demand personal sacrifice," preparation for it must begin at an early age. The GDR has therefore developed military-political and military-sports activities for the FDJ and Pioneers that are suitable for different age levels, beginning with mock maneuvers for ten year olds; in their summer encampments they may be visited by the ministers of defense and education, Heinz Hoffmann and Margot Honecker.[34] These war games are designed to appeal to the youthful need for adventure and fantasy, and they call upon reserves of courage, skill, and endurance.

An important aspect of youth policy is the integration of young people into the economic system, an activity in which the FDJ also plays a prominent part. Economic policy in this respect serves both as an incentive and as a means of control. Opportunities for training and advancement are offered to young people, but, at the same time, there are limits on the choice of occupation or profession and on admission to institutions of higher education, as well as pressure to volunteer for special projects involving considerable commitments of time and labor. In this last connection, however, there is also an opportunity for idealistic commitment, such that the interests of youth and regime may in fact converge.

One frequently used device is to declare a particular economic project a "Youth Objective" (*Jugendobjekt*). Such a project may involve existing enterprises with a predominantly youthful work force or, as with the Soviet gas pipeline project, may be staffed by specially recruited young workers from all sectors of the economy and all parts of the GDR, usually for a specified time. Some recent *Jugendobjekte* include

1. the "FDJ Berlin Initiative," in which Berlin youth together with more than 14,000 colleagues from throughout the GDR work on 377 *Judgendobjekte*, including housing construction in the new Berlin borough of Marzahn;
2. the Soviet natural gas pipeline;
3. since 1976, the 92 projects that have been assigned to the FDJ by the Ministry of Science and Technology (since 1981, these projects have focused on industrial robots and microelectronics);
4. capital improvements (there are seventeen such projects);

5. microelectronics (in several factories, 480 FDJ members are at work to raise output of this branch of production); and
6. "Havelfruit" (in the Havel River Valley, the largest fruit-growing region of the GDR, 25,000 FDJ members are at work).[35]

The regime seems to find that such crash programs of labor inputs pay off, either economically or politically, because their numbers have risen steadily over the years—from 23,000, with a third of a million participants in 1971, to over 98,000, with more than a million participants in 1981.[36]

The youth of the GDR has been provided with incentives through opportunities and subsidies in a number of fields. According to Honecker, the period 1976–1980, for example, saw the expenditure of 640 million Mark for school equipment; 104,854 places became available in day care centers; and openings in kindergarten were made available to all children whose parents requested it.[37] At the other end of the educational spectrum, 76 percent of all university students moved into dormitories. With the start of the 1981 academic year, the students enrolled and in residence at universities were entitled to receive a monthly stipend of 200 Mark; the size of special stipends for academic achievement was raised as well. Finally, pupils in the last two classes of secondary school were granted scholarship help (if needed), and apprenticeship stipends were increased.[38]

In 1981, the state subsidized young people's theater, concert, and movie tickets by an amount of 23 million Mark, substantially increased the number of youth clubrooms and of dances, and spent more money on sports facilities. Youth travel was encouraged: in 1979 some 291,830 people traveled abroad or in the GDR with the FDJ travel organization.[39]

Young people on the threshold of adult life were also favored through the extension of credits for young couples and newly started families. Every fifth apartment built or renovated between 1971 and 1981 was assigned to a young couple. From 1972 to 1982, the government lent young couples 4.8 billion Mark in interest-free loans up to 5,000 Mark each. About a fourth of this total amount did not have to be paid back, as it was waived following the birth of children.[40]

In addition to an excellent, if stressful, educational system and an active social benefits policy, the regime has been quite forthcoming regarding the sexual interests and behavior of young people. Unlike certain other East bloc countries, for example, official GDR scholarship on youth questions regards early sexual activity as socially acceptable.[41]

The GDR's adult authorities have also recognized that "entertainment, dancing, companionship are indispensable components of a cultivated socialist life style." The need to relax after intensive work or study is acknowledged as real; "it is all the more important, therefore, to overcome still existing tendencies toward an underestimation of youth's need for entertainment."[42] This admonition seems to have been taken to heart by the regime; it wishes to combat the insinuation that only Western society is characterized by "sensuality [*Sinnesfreuden*] and pleasure, by color and playfulness."

To persuade people of the superiority of the "actual socialism" of the GDR requires acceptance of young people's tastes in light amusement. The humorless denunciations of jeans or rock music have been replaced by the boast that

> we value the achievements of our rock musicians very highly. Their accomplishment is not only to be seen in the fact that rock in the German style had its birthplace in the GDR, but that in the past 15 years we have seen developed dance music which is relevant, which captures our young people's feeling for life, with which almost every young person in our country can identify, and which has won international recognition.[43]

To play this music there now exist professional discotheques, with officially trained disc jockeys, in addition to over six thousand amateur discos.

As social research has shown the attachment of young people to popular entertainment, the regime has decided to offer them their favorite forms; it has also sought to adapt it to official purposes. After all, rock groups can (and do!) sing in praise of GDR policy on nuclear arms as well as on other subjects.[44]

As the recent political advancement of Egon Krenz demonstrates, the regime is fairly well satisfied with its youth policy over the past decade. Does the growing involvement of young people in alternative peace and environmental movements, in church activities, and—from a very different perspective—in alternative life styles or asocial behavior mean that this satisfaction is premature? It is not possible to give a definite answer to such a question. One can only note that the regime is keenly aware of the importance of successful socialization of the GDR's young people. Its policies in the fields of education and sports, to which we now turn, give eloquent proof of that.

EDUCATION AND SPORTS

The social policies most relevant to young people in the GDR are those dealing with education and sports. They provide opportunities for advancement as well as positive entertainment, and they are generally regarded as two of the GDR's more successful policies. Whereas educational investment is a prominent feature of modern societies, and an especially important one for a resource-poor, advanced society like the GDR, the sports program is a clear example of shrewd and effective commitment of resources for the enhancement of the regime's stability and legitimacy. In fostering both mass sports and world-class championship performances, the GDR is, of course, emulating the Soviet example. At the same time, however, the GDR has attained global stature in sports, as at the Olympics, with a population less than a tenth of the Soviet figure, and with but a fraction of Soviet resources. These two programs, then, form an essential and successful component of the GDR as a modern society.

The Educational System

One of the first measures undertaken to reform society in the Soviet Zone of Occupation was the "Democratic School Reform" of June 1946. Such a reorganization was part of the Communist and Social Democratic programs as well as a long-standing goal of German reformers. The highlights of this reform were the creation of a single school system (*Einheitsschule*), a reorientation of the curriculum to do away with "militarism, racism, imperialism and ethnic prejudice (*Völkerverhetzung*)," and a wholesale purge of Nazi and reactionary teachers and their replacement by forty thousand "New Teachers."[45]

School policy was thus from the start an instrument of both pedagogical and sociopolitical reform, and its goal was to mold "highly educated, progressive persons, who are trained in deep love for their socialist fatherland, respect for people, love of work, class solidarity."[46] During the period 1946–1965, the schools were infused with ideological content and modified to meet the regime's goals of social and economic development. The schools were to provide educational opportunities for children from all social classes, and the Pioneers and FDJ were encouraged to play an ever more active role in them. In addition, a ten-year school, which stressed technical training, was organized.

The educational system today, in the final form it achieved in the early 1960s, is that of the "integrated socialist educational system" (see Figure 7.1).[47] Its purpose is the nurturing of "well-rounded and harmoniously developed socialist personalities, who consciously build society, transform nature, and live a full, happy, humane, and worthy existence." This system extends from preschool education through adult and continuing education, combining study with practical experience and learning with moral development.[48]

The core of the educational system is the "ten-class general polytechnical secondary school." The aim of this school is to give each pupil a sound general education, impart an understanding of nature and of society, transmit an appreciation of art and literature, and teach foreign languages, particularly Russian, as well as to train young people for practical work in the economy and in Communist attitudes toward labor.[49]

The general polytechnical school is divided into three stages: grades one through three, four through six, and seven through ten. As of 1983, there were 5,183 such schools in the GDR, with an enrollment of 1,973,902 pupils. The "expanded" twelve-year schools for college-bound pupils numbered 214 and enrolled 44,985 pupils.[50]

The subjects to be taught in the general polytechnical schools are prescribed by the Ministry of Education. The greatest stress is placed

160

Figure 7.1
The Integrated Socialist Education System in the GDR

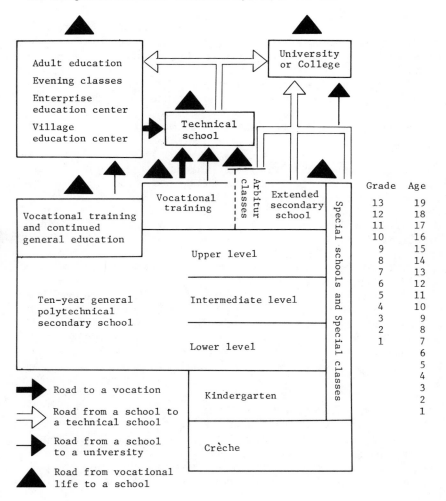

Source: Margrete Siebert Klein, _The Challenge of Communist Education:_
A Look at The German Democratic Republic, East European Monographs No. 70
(Boulder: Columbia University Press, 1980), p. 40.

throughout on the basic skills of the German languge and mathematics. As early as the first grade, for example, eleven of twenty-one weekly classroom hours are devoted to German and five to mathematics. By the fifth grade, classes in Russian, biology, geography, and history have already begun. Beginning with grade seven, polytechnical instruction as such is introduced, although manual training of some sort begins in grade one. Such instruction includes technical drawing, "introduction to socialist production, and productive work done by pupils." In the latter years of schooling (corresponding roughly to the secondary-school phase in the United States), 22 percent of formal instruction time is devoted to science, 15 percent to mathematics, 34 percent to the German language and to history, 14 percent to polytechnical education, 9 percent to Russian, and 6 percent to sports. The paramilitary training introduced to the ninth and tenth grades in 1978 includes twelve days in camp (eight hours per day) and involves some weapons training. For girls, and for some boys, there is an alternative civil defense program that takes twelve days (six hours daily) to complete. These seventy-two hours include twenty hours of practical instruction.[51]

Although it is possible to leave after the eighth grade and receive vocational training, more than 93 percent of all pupils enrolled in the general polytechnical schools finish ten grades. By contrast, only about 9 percent of those finishing the tenth grade go on to receive their twelfth-grade academic diploma (the *Abitur*).

Admission to the twelve-year school (*erweiterte Oberschule*) is, by the terms of the GDR constitution, open on the basis of "ability, society's needs, and the social structure of the population." In applying these criteria, the regime has acquired considerable leeway in regulating the numbers and kinds of entrants for reasons of social planning, in reducing the numbers of underemployed academics, and in increasing the proportion of students from worker and peasant backgrounds. In fact, the number of pupils in these schools dropped from 1971 to 1981.[52] The course of study introduces an obligatory second foreign language as well as a variety of electives. The polytechnical education is aimed at "frontier" areas such as data processing. There are also special schools to which a pupil may go as early as from the fifth or sixth grade, and which specialize in such areas of study as sports, music, and art.

Universities

There are currently slightly more than fifty institutions of higher learning in the GDR. Eight of these have university status: the universities of Berlin, Dresden, Leipzig, Jena, Rostock, Greifswald, and Halle-Wittenberg, plus the Technical University at Dresden. Specialized pedagogical, fine arts, and music institutions also exist, in addition to a network of engineering schools. The official task of these institutions is to graduate "persons who are highly qualified scientifically and have socialist consciousness, and who can subsequently bring the latest attainments of science to bear on every aspect of life in the GDR."[53]

The entire university system is centrally directed by the Ministry of Higher and Specialized Secondary Education; the minister since 1970 has been Hans-Joachim Böhme, who had previously been active in university administration. The criteria for university education reflect "the needs of science, of the economy, and of society." The ministry has the basic jurisdiction over the structure of university life, including the setting up of new fields of study, the review of syllabi, textbooks, and new admissions, and the coordination of universities and government.

The existing process of admitting students to their fields of study seems to suit most applicants.[54] In 1983, there were 1.2 applicants for each place; three-quarters of all applicants were admitted into the majors of their choice. (Almost 60,000 were not allowed their choice of major, and some 2,000 places went unfilled. Medicine, pharmacy, and psychology were among the "over-subscribed" fields; mathematics, factory management, and the teaching of Marxism/Leninism were unpopular majors.)

One of the ministry's primary, and most difficult, tasks is to plan the convergence of the GDR's needs for trained personnel with the desires of incoming students for particular courses of study. Although in theory every student's admission is contingent upon the availability of a given position upon graduation, this end cannot be realized in every case. Every graduate is to be given a job "commensurate in status and remuneration" with the one not available to him or her.[55] The official party view is that "the principles of admission to universities . . . based on the applicant's achievements, the social structure of the population, and with concern for the needs of our society have proved themselves." But, given future trends, it is important to "improve vocational and academic counseling. Young people should be made aware at an early stage of society's needs and possibilities. Stress should be placed on the engineering professions."[56]

The actual placement of university graduates into jobs is the responsibility of special commissions composed of representatives of the FDJ, government, university faculty, and factory or farm administrations.[57] Although job placement is intended to occur through mutual agreement, the student is already on record as having pledged, at the time of university admission, to work at a job that is in "the interests of society." This initial work assignment commits both employer and applicant for at least three years.

The "needs of society" are, of course, interpreted to include ideological considerations. Leipzig's Karl Marx University tells prospective applicants that, while still in secondary school they should have demonstrated a commitment to the socialist state, as expressed by social action as well as by ideological consciousness. Moreover, applicants should show their willingness to "defend socialism." Men can do this by volunteering for reserve officers' training; women, by taking a civil defense training course. Students should be prepared "to bring their personal interests into line with social needs by taking up a field other than the one originally desired."[58]

Since the "Third University Reform" of 1968, the organizational structure of GDR universities has centered on the office of rector and on the academic departments.[59] The rector is central to the administration of the university and has a decisive voice in resolving all important policy questions. The rector is in fact appointed by the minister, though only upon recommendation by the Academic Council and after a certain amount of internal university lobbying.

Two institutions that derive especially from the social-ideological character of the GDR universities are the Societal Council and the Scientific Council. The former is concerned with the university's relations with military, economic, and political institutions; the Scientific Council is the more traditional university body, consisting of representatives of the faculty, in addition to some students, and headed by the rector. This council awards degrees and formally approves teaching appointments.

What do the students study? Required courses include Marxist-Leninist ideology (the "essential prerequisite for a scientific education"); two foreign languages, of which one must be Russian; physical education; and "socialist military science and acquisition of military skills [which] are to be indissolubly linked to the entire educational process." The choice of a major is subject to counseling and is linked to manpower planning (see Table 7.2).

The students are from diverse social backgrounds, which, in turn, have undergone dramatic shifts throughout the history of the GDR.[60] In 1951, after several years of encouraging the "breaking of the educational monopoly," students from worker and peasant backgrounds still accounted for less than half of the total number enrolled. By 1960, the proportion of such students had risen moderately, only to decline thereafter. Although no figures on this subject have been published recently, indications from GDR policy discussions are that, after a brief spurt of "social" admissions in the early 1970s, the GDR has decided on a policy of strict performance criteria as essential for ensuring technical progress.

Even during the height of political struggles over the nature and future of the GDR universities, struggles that often saw the authorities in conflict with traditionally minded faculty (as well as with opponents of political and ideological regimentation),[61] the GDR was never hostile to the professoriate as such, and especially not toward those professors doing advanced research. A scientist such as Manfred von Ardenne, who had done nuclear research in the USSR until 1955, has headed his own research institute outside Dresden ever since. Even at the height of the campaign for a "socialist university" in the 1950s, the regime raised the salaries of professors quite substantially, and today an average monthly salary for a professor is double that of teachers or skilled workers. Although each member of a university faculty must, of course, "not take a special position above the classes" and assume a "clear political position for socialism," the authorities have recognized the

TABLE 7.2
Number of Students in Varying Fields at Start of Honecker Era and Today

Field of Study	1970	1983
Sciences		
Mathematics	3,675	1,037
Physics	2,746	1,591
Chemistry	4,386	2,664
Biology	959	957*
Engineering and other "technical" disciplines		
All	45,967	39,349
Electronics	15,108	10,898
Medicine	9,560	13,720
Agricultural sciences	6,946	7,849
Economics	20,583	17,118
Philosophy, history, sociology, political and juridical sciences	7,149	7,940
Literature/linguistics	1,299	2,153
Pedagogy	33,202	27,128

Sources: Statistisches Taschenbuch der DDR 1984 (Berlin: Staatsverlag der DDR, 1984), p. 124; Statistisches Jahrbuch der DDR 1983 (Berlin: Staatsverlag der DDR, 1983), p. 306.

*1982 figure

specific needs of the academic work and life-style; indeed, dedicated professors should be freed from excessive attendance at political and administrative meetings.[62]

Such official concern is due to the stress that the GDR, as a relatively resource-poor but highly industrialized country, has placed on applied science. In recent years, science has been upgraded to the level of prime generator of economic development. In the official view, "science has developed into a fundamental productive force as well as an instrument for shaping, planning and guiding social forces."[63] Any recent Honecker speech will have included an exhortation to improve the educational system's capacity for relevant research.

This emphasis on the social significance of higher education has been reflected in state expenditures, which have risen steadily in recent years. In the five years between 1977 and 1982, total expenditures for all aspects of higher education increased by just over one-fourth, to a total of roughly 2.33 billion Mark (of which 991 million were earmarked for universities).[64]

In keeping with the general practice of Communist countries, a major portion of scientific research in the GDR is carried on in institutions outside the universities, especially in units of the Academy of Sciences.[65] Most of the Academy's work is carried on through fifty-odd institutes and ad hoc research laboratories. These research institutions currently engage about 20,000 scientists. In 1980, the Academy worked on 137 research projects of its own, plus another 84 from the State Research Plan (of which 49 are directly related to industrial problems).

In the work of the Academy there is an inevitable tension between its main mission of fundamental research (as laid down in the State Council resolution of 1970) and the commitment it has undertaken to support industrial progress. In 1980, as noted earlier, roughly a third of all Academy research came from industrial contracts. In recent years, there has also been a shift toward encouraging basic research at the university level, or at least toward reaching a "balanced relationship" between basic and applied research and between research and teaching. Research cooperation between the Academy and the universities is increasing.

Sports

The material dimensions of the national, centrally directed development of the GDR sports program are truly impressive. The public displays of support and approval for championship athletes are a telling indication of the political and social purposes of the program.

Modern sports represent a major mass phenomenon—particularly as a spectator diversion but also as a participant movement. The GDR has in the Soviet Union a model of a determined, centrally directed, and politically motivated promotion of sports. It has also derived from the Communist and Socialist movements of the late nineteenth and early twentieth centuries a lively tradition of workers' sports activities. (Ulbricht's enthusiasm for fitness and exercise almost surely stemmed from this source.) The choice of sports as a policy designed to appeal to the youth of the GDR and to upgrade the GDR's international image was thus a logical one.

Despite the difficult economic circumstances of the early postwar years, by 1952 the regime had built some 122 sports stadiums, 1,122 large indoor fieldhouses, 47 indoor swimming pools, and other sports facilities.[66] The current center for physical education training and research, the College of Physical Education (Hochschule für Körperkultur) in Leipzig, was founded in 1950. The National Olympic Committee was founded in 1951 and received de facto international recognition in 1955. Thus both the policy of furthering sports activity at home and the use of sports on the international level as a legitimating activity go back to the earliest days of the regime.

The contemporary GDR sports program has two major components: a widespread mass physical education and fitness program, and an

Marita Koch is a GDR Olympic champion in track. Photo courtesy of the GDR Embassy, Washington, D.C.

elaborate and sophisticated training program for championship athletes. The mass fitness program begins with compulsory physical education classes in the schools—at every level. It continues with the manifold activities of the official GDR sports organization, the German Gymnastic and Sports Federation of the GDR (DTSB), which, in 1982, had 3,312,319 members, or almost a fifth of the GDR population. Millions participate in sports activities organized by the DTSB, through its more than nine thousand clubs and over three hundred thousand officials and trainers, with soccer, fishing, and gymnastics (in that order) as the three most popular activities. A vivid example of this mass sports program was the National Festival of Sports and Fitness held in Leipzig in July 1983.[67] This combination junior Olympics ("Spartakiad") and fitness festival witnessed the participation of tens of thousands of athletes and ordinary people working out in their spare time. The authorities, with Honecker presiding, turned the event into an international festival—complete with resolutions of support for GDR foreign policy.

As with every other facet of life in the GDR, this manifold sports activity comes under the direction of party and state institutions. Among the party leadership there is a Department for Sports in the apparatus of the Central Committee Secretariat. In the state apparatus, there is the State Secretariat for Physical Education and Sports; in addition, the Ministries of Health and Education oversee school physical education and sports medicine training and research. Finally, there is the DTSB itself, which has been headed since 1961 by an experienced GDR sport official, Manfred Ewald (who has also headed the Olympic Committee since 1973).[68]

The aspects of GDR sports that attract the most attention, both at home and abroad, are those pertaining to the success of GDR athletes at the championship level. However one measures sports results, the achievements of athletes from a nation of under seventeen million total population are impressive. Performance at the Olympics is perhaps best known: 116 gold medals in the four summer games and 31 in five winter games since a separate GDR team has been allowed to enter. The GDR teams have consistently finished among the top three countries in total points.[69] GDR performances are also impressive at world and European championships, winning 79 gold, 68 silver, and 58 bronze medals at such events in 1983.[70]

The foundation of such achievements is a systematic fostering of sports excellence.[71] Children who show promise in sports are identified by teachers and coaches while still in elementary school and shunted into one of nineteen special sports schools, where a normal curriculum is presented in a way that allows for several hours of daily intensive sports training. In some cases, pupils board in cities distant from their families or live in dormitories. Their training is designed to fit criteria developed through systematic research into the physiological parameters of championship performance. Further training is provided at elaborate sports facilities such as the East Berlin Sports and Gymnastics Club, with its $500,000 annual budget (in 1976), its modern imported equipment, its six hundred members, and thirty-two professional coaches. In common with Soviet practice, many enterprises, state institutions, and military units sponsor sports clubs whose members, ostensibly amateurs working at the respective tasks, in reality spend most of their time in training.

The scientific center of this multifaceted sports enterprise is the Leipzig Sports and Physical Education College, with its attached Institute for Sports Medicine. (The institute's director, Dr. Kurt Tittel, was trained as a surgeon and has an advanced degree in sports medicine.) It has a staff of eighty-five, and has graduated over seven thousand coaches and trainers from its five-semester sports medicine program.

The system works to the advantage of the athlete participants, although not without drawbacks. There have been repeated charges, in some cases by defecting athletes, of excessive use of drugs to produce better performances; however, the chief problem seems to be the social isolation from family and neighborhood friends and the intensive training program to which very young children are subjected. Yet, if the par-

ticipants can overcome those obstacles, the rewards—in the form of
more liberal career choices, foreign travel, grants of apartments, and
other material goods—are quite extensive.

The great expense of this whole system is borne by the regime
precisely because of the legitimating purposes served. Sports are widely
publicized in the GDR. For example, each medal winner in recent
Olympics had her or his picture in the pages of *Neues Deutschland*;
given that this is normally an eight-page newspaper, such publicity can
run to 50 percent of available space! In general, star athletes are feted
and given medals and awards at national political ceremonies.[72]

GDR leaders have made it clear on many occasions that they regard
GDR sports performances as a way of advancing GDR interests and
reputation. Thus at a ceremony in December 1982, Honecker told the
assembled athletes and coaches that "as symbols of the German Democratic Republic, you have represented our socialist fatherland with honor
at many international competitions. . . . Your successes are a valuable
contribution to strengthening our workers' and peasants' state and to
its international reputation."[73]

During the long years in which the GDR lacked international
diplomatic recognition, one of the few arenas of international participation
open to it was that of sports contacts. Moreover, sports were a vehicle
for recognition of the GDR apart from West Germany. The contacts of
the two Germanys in sports affairs involved questions of recognition
of flags and anthems, personal liability of GDR and FRG athletes in
the other German state, and the implicit recognition involved in dealing
with national sports associations. During the Adenauer era, for example,
the Bonn government was hostile to formal East–West German sports
arrangements. Only after the signing of an inter-German sports agreement
between the two states' respective sports federations in 1974 did the
tempo of inter-German sports competition increase.

Sports are intended to serve as a visible sign of success both at
home and abroad. Abroad, they "[increase] the esteem in which the
GDR is held" (in the United States after the 1980 winter Olympics,
according to the GDR ambassador here),[74] and at home they constitute
a social policy that the regime has provided for youthful sports participants
and fans as well as for the public at large.

NOTES

1. *Neues Deutschland*, 31 December 1982, p. 1.

2. An excellent comparative survey, with much data, is Gisela Helwig,
Frau und Familie in beiden deutschen Staaten (Cologne: Verlag Wissenschaft und
Politik, 1982).

3. *Verfassung der Deutschen Demokratischen Republik* (Berlin: Staatsverlag
der DDR, 1975), pp. 24, 33–34.

4. Harry G. Shaffer, *Women in the Two Germanies* (New York: Pergamon Press, 1981), pp. 104–106; Authors' Collective, *Die Frau in der DDR* (Dresden: Verlag Zeit im Bild, 1978), pp. 147–148, 153, 181.

5. Ilse Thiele, in *Neues Deutschland,* 5 March 1982; Joan Levin Ecklein and Janet Zollinger Giele, "Women's Lives and Social Policy in East Germany and the United States," *Studies in Comparative Communism* 14 (Summer-Autumn 1981):202–203.

6. Ecklein and Giele, "Women's Lives," pp. 201–202; Authors' Collective, *Die Frau in der DDR,* p. 146.

7. *Frankfurter Allgemeine Zeitung,* 18 May 1981, p. 9. This article was based on a GDR radio interview with a doctor identified in the newspaper story as "Dr. Hennig, Director of a Study Group for Social and Ethical Questions of Gynecology and Natal Care at the Department of Medicine" of Leipzig's Karl Marx University.

8. Herta Kuhrig, "Liebe und Ehe im Sozialismus," *Einheit* 37 (July-August 1982):800–808. Kuhrig heads the Scientific Council on "Women and Socialism." The divorce rate for 1982 was 3.0 per 1,000 (*Statistisches Taschenbuch der DDR 1983* [Berlin: Staatsverlag der DDR, 1983], p. 144).

9. Kuhrig, "Liebe und Ehe im Sozialismus," p. 807; Shaffer, *Women in the Two Germanies,* pp. 146–149. According to a GDR survey, men share in household tasks to an appreciable extent in only one-third of households (see *Frankfurter Allgemeine Zeitung,* 11 February 1983, p. 9.)

10. Marilyn Rueschemeyer, *Professional Work and Marriage: An East-West Comparison* (New York: St. Martin's Press, 1981), p. 174.

11. Marilyn Rueschemeyer, "Social Work Relations of Professional Women: An Academic Collective in the GDR," *East Central Europe* 8, nos. 1–2 (1981):33–35.

12. Gabriele Gast, *Die politische Rolle der Frau in der DDR* (Düsseldorf: Bertelsmann, 1973), p. 15.

13. Ibid., pp. 92–95; Christiane Lemke, "Frauen in leitenden Funktionen," *Deutschland Archiv* 14 (September 1981):973; "Kaum Veränderungen nach Parteiwahlen," *Frankfurter Allgemeine Zeitung,* 21 February 1984, p. 5.

14. Authors' Collective, *Die Frau in der DDR,* p. 168.

15. Ilse Thiele, in *Neues Deutschland,* 5 March 1982: Thiele has been the head of the DFD since November 1953 and is a member of the SED Central Committee and (since 1971) of the *Staatsrat.* Four of her five deputies at the DFD are from parties other than the SED. There is a six-woman Secretariat and thirty-woman Praesidium. DFD membership (in 1982) was 1.4 million, of whom 77 percent were over thirty-five years old and of whom 72.3 percent were employed. See *Neues Deutschland,* 6 March 1982, p. 3; *Statistisches Taschenbuch der DDR 1983,* p. 21.

16. Shaffer, *Women in the Two Germanies,* p. 73. *Frankfurter Allgemeine Zeitung,* 11 February 1983, pp. 9–10. Irene Böhme, *Die Da Drüben. Sieben Kapitel DDR* (Berlin: Rotbuch Verlag, 1983), pp. 82–109, argues that as GDR society recovers from the gender-distribution and abnormal demographic ties of the early years, sexist arguments against women's participation have become more frequent; on the other hand, women see the relative impotence of all but a handful of leading positions and therefore prefer to stay in "low"-level jobs, where they can exercise a direct influence on daily life.

17. Lemke, "Frauen in leitenden Positionen," pp. 971–972.

18. Authors' Collective, *Die Frau in der DDR*, pp. 172–173; *Statistisches Taschenbuch der DDR 1984*, p. 123.
19. *Neues Deutschland*, 5–6 March 1983, p. 11.
20. *Neues Deutschland*, 9 March 1983, p. 3.
21. Wolfgang Herger, "Lebenssinn der Kommunisten—Massstab für die heranwachsende Generation," *Einheit* 37 (October 1982):983. Herger is a department head (presumably of youth affairs) of the Central Committee Secretariat.
22. The Youth Law of 1974, quoted in Gunter Erbe et al., *Politik, Wirtschaft und Gesellschaft in der DDR* [hereafter cited as *PWG*], 2d ed. (Opladen: Westdeutscher Verlag, 1980), p. 328.
23. For information on the rise in juvenile crime, see the sources cited by Wolf Oschlies in "Jung sein in der DDR," paper presented at the Seventeenth DDR-Forschertagung, Lerbach (June 1984), pp. 18–19.
24. For a discussion of drunkenness among troops, see *Frankfurter Allgemeine Zeitung*, 21 March 1983, p. 6.
25. *New York Times*, 1 August 1978, p. 12; *Frankfurter Allgemeine Zeitung*, 22 November 1980, p. 10.
26. Named after Ernst ("Teddy") Thälmann, the Communist leader during the latter years of the Weimar Republic. Thälmann spent the period after 1933 in Nazi prisons before being murdered at the Buchenwald camp in August 1944.
27. *Statistisches Taschenbuch der DDR 1983*, p. 21.
28. Arnold Freiburg, "'Freie Deutsche Jugend.' Aufgaben und Strukturen der FDJ," *Deutsche Studien* 19, no. 76 (December 1981):360; Heinz Lippmann, in *Honecker. Porträt eines Nachfolgers* (Cologne: Verlag Wissenschaft und Politik, 1971), pp. 49–66 and passim, discusses Honecker's role as FDJ leader in dealing with non-Communists; for an example of the FDJ's role in implementing the SED's economic policy, see Werner Haltinner, "Arbeit zum Wohle des Volkes—eine Kernfrage kommunistischer Erziehung der Jugend," *Einheit* 36 (July 1981):679–685. Membership data are taken from Freiburg, "'Freie Deutsche Jugend,'" and "FDJ in Zahlen und Fakten," *Einheit* 37 (October 1982):1019.
29. Freiburg, "'Freie Deutsche Jugend,'" p. 363; *PWG*, p. 167.
30. Freiburg, "'Freie Deutsche Jugend,'" p. 367; *Neues Deutschland*, 6–7 June 1981, p. 5.
31. Herger, "Lebenssinn der Kommunisten," p. 685.
32. *Neues Deutschland*, 5–6 March 1982, p. 9; *Süddeutsche Zeitung* (Munich), 5 May 1976, p. 3; *Frankfurter Allgemeine Zeitung*, 4 May 1982, p. 10. See also *Neues Deutschland*, 16 November 1984, p. 3, and 28 May 1984, p. 1.
33. For an overview of FDJ activity designed to foster military preparedness, see Karl-Heinz Borgwardt and Peter Miethe, "FDJ and Sozialistische Landesverteidigung," *Einheit* 36 (October 1982):1008–1013.
34. *Neues Deutschland*, 28–29 June 1980, p. 5.
35. See Herger, "Lebenssinn der Kommunisten," pp. 988–990.
36. *PWG*, p. 169; *Einheit* 37 (October 1982):1019. For details on a new series of projects in connection with the SED Eleventh Congress in 1986, see *Neues Deutschland*, 26 November 1984, p. 3.
37. *Neues Deutschland*, 12 April 1981, pp. 9–10.
38. *Frankfurter Allgemeine Zeitung*, 20 June 1981, p. 4.
39. *Neues Deutschland*, 22 October 1982, p. 5; *PWG*, p. 170; Herger, "Lebenssinn der Kommunisten," p. 990.
40. Herger, "Lebenssinn der Kommunisten," p. 989; *Neues Deutschland*, 8 March 1979, p. 3.

41. Oschlies, "Jung sein in der DDR," pp. 8–11.

42. Lothar Bisky and Dieter Wiedemann, "Geistig-Kulturell Ansprüche und Aktivitäten der Jugend," *Einheit* 36 (October 1982):1014–1018.

43. *Neues Deutschland*, 22 October 1982, p. 5.

44. For an interesting discussion of the political significance of mass culture in the GDR, see Olaf Leitner, "Ideologische Aspekte sozialistischer Unterhaltungskunst," *Die DDR vor den Herausforderungen der achtziger Jahre . . . Mai 1983* (Cologne: Edition Deutschland Archiv, 1983), pp. 167–180.

45. Weber, *Kleine Geschichte der DDR* (Cologne: Edition Deutschland Archiv, 1980), p. 29; *PWG*, p. 328.

46. Margot Honecker, in *Neues Deutschland*, 13 June 1980, p. 3.

47. For a perceptive analysis of GDR education policy in a wider socio-political setting, see Gert-Joachim Glaessner, "The Education System and Society," in Klaus von Beyme and Hartmut Zimmerman, eds., *Policymaking in the German Democratic Republic* (New York: St. Martin's Press, 1984), ch. 5.

48. *Gesetz über das einheitliche sozialistische Bildungssystem der DDR* (Berlin: Staatsverlag der DDR, 1971), pp. 13–15; Margarete Siebert Klein, *The Challenge of Communist Education: A Look at the German Democratic Republic*, East European Monographs No. 70 (Boulder, Colo.: Columbia University Press, 1980), especially pp. 39–60.

49. *PWG*, p. 334; *Programm der Sozialistischen Einheitspartei Deutschlands* (Berlin: Dietz Verlag, 1976), pp. 66–68.

50. *Statistisches Taschenbuch der DDR 1984*, p. 119.

51. Klein, *Challenge of Communist Education*, p. 93; *PWG*, pp. 340–342.

52. See *PWG*, pp. 343–344; see also Article 26 of the constitution, in *Verfassung der Deutschen Demokratischen Republik* (Berlin: Staatsverlag der DDR, 1975), p. 28.

53. *Gesetz über das einheitliche sozialistische Bildungssystem der DDR*, p. 49.

54. Ralf Rytlewski and Gabrielle Husner, "Zwischen permanenter Zuwendung und sanftem Zwang—Studenten in der DDR seit dem VIII. Parteitag der SED," paper delivered at the XVII DDR-Forschert gung, Lerbach (June 1984), p. 6.

55. Geoffrey J. Giles, "The Structure of Higher Education in the German Democratic Republic," Yale Higher Education Program Working Paper no. 12, October 1976, pp. 21–22.

56. *Neues Deutschland*, 20 March 1980, p. 3.

57. Glaessner, "The Education System and Society," p. 16.

58. *PWG*, pp. 373. *Karl Marx Universität Leipzig Universitätsführer* (Leipzig: KMU, 1976), pp. 33–35.

59. See Giles, "Structure of Higher Education in the German Democratic Republic," pp. 12, 18–19; *Karl Marx Universität Leipzig Universitätsführer*, p. 23. See also the KMU's *Studienführer 1971/73* (Leipzig: KMU, 1970), pp. 56–57.

60. Between 1949 and 1965, a special channel into higher education was provided for children from worker and peasant backgrounds: the "Workers' and Peasants' Faculties" (Arbeiter- und Bauernfakultäten, or ABF).

61. For an account of the early political struggles, see Ernst Richert, "Sozialistische Universität": Die Hochschulpolitik der SED (Berlin: Colloquium Verlag, 1967).

62. See the remarks of Kurt Hager in *Neues Deutschland*, 6–7 September 1981, pp. 3–4; and in *Einheit* 36 (November 1981):752.

63. *Neues Deutschland,* 20 March 1980, p. 3.

64. *Neues Deutschland,* 28 October 1983, p. 3; *Statistisches Jahrbuch der DDR 1980* (Berlin: Staatsverlag, 1980), p. 253.

65. This discussion is based on Peter C. Ludz et al., eds., *DDR Handbuch,* 2d ed. (Cologne: Verlag Wissenschaft und Politik, 1979), pp. 32–33; and on articles in *Neues Deutschland,* 7–8 July 1979, p. 5; 22 January 1980, p. 3; 5 September 1980, p. 3; and 22 January 1980, p. 1.

66. Gunter Holzweissig, *Diplomatie im Trainingsanzug* (Munich: R. Oldenbourg, 1981), p. 199. The continuing coverage of DDR sports by Willi Knecht in *Deutschland Archiv* was used for this section as well.

67. Of the extensive press coverage, see especially *Neues Deutschland,* 26 July and 1 August 1983, as well as (in color and several languages) DTSB, *Fest des DDR-Sportes* (Dresden: Verlag Zeit im Bild, 1983).

68. *Neues Deutschland,* 17 December 1982, pp. 1, 3, and 21–22 March 1981, pp. 3, 8.

69. The GDR withdrawal from the 1984 Summer Games in Los Angeles was surely a painful decision, taken under heavy Soviet pressure. Once announced, however, it was of course "greeted" by Olympic hopefuls. See *Neues Deutschland,* 11 May 1984, pp. 1–2; *New York Times,* 11 May 1984, p. A12.

70. *Neues Deutschland,* 17 December 1982, p. 3, and 19 January 1984, p. 1.

71. See the excellent series by Craig Whitney in the *New York Times,* 20, 21, 22, December 1976, and the equally interesting article by James Markham, *New York Times,* 1 August 1983, pp. 1–2, for the material in the following three paragraphs.

72. *Neues Deutschland,* 8 August 1980, pp. 3–6; 26 February 1980, p. 7; and 21 February 1984, p. 7.

73. *Neues Deutschland,* 17 December 1982, p. 3.

74. *Neues Deutschland,* 26 February 1980, p. 7.

8

Facing the Future

In its proclamation for the thirty-fifth anniversary of the republic, the GDR leadership declared that "the ground on which we stand is solid. On it, we can continue to build."[1] The grounds for confident self-assertion are evident. They reflect the considerable successes of the GDR in international relations, economic growth, social development, and foreign relations. After a long and difficult process of consolidation, the GDR enters the second half of the 1980s as an important and established European state. By no means, however, does this signify a time of rest in which the GDR will cease to be faced with serious problems. Rather, it is that the problems with which the GDR will be faced in the near and middle-term future are those resulting from its successes. These may be summed up under four categories:[2]

1. Continuing problems in defining national identity (a resolution of which will be essential in strengthening the regime and establishing a satisfactory relationship with West Germany).
2. Growing difficulty in securing the resources for the economic growth needed to sustain the GDR's welfarist socialism.
3. The need to regulate increasingly active and restive social and intellectual forces.
4. The need to ensure that a stable and effective political leadership will be in place to guide the GDR effectively toward resolution of these difficulties.

Although the roots of many of these problems naturally reach back to the beginnings of the GDR, they represent, in their current incarnations, the difficult choices the GDR faces now that the basic requirements of international acceptance, minimal domestic legitimacy, and steady economic growth have been achieved.

Among the problems that will require decisions of the GDR leadership, the most concrete is that of economic policy. It is clear that the political leadership generally, and Honecker in particular, has made continued success in economic policy an essential element in maintaining its positions.[3] This success, in turn, requires continued growth in the

GDR economy, not only in productive capacity but also in output of consumer goods and in the expansion of export capacity. Here the GDR faces a series of interrelated difficulties, beginning with the increased dependence of the economy on external markets. The GDR buys energy and raw materials in the East, at ever higher prices. Even assuming a continuing, politically inspired willingness on the part of the USSR to carry the GDR's economy, there are problems of availability of supply and price that will motivate the GDR to reduce further the consumption of energy and imported raw materials.[4] At the same time, imports of technology and consumer goods from the West will have to be paid for, either with export surpluses that have the unwanted effect of reducing consumption, or with loans that unfortunately need repayment. To maintain its creditworthiness, the GDR must make strenuous efforts to service its hard-currency debt—a major purpose, apparently, behind the blockbuster loan arranged by Bonn and Munich in 1983. Such a practice, in turn, gives West Germany a politically uncomfortable influence on East Berlin's policies.

Moreover, the stress on increased productivity has had significant social consequences. In order to benefit from the advances in productivity and product development that proceed from application of advanced techniques in science and industry, the GDR must foster and reward people of unusual skills. Performance and the social standing that must accompany it as a necessary stimulus are seen as the motors for economic success. But this emphasis on accomplishment in turn exposes one of the basic social tensions of socialist societies: that between "to each according to his work" and the thrust toward egalitarianism, or, in specific social terms, that between the working class and the scientific-technical intelligentsia. One of the political dimensions of the transition from Ulbricht to Honecker was a renewed emphasis on the role of the working class and on the welfarist stimulus of the economy. The recent attention paid to differentiation as an untapped economic resource casts this line of the 1970s into doubt.[5]

Already the minister of higher education has complained of a lack of young scholars willing to teach basic ideological subjects and, hence, threatens to appoint graduates in philosophy, political economy, and history only as instructors in Marxism-Leninism![6]

Economic planning in the GDR has tried to take account of these pressures.[7] On the one hand, economic targets have become more modest and attainable; at the same time, the rate of growth of private consumption has been held down below the planned increases in produced national income—unlike the policy of the early 1970s. As far as the economy is concerned, therefore, the prospects for the GDR are such that ever more strenuous efforts are required to squeeze the socially needed increment of production out of a strained economy increasingly dependent on external conditions. The GDR will have to continue its reliance on the ingenuity, diligence, and willingness to postpone gratification of its labor force. It may well succeed in this—but the lessons of similar trends in other countries are not encouraging.

As a consequence of the GDR's successes in social policy, a well-educated and politically and socially aware generation has come into being. Dealing with such a generation will require more imagination and patience than that displayed in allowing rock concerts and Western styles. As the continued strength of the peace movement shows, autonomous social forces have become a fixture of life in the GDR. Popular interest in peace, the environment, religious life, women's roles, and cultural forms is certainly growing. Much of this activity takes place in the private niches of the social order; only later, when it has surfaced or been recorded by outsiders,[8] do we become aware of it. Still, GDR society shows occasional unexpected flashes of vigorous public opinion; one example has been the public defense of Christa Wolf by members of the reading public against dogmatic ideological attack.[9]

Of course, the regime may, and undoubtedly will, exercise its capacity for repression.[10] Within rather narrow limits, it can maintain its monopoly over political initiatives and channel the direction of intellectual development. However, repression cannot solve the basic tensions between an authoritarian regime and an increasingly capable citizenry; thoughtful GDR scholars recognize this. Uwe-Jens Heuer has spoken of "socialist democracy" as a source of reserves for economic growth. He argues that subjectivism and bureaucratism must be replaced by democratic mass participation (but in a dialectical unity of discipline, of course).[11]

If the GDR cannot satisfy such economic or social demands, then its citizens retain a destabilizing option; they can try to go to West Germany, or, at least, they can regard themselves as "Germans" plain and simple, thereby depriving the GDR of national legitimacy.

The ambitious program of linking the GDR to all Germany history makes a great deal of plain sense and has political advantages for the GDR as well.[12] Nevertheless, the relationship of the GDR to its German past remains an ambiguous one, fraught with political perils for the GDR. If the GDR is truly the heir of all that at any historical stage may have been progressive, then this mixed (albeit realistic) heritage is also present in West Germany. Further, these progressive elements are not necessarily beneficial to the GDR unless they can be transformed by the exercise of party leadership, whereas traits (such as proletarian industriousness) cultivated originally for bourgeois purposes are now to the GDR's advantage. Conversely, politically undesirable aspects of the German past, which had hitherto been excluded by political fiat from the GDR's heritage, are now being reconsidered as potential influences on the GDR. Most pointedly, writers are questioning the shibboleth that the GDR—and everyone in it—had permanently broken with the Nazi past.[13]

What gives these intellectual disputes particular relevance is the degree of dependence on the Federal Republic that economic pressures have forced on the GDR. Both domestic economic discontent and the need to be accommodating to West German creditors presumably lay behind the (unannounced) apparent decision to allow legal emigration from the GDR in unprecedented numbers,[14] while others (such as Stoph's niece and her family, to the intense embarrassment of the GDR) were allowed to emigrate after "sitting in" at the FRG Embassy in Prague, the Bonn mission in East Berlin, and the U.S. Embassy there. (See chapter 4 for details.) Although East Berlin may be allowing only applicants of long standing to emigrate, the experience of flight just prior to construction of the Berlin Wall, or of applications for Jewish emigration from the USSR, suggests the existence of a possible panic reaction whereby people decide to apply to leave just in case it will not be allowed later on.

From a public relations perspective, this surge of desire to flee the GDR could not have come at a worse time. These GDR citizens are going to the land of high unemployment, to the land that has become "a launching ramp for American first-strike weapons"—in short, to the land that should not be attracting them but *is* doing so, partly for economic reasons but undoubtedly also because it is German.

Can the party and state leadership of the GDR cope with these problems? Any estimate of the future of political leaders in the GDR is difficult at best. GDR leaders are necessarily dependent on at least passive Soviet acceptance. Honecker came through the transition from Brezhnev to Andropov to Chernenko with his power secure; how he will fare with Gorbachev remains to be seen. Then again, Honecker will be seventy-three years old in August 1985; although he is in good health, he is presumably mortal—and although there is a plausible successor on the scene in Krenz (as Honecker was in 1971), there is no assured succession.

In fact, the most notable feature of the Honecker era with respect to political personalities is the extraordinary stability of the leadership. As of early 1985, ten of the sixteen *Bezirke* party secretaries have been in office for at least a decade, and the two most recent replacements were brought about as a consequence of death and promotion at higher levels. The state leadership (Stoph, Hoffmann, Mielke) has been equally unchanging. Moreover, the public praise for Honecker at the most recent Central Committee meetings, as well as the promotion of Egon Krenz to a crucial party position, indicates Honecker's continued preeminence. Judging from leaders' speeches in the winter of 1983–1984, the present incumbents of party and state positions are committed to continuing the present policies.

Could this change? Could a political challenge to the Honecker leadership be mounted from within the SED and receive Soviet backing? To imagine the circumstances leading to such a policy change, and its consequences, we may find it helpful to picture the GDR's future along three possible lines of development. We may call these the Polish, Austrian, and GDR perspectives.

The Polish perspective opens onto a picture of economic collapse, including heavy foreign debt without available credit. Under such circumstances, with disgruntled consumption-minded citizens ever less amenable to party discipline, that wing of the leadership (Berlin First Secretary Konrad Naumann comes to mind) that dislikes "bribing" the population on ideological as well as fiscal grounds would present itself to the USSR as the only reliable leadership. In effect, it would be replaying Ulbricht's maneuvers in 1953 and 1956, but the consequences would be devastating for the GDR's legitimacy, as the hopes generated by more than a decade of *Ostpolitik* would be dashed.

A second perspective would see the GDR slowly transformed into a very "German"—albeit still independent—state, economically and culturally ever more closely linked to the Federal Republic. In short, the Willy Brandt–Egon Bahr notion of "change through close relations" would take place. This would allow the regime to release the pressure of peace, church, and environmental groups, and to satisfy cultural and perhaps even travel longings—granting such frequent passes, for example, as to render the Wall irrelevant. The GDR would be stable and peaceful while remaining, in effect, Bonn's cultural-economic protectorate.

If the first perspective would be politically and economically destabilizing for both Moscow and Bonn, and the second politically and militarily a setback for the USSR, we are left with the third, or GDR, perspective. This seems the most probable one, not only because it is easiest to imagine an extrapolation of the present, but also because the present GDR leadership would favor it and both West Germany and the Soviet Union have an interest in maintaining it.[15] In this perspective, the GDR steadily if slowly improves its economic performance and consequently its standard of living. Contacts with West Germany are maintained but remain closely monitored. Social groups are co-opted to the maximum extent possible, and this is sufficient to make more vigorous dissent seem a poor choice. Cultural life is allowed freer development, and it becomes a distinctive part of a broader Germanic culture. The two German states cooperate in the less sensitive areas of international life, possibly acting as moderating influences within their respective alliances.

Three factors, in turn, are the necessary underpinnings for this perspective. One is the requirement that Soviet–United States relations get no worse than they had been in late 1983, and, in fact, that they improve somewhat. Second is the requirement that West Germany's economic power remains sufficient to play its role toward the GDR in terms of granting credits, buying prisoners, and so on. Finally, both Germanies must remain economically and technologically important to the USSR. A stable GDR is of economic and political-military importance to the Soviet Union; this stability is, however, a very expensive prize. Sharing the cost of economic growth in the GDR with the West Germans makes sense in Moscow, especially if the USSR has strategic and commercial interests to be served in Bonn; such Soviet interests will be more readily accommodated in Bonn when Soviet policy allows a measure of intra-German relaxation.

It seems, therefore, that the relatively favorable international constellation that made the Honecker era possible is likely to continue. Policymakers in Moscow, East Berlin—and, judging by their actions in 1983–1984, in Bonn as well—have a well-defined stake in a stable GDR. What remains is the task of political leadership: to convince the GDR population that socialism with a German face is an acceptable way of life.

NOTES

1. *Neues Deutschland,* 21–22 January 1984, p. 1.

2. Dietrich Staritz, "DDR: Herausforderungen der achtziger Jahren," *Die DDR vor den Herausforderungen der achtziger Jahre . . . Mai 1983* (Cologne: Edition Deutschland Archiv, 1983), pp. 21–32.

3. See, for example, the multipage coverage on the occasion of the completion of the two-millionth new apartment built in the GDR since 1971, in *Neues Deutschland,* 10 February 1984, pp. 1–3.

4. Hans-Dieter Schulz, "Wachstumsquellen 'wie noch nie.'" *Deutschland Archiv* 17 (January 1984):5–9.

5. Katharina Belwe, "Soziale Differenzierung der wissenschaftlichen Intelligenz in der DDR-Diskussion," *Die DDR vor den Herausforderungen der achtziger Jahre . . . Mai 1983* (Cologne: Edition Deutschland Archiv, 1983), pp. 106–123, and especially pp. 110–111.

6. Cited in Hans-Joachim Böhme, *DDR-Report* 16 (1983):686.

7. Schulz, "Wachstumsquellen 'wie noch nie.'"

8. See, for example, the youth activities cited in Norbert Haase, Lothar Reese, and Peter Wensierski, ed., *VEB Nachwuchs. Jugend in der DDR* (Hamburg: Rowohlt, 1983).

9. See the letters cited in *DDR-Report* 16 (1983):697–698.

10. In July 1984, the GDR strengthened legal bans on "offenses against public order" (*Ordnungswidrigkeiten*) to criminalize "gatherings" or "use of symbols or objects" that run counter to state or social interests. There is in this connection a clear threat of action against, for example, peace activists. See "Verschärfte Ahndung von Ordnungswidrigkeiten in der DDR," *Deutschland Archiv* 17, no. 8 (August 1984):805–806.

11. See, *DDR-Report* 16 (1983):694.

12. For an example of West German concerns about this policy, see "Alleinvertretungs-Anspruch für die ganze deutsche Geschichte," *Frankfurter Allgemeine Zeitung,* 30 August 1983, p. 11.

13. See the resume of an article on this theme in *Deutschland Archiv* 16 (October 1983):1035–1036; Ralf Badstubner, *DDR-Report* 16, no. 7 (1983):406.

14. See "A Tidal Wave of Germans Is Sweeping Westward," *New York Times,* 2 March 1984, p. A3; stories about Stoph's relatives appeared in *New*

York Times, 29 February 1984, p. A3, and 2 March 1984, p. A3, and the official GDR rejoinder appeared in "Ein untauglicher Versuch," *Neues Deutschland,* 29 February 1984, p. 2.

15. "Bonn Fears East Germans' Flight Will Spoil Ties," *New York Times,* 28 February 1984, p. A3.

Selected Bibliography

This bibliography is limited to relatively recent works in English. Historically, and perhaps understandably, most writing on the GDR has been done in German; accordingly, several of the titles listed below are of works translated from the German.

In recent years, a marked increase has occurred in the number of high-quality English-language works written about the GDR. I have attempted to demonstrate this trend by citing material from scholarly journals and anthologies written, in many cases, by younger scholars.

The purpose of this bibliography is to provide a representative introduction to GDR politics and society. It does not include works of literature and literary criticism. Readers wishing to pursue the subject in German should consult two indispensable West German journals—*DDR-Report* and *Deutschland Archiv* (both of which appear monthly)—and the latter's annual special issue, *Sonderheft* (which presents the papers given at the annual West German meeting on GDR studies).

GENERAL WORKS ABOUT THE GDR

Childs, David. *The GDR: Moscow's German Ally.* London: Allen & Unwin, 1983.
Keefe, Eugene K. *East Germany: A Country Study.* 2d ed. Washington, D.C.: Government Printing Office (Department of the Army), 1982.
Legters, Lyman H., ed. *The German Democratic Republic: A Developed Socialist Society.* Boulder, Colo.: Westview Press, 1978.
McCauley, Martin. *The German Democratic Republic Since 1945.* New York: St. Martin's Press, 1983.
Scharf, C. Bradley. *Politics and Change in East Germany.* Boulder, Colo.: Westview Press, 1984.

ORIGINS AND DEVELOPMENT OF THE GDR

Krisch, Henry. *German Politics Under Soviet Occupation.* New York: Columbia University Press, 1974.
Ludz, Peter C. *The German Democratic Republic from the Sixties to the Seventies.* Cambridge, Mass.: Harvard University Press, 1970, 1984.

Nettl, J. Peter. *The Eastern Zone and Soviet Policy in Germany, 1945–1950.* London: Oxford University Press, 1951.
Sandford, Gregory W. *From Hitler to Ulbricht.* Princeton, N.J.: Princeton University Press, 1983.

GDR GEOGRAPHY AND ECONOMY

German Institute for Economic Research. *Handbook of the Economy of the German Democratic Republic.* London: Saxon House, 1979.
Leptin, Gert, and Manfred Melzer. *Economic Reform in East German Industry.* Oxford: Oxford University Press, 1978.
Melor, Roy E. H. *The Two Germanies: A Modern Geography.* New York: Barnes & Noble, 1978.
U.S. Congress, Joint Economic Committee. *East European Economic Assessment: Part 1—Country Studies; Part 2—Regional Assessments.* 97th Cong., 1st sess., 1981.

GDR POLITICAL SYSTEM

Baylis, Thomas A. *The Technical Intelligentsia and the East German Elite.* Berkeley: University of California Press, 1974.
von Beyme, Klaus, and Hartmut Zimmermann, eds. *Policymaking in the German Democratic Republic.* New York: St. Martin's Press, 1984.
Foster, Thomas M. (pseud.). *The East German Army.* London: Allen & Unwin, 1980.
Herspring, Dale R. *East German Civil-Military Relations: The Impact of Technology.* New York: Praeger Publishers, 1973.
Honecker, Erich. *From My Life.* London: Pergamon Press, 1980.
Krisch, Henry. "Political Legitimation in the German Democratic Republic." In T. H. Rigby and Ferenc Feher, eds., *Political Legitimation in Communist States.* London: Macmillan Publishers, 1982.
Lippmann, Heinz. *Honecker and the New Politics of Europe.* New York: Macmillan Publishing Co., 1972.
Ludz, Peter C. *The Changing Party Elite in East Germany.* Cambridge, Mass.: MIT Press, 1972.
Stern, Carola. *Ulbricht: A Political Biography.* New York: Praeger Publishers, 1965.

THE GDR IN THE WORLD

Asmus, Ronald D., ed. *East Berlin and Moscow: The Documentation of a Dispute.* Radio Free Europe Occasional Papers, no. 1. Munich: Radio Free Europe, 1985.
Croan, Melvin. *East Germany: The Soviet Connection.* Washington Papers, no. 36. Beverly Hills, Calif.: Sage, 1976.
Moreton, N. Edwina. *East Germany and the Warsaw Alliance: The Politics of Detente.* Boulder, Colo.: Westview Press, 1978.
Schulz, Eberhard, et al. *GDR Foreign Policy.* White Plains, N.Y.: M. E. Sharpe, 1982.

Sodaro, Michael, "The GDR and the Third World: Supplicant and Surrogate."
    In Michael Radu, ed., *Eastern Europe and the Third World*. New York:
    Praeger Publishers, 1981.
Wittig, Gerhard. *Community and Conflict in the Socialist Community, 1965–1972*.
    New York: St. Martin's Press, 1975.

THE GDR IN GERMANY

Bailey, Anthony. *Along the Edge of the Forest*. New York: Random House, 1983
Bark, Dennis L. *Agreement on Berlin*. Washington, D.C.: American Enterprise
    Institute, 1974.
McAdams, A. James. "Surviving the Missiles: The GDR and the Future of Inter-
    German Relations." *Orbis* 27 (Summer 1983):343–370.
Schweigler, Gebhard. *National Consciousness in a Divided Germany*. Beverly Hills
    and London: Sage, 1975.
Whetten, Lawrence L. *Germany East and West: Conflicts, Collaboration, and
    Confrontation*. New York: New York University Press, 1980.

CULTURE AND SOCIETY

Asmus, Ronald D. "Is There a Peace Movement in the GDR?" *Orbis* 27 (Summer
    1983):301–341.
Bahro, Rudolph. *The Alternative in Eastern Europe*. New York: Shocken Books,
    1981.
Gerber, Margy, ed. *Studies in GDR Culture and Society*. Lanham, Md.: University
    Press of America, 1982, 1983, 1984.
Goeckel, Robert F. "The Luther Anniversary in East Germany," *World Politics*
    37 (October 1984):112–133.
Klein, Margarete S. *The Challenge of Communist Education: A Look at the German
    Democratic Republic*. East European Monographs, no. 70. New York: Co-
    lumbia University Press, 1980.
Mushaben, Joyce M. "Swords to Ploughshares: The Church, the State, and the
    East German Peace Movement." *Studies in Comparative Communism* 17
    (Summer 1984):123–136.
Rueschemeyer, Marilyn. *Professional Work and Marriage: An East-West Comparison*.
    New York: St. Martin's Press, 1981.
_____ . "Social Work Relations of Professional Women: An Academic Collective
    in the GDR." *East Central Europe* 8 (1981):33–55.
Sodaro, Michael. "Limits to Dissent in the GDR: Fragmentation, Cooptation,
    and Repression," ch. 6 in Jane Leftwich Curry, ed., *Dissent in Eastern
    Europe*. New York: Praeger Publishers, 1983.

Acronyms

ABF	Arbeiter- und Bauernfakultäten
AbtO	Abteilungsorganisationen
ACC	Allied Control Council (four-power occupation authority for Germany)
AKB	Allied Kommandatura Berlin (four-power Berlin authority)
ANC	African National Council
BL	Bezirksleitung (regional party leadership)
CC	Central Committee
CDU	Christian Democratic Union
CMEA	Council for Mutual Economic Assistance
CPSU	Communist Party of the Soviet Union
CSCE	Conference on Security and Cooperation in Europe
DBD	Demokratische Bauernpartei Deutschlands (GDR peasants' party)
DDR	Deutsche Demokratische Republik (German Democratic Republic)
DFD	Demokratischer Frauenbund Deutschlands (Democratic Womens' Federation of Germany)
DM	Deutsche Mark (West German currency)
DTSB	German Gymnastic and Sports Federation
FDGB	Freier Deutscher Gewerkschaftsbund (Free German Trade Union Federation)
FDJ	Freie Deutsche Jugend (Free German Youth)
FDP	Freie Demokratische Partei (Free Democratic party)
FRELIMO	Mozambique Liberation Front
FRG	Federal Republic of Germany

GDR	German Democratic Republic (Deutsche Demokratische Republik)
GO	Grundorganisationen
GSSD	Gruppe Sowjetischer Streitkräfte in Deutschland (Group of Soviet Forces in Germany)
KL	Kreisleitung (district party leadership)
KPD	Communist Party of Germany
KVP	Kasernierte Volkspolizei
LDPD	Liberal Demokratische Partei Deutschlands
LPD	Liberal Democratic party
LPG	Landwirtschaftliche Produktionsgenossenschaft
M	Mark (East German currency)
MfS	Ministerium für Staatssicherheit (Ministry for State Security)
MPLA	Popular Movement for the Liberation of Angola
NDPD	National-Demokratische Partei Deutschlands (National Democratic Party of Germany)
NÖSPL	New Economic System of Planning and Leadership
NVA	Nationale Volksarmee (National People's Army)
OECD	Organization for Economic Cooperation and Development
RFE-RL	Radio Free Europe–Radio Liberty
RgW	Rat für gegenseitige Wirtschaftshilfe (CMEA)
SAGs	Sowjetische Aktien-Gesellschaft (Soviet-German joint stock companies)
SBZ	Sowjetischer Besatzungszone (Soviet Occupation Zone)
SED	Sozialistische Einheitspartei Deutschlands (Socialist Unity Party of Germany)
SMAD	Sowjetischer Militar-Administration Deutschland (Soviet Military Administration in Germany)
SPD	Sozialdemokratische Partei Deutschlands (Social Democratic Party of Germany)
SPK	Staatliche Plankommission (State Planning Commission)
SSD	State Security Service
UNCTAD	United Nations Conference on Trade and Development

VE	Verrechnungseinheiten
VEB	Volkseigenes Betrieb (People's Own Enterprise)
VEG	Volkseigenes Gut (state farm)
VELK	Vereinigte Evangelisch-Lutherische Kirche
VVB	Vereinigung volkseigener Betriebe (association of VEBs)
VW	Volkswagen
WTO	Warsaw Treaty Organization
ZK	Zentralkommittee (Central Committee)

Index

187